Men and Women in the Fourth Gospel

SOCIETY
OF BIBLICAL
LITERATURE

DISSERTATION SERIES
Michael V. Fox, Old Testament Editor
Mark Allan Powell, New Testament Editor

Number 167
MEN AND WOMEN
IN THE FOURTH GOSPEL
Gender and Johannine Characterization

by
Colleen M. Conway

Colleen M. Conway

MEN AND WOMEN IN THE FOURTH GOSPEL
Gender and Johannine Characterization

Society of Biblical Literature
Atlanta, Georgia

MEN AND WOMEN
IN THE FOURTH GOSPEL
Gender and Johannine Characterization

by
Colleen M. Conway

Ph.D., 1997   Advisor:
Emory University   Hendrikus Boers

Library of Congress Cataloging-in-Publication Data

Conway, Colleen M.
    Men and women in the Fourth Gospel : gender and Johannine
    characterization / by Colleen M. Conway.
        p. cm. — (Dissertation series / Society of Biblical Literature ; no. 167)
    Includes bibliographical references.
    ISBN 0-88414-002-4 (cloth : alk. paper)
    1. Men in the Bible. 2. Women in the Bible. 3. Bible. N.T. John—Criticism
    interpretation, etc. I. Title. II. Dissertation series (Society of Biblical
    Literature) ; no. 167.

BS2615.6.M39 C66 1999
226.5'083053—dc21
                                                              99-045667
                                                              CIP

08 07 06 05 04 03 02 01 00 99   5 4 3 2 1

Printed in the United States of America
on acid-free paper

For Ian and Madelyn

Table of Contents

Introduction

Is there a difference between the men and women in the Fourth Gospel and if so, what is the nature of this difference? These questions are the motivating force behind this dissertation. They are also the result of my uneasiness with the way that the subject of women in the Fourth Gospel has been treated over the past two decades. As the review in chapter one will show, the answer to the first question frequently has been that in terms of what is crucial in the Gospel, there is no distinction between women and men. Any special attention the Gospel writer gives to women is, in effect, to raise them up to the level of men so that both are equally portrayed as faithful disciples of Jesus. In short, the question of gender difference has been answered in terms of equal discipleship. Moreover, the notion of equal discipleship is most often seen as a reflection of the historical Johannine community.

That this answer came from work generated in the midst of the revitalized women's movement is not surprising. Much of the feminist movement, especially in America, was engaged in precisely this struggle—to elevate people's perceptions of women and women's abilities so that men and women could be seen as equal players in both public and private domains. This included, of course, women's roles in the church. Eager to find support for active participation in the leadership of the church, feminist advocates quite naturally sought biblical support for their views. The Gospel of John, populated with unique and interesting women characters, readily lends itself to such support.

It is in light of this trend to read Johannine female characters largely as proof of an egalitarian Johannine community that I raise the question concerning the possibility of different and perhaps contrasting portrayals of men and women in the Gospel. I realize that by framing the question around the issues of difference and equality I may well be stirring the waters of feminist critical debate around these two terms.[1]

---

[1] Historian Joan W. Scott summarizes the debate this way: " 'equality-versus-difference' has been used as a shorthand to characterize conflicting feminist positions and political strategies. Those who argue that sexual difference ought to be an irrelevant consideration in schools, employment, and courts are put in the equality category. Those who insist that appeals on behalf of women ought to be made in terms of the needs, interests, and characteristics common to women as a group are placed in the difference category" ("Deconstructing Equality-Versus-

This is not my intention. In asking about the difference between women and men in the Fourth Gospel, I do not mean to imply theoretically that these differences would negate the possibility that the Gospel is presenting images of equal discipleship. Indeed, as I point out in chapter one, the studies that have convincingly demonstrated the model discipleship of women in the Gospel have done an important service for women in the contemporary Christian community. I do not understand this dissertation to be supplanting them but rather supplementing them. Fundamentally, I believe that the feminist positions represented in the "equality versus difference" formulation need not be understood as conflicting. Indeed, Joan Scott has suggested that a resolution to the "difference dilemma" lies in first systematically exposing the ways in which sexual difference creates hierarchies and then refusing the ultimate truth of these hierarchies. "A refusal, however, not in the name of an equality that implies sameness or identity, but rather...in the name of an equality that rests on differences—differences that confound, disrupt, and render ambiguous the meaning of any fixed binary opposition."[2] It is my contention that in previous studies on women in the Fourth Gospel critics have not dwelled long enough with the idea of difference and moved too quickly to an insistence on equality. In doing so, they may have cut short certain avenues of investigation that would enhance our understanding of both female and male characters in the Gospel.

Thus, for several reasons, both textual and theoretical, I suggest that the time has come to revisit the question of women's roles in the Gospel. First, on the textual side, despite the substantial number of studies on women in the Fourth Gospel, few have undertaken a careful examination of women's roles in the narrative itself. Instead, the

---

Difference: Or, the Uses of Poststructuralist Theory for Feminism," *Feminist Studies* 14 [1988]: 38). In other words, the first position considers sexual difference irrelevant to feminist political agendas and the second position emphasizes sexual difference and lobbies for change in the situation of women precisely on the basis of this difference.

[2]Scott, "Deconstructing Equality-Versus-Difference," 48. Cf. also Showalter, ("Feminism and Literature," in *Literary Theory Today* [Peter Collier and Helga Geyer-Ryan, eds. New York: Cornell University Press, 1990], 195–196)

> To talk about 'difference' is not to declare an essentialist belief; differences always have to be defined contextually. Thus to demand equality for women does not mean to say that women are identical to men, nor that all women are alike. Similarly, to investigate difference is not to insist that all women are different from men in the same way, or to celebrate motherhood or any other trait as the fundamental condition of femininity.

motivation to find historical examples of equal discipleship and active participation of women in the church has meant that the women characters in the Fourth Gospel have largely been read as representatives of real women in the historical Johannine community. As I will discuss in chapter one, this move has been advantageous in certain respects, but problematic as far as understanding the role of women (and men) in the Gospel narrative. Indeed, the literary role of the female characters, particularly in relation to the male characters, has not yet been adequately studied.

This leads to a second textual consideration. Because the focus on women has tended to demonstrate their equality with men, the possibility of contrast between the categories of male and female in the Gospel has been largely overlooked. This is true despite the fact that the Gospel is thoroughly infused with dualistic language and perspective. Is it not possible that in a world of light and dark, above and below, life and death, the categories of male and female may also stand in contrast? To be sure, there is no explicit male/female language that compares with other terms of opposition in the Gospel, and I do not suggest that such a contrast would be on the same level as these more explicit oppositions. However, at a structural level, there is a clearly drawn contrast between Nicodemus and the Samaritan woman, as well as possible polarities drawn between Martha and Peter, Mary of Bethany and Judas, and Mary Magdalene and the two disciples at the tomb. Do such pairings suggest that a sort of incipient gender dualism may also be part of the literary matrix of the Fourth Gospel? Such a question demands thoughtful consideration that can only be done in a detailed look at both women and men in the Gospel.

On the theoretical side, recent developments in feminist criticism suggest that studying gender roles whether in life or literature must be a carefully nuanced undertaking. Most feminist critics now realize that simply arguing for the equal status of women does not address the deeper question of how men and women are perceived in the first place. In light of this, critics have begun to analyze the epistemological structures that undergird particular perceptions of men and women, and particular understandings of gender identity. This work is being done from a whole range of theoretical perspectives, including historical, anthropological, sociological, psychological, and literary critical.[3]

---

[3]I cite here only a sampling of the variety of work being done over the past two decades using gender as an analytic category: Caroline Walker Bynum, Stevan

Within this range of perspectives, gender critical theories are becoming increasingly varied and complex, as the notion of what constitutes gender and sexuality continues to be debated. Nevertheless, at the root of most gender critical approaches is the idea that gender identity is a social construct or performance.[4] One's understanding of what it means to be male or female is determined by one's particular social and historical location. Furthermore, when the role of gender is examined within various epistemological systems, it becomes clear how the categories of women and men are intricately interwoven. Women and men are defined in relation to and over against one another.

This observation is of fundamental importance for my own study of women and men in the Gospel of John. I want to move beyond previous studies of women by incorporating such a relational understanding of gender categories into the analysis. This will mean that both women and men will be examined with respect to their functions in the narrative as well as the way they define one another. To this end, the study will use a literary critical approach, with an emphasis on characterization. My aim is to study men and women in the Fourth Gospel with the specific goal of understanding the significance of gender identity in Johannine characterization. This, I hope, will be the dissertation's contribution to Johannine studies.

Harrell, Paula Richman, eds. *Gender and Religion: On the Complexity of Symbols* (Boston: Beacon Press, 1986); Nancy K. Miller, ed. *The Poetics of Gender* (New York: Columbia University Press, 1986); Joan Wallach Scott, *Gender and the Politics of History* (New York: Columbia University Press, 1988); Elaine Showalter, ed. *Speaking of Gender* (New York: Routledge, 1989); Judith Butler, *Gender Trouble: Feminism and the Subversion of Identity* (New York: Routledge, 1990), also Butler, *Bodies that Matter: On the Discursive Limits of 'Sex'* (New York: Routledge, 1993); Thomas Laqueur, *Making Sex: Body and Gender from the Greeks to Freud* (Harvard University Press, 1990); Eve Sedgwick, *Epistemology of the Closet* (Berkeley: University of California Press, 1992); Sandra Lipsitz Bem, *The Lens of Gender: Transforming the Debate on Sexual Inequality* (New Haven/London: Yale UP, 1993); Ursula King, ed. *Gender and Religion* (Cambridge, MA: Basil Blackwell, 1995); Lisa Sowle Cahill, *Sex, Gender and Christian Ethics* (Cambridge/New York: Cambridge University Press, 1996). Mary Jo Maynes, et. al., eds. *Gender, Kinship and Power: A Comparative and Interdisciplinary History* (New York: Routledge, 1996) Sabrina Petra Ramet, ed. *Gender Reversal and Gender Culture: Anthropological and Historical Perspectives* (New York: Routledge, 1996); Brackette F. Williams, ed. *Women Out of Place: The Gender of Agency and the Race of Nationality* (New York: Routledge, 1996).

[4]For a biological approach to understanding gender identity see Steven Pinker, *How the Mind Works* (New York W.W. Norton & Co., 1997).

It is also my hope that the study will further the work of literary criticism of the Gospels. While great advances have been made in understanding the literary aspect of the Gospel narratives, little effort has been made to incorporate gender as part of such analysis. Along this line, in an article on literary criticism of the Bible, Elizabeth Struthers Malbon and Janice Capel Anderson state that more work needs to be done linking the elements of narrative (i.e., settings, characters, plot and rhetoric) to gender as an analytic category.[5] Hopefully, providing such a link will be a byproduct of this investigation as I introduce gender as an analytic category to a discussion of Johannine characterization.

The dissertation will proceed in the following way. Chapter one will provide the background for the project, first situating the study within twentieth century Johannine scholarship and then tracing the work that has particular importance to the topic—research on women in the Fourth Gospel and literary critical analyses of the Gospel. Concerning the latter, special attention will be given to studies on Johannine characterization.

In chapter two, I will outline the theoretical grounding for my work. Because my primary category of analysis is character as a literary feature, I will begin with a discussion of character and characterization. The chapter will consist of two parts. In the first part, I will draw on contemporary character theory to explain my understanding of the nature of Johannine characters and characterization. Of particular interest will be the work of Seymour Chatman and Baruch Hochman, literary critics who steer a middle course between the functional and mimetic understandings of character, a course that well suits my understanding of character in the Fourth Gospel. Even more significantly for my purposes, Hochman articulates a relational view of character that will serve this investigation well. He argues that a key component to characterization is

---

[5]"Literary–Critical Methods," in *Searching the Scriptures: A Feminist Introduction* ed. Elisabeth Schüssler Fiorenza (Crossroad, New York, 1993) 241–254. For more general reviews of the development of feminist literary criticism cf. Pam Morris, *Literature and Feminism: An Introduction* (Oxford/Cambridge, MA: Blackwell, 1993); Jane Gallop, *Around 1981: Academic Feminist Literary Theory* (New York/London: Routledge, 1992); Mary Eagleton, "Introduction," *Feminist Literary Criticism* (ed. M. Eagleton; London/New York: Longman, 1991) 1–23; Mary Todd, *Feminist Literary History* (New York: Routledge, 1988); Maggie Humm, *Women as Contemporary Critics* (Sussex: Harvester Press, 1986): 3–41; Toril Moi, *Sexual/Texual Politics: Feminist Literary Theory* (Methuen & Co., 1985), Elaine Showalter, "Women's Time, Women's Space: Writing the History of Feminist Criticism," *Tulsa Studies in Women's Literature* 3 (1984): 29–34.

the way in which characters are constructed in relation to the other structures of meaning that make up the narrative. Exploring this idea with respect to the women and men of the Fourth Gospel will be essential to my analysis. Also involved in this first part will be a discussion of E. M. Forster's famous flat/round dichotomy, since it has had a significant role in the discussion of biblical characterization.

Finally, the first part of chapter two will consider techniques of characterization that are particular to biblical texts. Here the work of Robert Alter will be especially important, as he points to the subtle means by which the biblical writers construct their characters. Attending to these techniques will strengthen the analysis of characters and characterization in the Fourth Gospel.

The second part of chapter two will suggest ways in which gender can function as a category of analysis within the framework of a study on characters and characterization. Here I will draw on the use of gender as a term that introduces a relational notion to the categories of male and female. I argue that gender is not simply a given for the author of the Fourth Gospel but a deliberate component of Johannine characterization. Therefore, the gender identity of each character demands consideration in terms of individual presentations, relationships between characters, and the narrative structure of the Gospel.

Chapter three will comprise the bulk of the study. Here, based on the discussion of character and gender developed in the previous chapter, I will undertake a study of ten minor characters in the Gospel—five female (the mother of Jesus, the Samaritan woman, Martha and Mary of Bethany, and Mary Magdalene) and five male (Nicodemus, the man born blind, Peter, the Beloved Disciple, and Pilate). My goal will be an analysis of these characters on several levels. I will be interested first in their immediate functions in the various scenes in which they appear. Second, I will look at the ways in which the characters contribute to meaning in the narrative as a whole. Along these lines, it will be important to ask, how do individual characters appear in relation to other characters in other scenes in the Gospel? Furthermore, in what ways are individual characters related to other systems of meaning that make up the overall structure of the narrative? Most important, are any patterns evident in the presentation of women and men, which may shed light on the significance of gender categories in Johannine characterization? It is hoped that these, and other questions, will open the way toward a deeper understanding of the role of characters—both men and women—in the Fourth Gospel.

Finally, a word about footnotes: in most cases once a full reference has been provided, future references will include the name of the author, an abbreviated title, and the page number. The exception is commentaries on the Gospel of John. To avoid wearisome repetition of "John" or "Gospel of John," once full reference to the commentary has been cited, future references will include author and page number only.

Chapter One
History of Research

INTRODUCTION

The purpose of this chapter is to situate this dissertation within the context of twentieth century Johannine studies and more specifically within the areas of Johannine research that pertain most immediately to the topic. Along this line, I begin with a brief review of the issues that have been at the forefront of Johannine research in the twentieth century.[1] Here I am particularly interested in tracing the emergence of interest in the Johannine community, an interest that has dominated scholarly discourse over the past three decades. I then move to a survey of research on women in the Fourth Gospel that will provide important background for my own study. Finally, I conclude with a discussion of literary critical studies of the Gospel, with focused attention on investigations of Johannine characters and characterization.

---

[1]For a review of earlier scholarship on the Gospel see: W. F. Howard, *The Fourth Gospel in Recent Criticism and Interpretation* (London: Epworth Press, 1931); J. N. Sanders, *The Fourth Gospel in the Early Church: Its Origin and Influence on Christian Theology up to Irenaeus* (Cambridge: Cambridge University Press, 1943); Maurice F. Wiles, *The Spiritual Gospel: The Interpretation of the Fourth Gospel in the Early Church* (Cambridge: Cambridge University Press, 1960); Emil Schürer, "Über den Gegenwärten Stand der Johanneischen Frage," *Johannes und Sein Evangelium* (Wege der Forschung 82; Darmstadt: Wissenschaftlich Buchgesellschaft, 1973).
The following are some of the many reviews available on twentieth century research on the Gospel of John: Robert Kysar, *The Fourth Evangelist and His Gospel: An Examination of Contemporary Scholarship* (Minneapolis: Augsburg, 1975); "The Gospel of John in Current Research," *RelSRev* 9/4 (1983): 314–23; "The Fourth Gospel: A Report on the Current Research," (Aufstieg und Niedergang der Romanischen Welt II, 25.3; Berlin/New York: Walter de Gruyter, 1985) 2391–480; Jürgen Becker, "Aus der Literatur zum Johannesevangelium (1978–1980)" *TRu* 47 (1982): 279–301, 305–47; "Das Johannesevanglium im Streit der Methoden (1980–1984)" *TRu* 51 (1986): 1–78; Gerard S. Sloyan, *What are they saying about John?* (New York: Paulist Press, 1991); John Ashton, *Understanding the Fourth Gospel* (Oxford: Clarendon Press, 1991) 3–117; Jean-Pierre Lemonon, "Chronique Johannique (1981–1992)," *LV* 41 (1992): 95–104.

TWENTIETH CENTURY TRENDS IN JOHANNINE SCHOLARSHIP

In many ways, the shift to new trends in twentieth century scholarship on the Gospel of John began with Rudolf Bultmann.[2] Nineteenth century research had been primarily concerned with debates on the authenticity and integrity of the Gospel. In the early part of the twentieth century, research continued on the individual aspects of the Johannine problem–the question of the Gospel's authorship, its literary integrity and its relationship to the synoptic Gospels dominated the scholarly conversation. But it was Rudolf Bultmann who proposed a coherent solution, tackling all of the issues in his commentary and adding to them interests in the history of religion behind the Gospel and the Gospel's theological meaning.[3] His careful source critical work, combined with an often astute theological interpretation marks Bultmann's commentary as a watershed in Johannine scholarship.[4] It is not too much to say that all subsequent historical research on the Gospel has its roots in one way or another in the work of Bultmann, making it the essential starting point of this survey of the history of research on the Fourth Gospel.

While his work on the Gospel is too extensive to detail here, the main points of his source critical theory may be sketched.[5] In brief, Bultmann argued that he could identify four distinct sources that were at the disposal of the evangelist as he crafted the Gospel—a semeia source,

[2]Bultmann's commentary was not published until 1941 but his work on John had dates back to the 1920's during which he published several influential articles: "Der religionsgeschichtliche Hintergrund des Prologs zum Johannes-Evangelium," *Eucharistërion: Studien zur Religion und Literatur des Alten und Neuen Testament* (Festschrift für Hermann Gunkel; Göttingen: Vandenhoeck & Ruprecht, 1923) 3–26; "Die Bedeutung der neuerschlossenen mandäischen und manichäischen Quellen für das Verständnis des Johannesvangeliums," *ZNW* 24 (1925): 100–146; "Untersuchungen zum Johannesevangelium," *ZNW* 27 (1928): 113–163. "Die Eschatologie des Johannesevangelium," *ZwZ* 6 (1928): 4–22.

[3]*Das Evangelium des Johannes* (Göttingen: Vandenhoeck & Ruprecht, 1941); Eng Tr., *The Gospel of John: A Commentary* (Philadelphia: Westminster Press, 1971).

[4]Note the tripartite structure of John Ashton's review of history of interpretation of the Gospel—before Bultmann, Bultmann, and after Bultmann (*Understanding the Fourth Gospel*, 9–111).

[5]D. Moody Smith offers a detailed summary and analysis in his published dissertation, *The Composition and Order of the Fourth Gospel* (New Haven: Yale University Press, 1965). A shorter summary can be found in Robert Kysar, *The Fourth Evangelist and His Gospel: An Examination of Contemporary Scholarship* (Minneapolis: Augsburg Publishing House, 1975) 14–17.

a collection of revelation discourses originating in a pre-Christian gnostic community, passion and resurrection stories, and some additional miscellaneous "Synoptic-like" traditions (e.g., 2:14–15; 12:1–7). At a later stage, the Gospel was subjected to an "ecclesiastical" redaction to align the Gospel unmistakably with Christian orthodoxy. Along with identifying these basic sources, Bultmann accepted the view that the Gospel manuscript had suffered some type of disruption, as his frequent rearrangement of the text makes clear.

Although the details of Bultmann's source theory have since been challenged, especially his claim that a pre-Christian gnostic redeemer myth lies behind the discourse material,[6] his ideas remain the starting point for discussion of the composition of the Fourth Gospel. His careful delineation of the Evangelist's editorial work from earlier and later material in the Gospel led the way to further source and redaction studies that have decisively influenced the twentieth century perspective on John.

Concerning Bultmann's source theory, it is his positing of a primitive signs source that has drawn the most attention. In the early seventies, three different monographs appeared that were based on the existence of a signs source. Robert Fortna,[7] W. Nicol[8] and W. Teeple,[9] each built on this theory in various ways to identify other sources within the Gospel. Others responded to Bultmann's multiple source theory with more skepticism, and opted for a developmental theory of composition. The analyses of M.-E. Boismard, R. Brown, and B. Lindars are representative of this approach, with Brown's five-stage story the most elaborate.[10]

---

[6]Bultmann lays out his theory of the redeemer myth and its background in Mandean and Manichean revelatory literature in his 1925 article, "Die Bedeutung der neuerschlossenen mandäischen und manichäischen Quellen." H. Becker, a student of Bultmann, develops the theory of a discourse source more fully in *Die Reden des Johannesevangeliums und der Stil der gnostischen Offenbarungsreden* (Göttingen: Vandenhoeck, 1956). Despite Becker's efforts, the theory has not gained wide acceptance.

[7]Robert Fortna, *The Gospel of Signs: A Reconstruction of the Narrative Source Underlying the Fourth Gospel* (Cambridge: Cambridge University Press, 1970). Cf. Kysar, *The Fourth Evangelist*, 17–24.

[8]W. Nicol, *The Semeia in the Fourth Gospel* (Leiden: Brill, 1972).

[9]Howard M. Teeple, *The Literary Origin of the Fourth Gospel* (Evanston: Religion and Ethics Institute, 1974).

[10]Marie-Emile Boismard, "L'Evolution du Thème Eschatologique dans les Traditions Johanniques," *RB* 68 (1961): 507–524. Raymond Brown, *The Gospel*

Bultmann's assessment of the history of religion behind John has also brought about much debate, particularly his understanding of the connection between John and gnosticism. On the one hand, as mentioned above, Bultmann finds evidence of the pervasive influence of gnostic thought on the Fourth Evangelist to the degree that "John manifests close contacts with the Gnostic conception of the world." On the other hand, he also detects a "pointed anti-Gnostic theology" seen most clearly in the emphasis on the Redeemer *becoming* flesh.[11] Interpreters have responded by stressing the first part of Bultmann's position,[12] or drawing out the second part,[13] or by suggesting that Johannine Christology actually influenced second century gnostic developments.[14] However, most scholars have moved away from the idea of gnostic influence in terms of a distinctly Hellenistic or Persian phenomenon. Instead, especially since the discovery of the Qumran scrolls, emphasis has fallen on the Jewish background of the Gospel, albeit a highly syncretistic, or perhaps heterodox Judaism.[15]

This emphasis on the Gospel's Jewish background, combined with the work on its composition history, brought the question of historical setting to the fore. It is at this point in the review that we come to research that forms a more immediate background for studies on the role of women in the Fourth Gospel. Without a doubt, the work that has

---

According to John, 2 vols. (AB; New York: Doubleday, 1966) xxxiv–xxxix. Barnabus Lindars, *Behind the Fourth Gospel* (London: SPCK, 1971). Cf. Kysar, "The Fourth Gospel: Current Research," 2402-2407.

[11]The quotations are taken from Walter Schmithals' introduction to the English edition of Bultmann's commentary (8–9).

[12]E.g., S. Schultz, *Das Evangelium nach Johannes* (Göttingen: Vandenhoeck and Ruprecht, 1972). L. Schottroff, *Der Glaubende und die feindliche Welt. Beobachtungen zum gnostischen Dualismus und seiner Bedeutung für Paulus und das Johannesevangelium* (Neukirchen: Neukirchener Verlag, 1970). Cf. Kysar, "The Fourth Gospel: Current Research," 2413–2416.

[13]E.g., Rudolf Schnackenburg, *The Gospel According to St. John* , 3 vols. (New York: Crossroad, 1990) 1.135–149, 169–172. German original, *Das Johannesevangelium* (Freiburg: Herder, 1965).

[14]E.g., Wayne Meeks, "The Man from Heaven in Johannine Sectarianism," *JBL* 91 (1972): 44–72; Helmut Koester, "The History-of-Religions School, Gnosis, and the Gospel of John," *ST* 40 (1986): 115–135; and François Vouga, "The Johannine School: A Gnostic Tradition in Primitive Christianity?" *Bib* 69 (1988): 371–385.

[15]Cf. Brown who states, "A large number of scholars are coming to agree that the principal background for Johannine thought was the Palestinian Judaism of Jesus' time. This Judaism was far from monolithic, and its very diversity helped to explain different aspects of Johannine thought," (lix).

most decisively influenced the question of the Gospel's historical setting has been that of J. Louis Martyn. His *History and Theology in the Fourth Gospel* was the first to engage in a thoroughly redaction critical study of the Fourth Gospel with a heavy emphasis on the community of the Fourth Evangelist.[16]

The title of his book indicates Martyn's main concerns. By concentrating on the stories of conflicts in chapters five, seven and nine and attempting to separate tradition from redaction, Martyn identifies both the historical situation of the Johannine church and the theology that guided the community. This is possible in his view, because the miracle stories in John represent a "two-level drama." At one level, they tell of an *einmalige* event in the life of Jesus, but at another, they are enactments of events that occurred in the life of the Johannine church.[17] Focusing on this second level, especially in the ninth chapter of John, Martyn concludes that the Gospel reflects an actual situation in which Jewish Christians were formally banned from the synagogue.[18] In his view, the author of the Fourth Gospel addressed Christians who were forced to choose between their traditional Jewish heritage and their new identity as Christians.[19]

---

[16]J. Louis Martyn, *History and Theology of the Fourth Gospel* (Nashville: Abingdon Press, 1968). Bultmann was not concerned with the community of the Fourth Evangelist presumably because he believed it was of little concern to the Evangelist himself. At one point Bultmann states, "the Evangelist's chief concern is not with his contemporaries but with the basic truth of the Gospel" (79). The statement reflects Bultmann's existentialist interpretation of Johannine theology. For Bultmann, the Gospel is always and only concerned with the immediate moment of encounter between the individual and the revelation of God in Jesus Christ.

[17]Martyn, *History*, 29–30. He suggests "back there" as opposed to "now and here" or "once upon a time" as possible English equivalents for *einmalig*.

[18]The external evidence adduced for this theory is based on a Talmudic reference to a reformulation of part of the Jewish Prayer known as The Eighteen Benedictions. Martyn dates the formulation of the *Birkath ha-minim* (Benediction against the Heretics), including a specific reference to Christians, to between 85 and 115 C.E., leaning more toward the early part of this range. According to Martyn, this addition to the Eighteen Benedictions amounted to a means of identifying Jewish Christians in the community in order to excommunicate them from the synagogue fellowship (*History and Theology*, 54–62). The attempt to link the Johannine community's experience to this particular prayer has proved to be the stumbling block for full acceptance of Martyn's theory, since the dating of both the prayer and its reformulation is by no means certain.

[19]In a later article, Martyn presents a detailed version of his proposed history of the community behind the Gospel. By isolating various literary strata in the text, he identifies an early, middle and late period of development. Cf. "Glimpses into the

For the most part, Martyn's theory has been received positively—though not always in all its details—since it accounts well for the obvious Jewish/Christian polemic in the Gospel. In more general terms, a significant result of Martyn's work has been a persistent interest in characterizing the so-called Johannine community. In the last twenty years, studies using a variety of different approaches have contributed to the picture of this community so that, for better or worse, it has become increasingly concretized in discussions of the Gospel.

One of the most specific and most speculative among these studies is the work of Raymond Brown in *The Community of the Beloved Disciple*. Brown is directly dependent on Martyn for his methodology, as is clear when he bases his work on the suggestion that "the Gospel must be read on several levels, so that it tells us the story both of Jesus and of the community that believed in him." He goes on to say: "*Primarily*, the Gospels tell us how an evangelist conceived of and presented Jesus to a Christian community in the last third of the first century, a presentation that indirectly gives us an insight into that community's life at the time when the Gospel was written."[20]

With this basic principle in mind, Brown proposes a four-phase rendering of the history of the Johannine community: 1) the pre-Gospel era; 2) the life situation of the Johannine community at the time the Gospel was written; 3) the life-situation of the divided Johannine communities at the time the Epistles were written 4) the dissolution of the two Johannine groups after the Epistles were written. Additionally, he describes each of these phases in detail, from the originating group, which claimed the Beloved Disciple as its authoritative link to Jesus, to the secessionists who split from the orthodox Johannine group. According to Brown, the remaining community, which had been theologically loyal to the author of I John, had "a pedigree or orthodoxy going back to 'apostolic'" times and eventually merged with the "Great Church."[21]

The work of Martyn and Brown has been included in some detail because it represents the dominant movement within Johannine studies

---

History of the Johannine Community," *L'Evangile de Jean: Sources, rédaction théologie* (ed. M. de Jonge; Gembloux: Duculot/Louvain: Leuven University Press, 1977).

[20]Raymond E. Brown, *The Community of the Beloved Disciple* (New York: Paulist Press: 1979) 17. Brown notes Martyn's work in a footnote, although he reminds the reader that in principle Martyn's suggestion is not new.

[21]Brown, *Community*, 150.

in recent years. Although not all scholars approach the level of speculation that especially Brown does, the search for the historical Johannine community has continued unabated since the late 1960's.[22] Writing in 1975, R. Alan Culpepper states, "Today most scholars are convinced that John was written in and for a definite community....One of the cutting edges of Johannine research is to learn more about this community."[23] Similarly, David Rensberger posits, "We have barely begun to realize what the awareness of John's communal setting may mean for our understanding and appropriation of Johannine theology."[24]

Assuming the existence of a distinct "Johannine" community, scholars have gone on to speculate about the precise nature of that community—what sort of group was it and how did it relate to its surrounding environment? Should it be called a sect, in the modern sociological sense of the term?[25] Is it better described as an ancient

---

[22]These are too numerous to detail here. Brown helpfully includes an appendix to *The Community of the Beloved Disciple* in which he reviews several reconstructions of Johannine community history that appeared in the 1970's. Along with Martyn, he includes the following: Georg Richter, "Präsentische und futerische Eschatologie in 4. Evangelium," *Gegenwart und kommendes Reich* (A. Vögtle Schülergabe; ed. P. Fiedler and D. Zeller; Stuttgart: Katholisches Bibelwerk, 1975) 117–52. English summary by A. J. Mattill, "Johannine Communities behind the Fourth Gospel: Georg Richter's Analysis," *TS* 38 (1977): 294–315; Oscar Cullman, *The Johannine Circle* (Philadelphia: Westminster, 1976); Marie-Emile Boismard, *L'Evangile de Jean*, Synopse des Quartres Evangiles en français, III, ed. M.-E. Boismard and A. Lamouille, (Paris: Cerf, 1977). For more recent work on community history cf. J. D. Kaestle, J. M. Poffet, J. Zumstein, eds. *La Communauté johannique et son histoire: la trajectoire de l'évangile de Jean aux deux preimers siècles* (Genève: Labor et Fides, 1990). Thomas L. Brodie, *The Quest for the Origin of John's Gospel* (New York: Oxford University Press, 1993).

[23]R. Alan Culpepper, *The Johannine School: An Evaluation of the Johannine School Hypothesis Based on an Investigation of the Nature of Ancient Schools* (Missoula: Scholars Press, 1975) 37.

[24]David Rensberger, *Johannine Faith and Liberating Community* (Philadelphia: Westminster, 1988) 24-25. Rensberger's first chapter is a review of the shift from the notion of John as a "spiritual Gospel" which required a focus on the Gospel's ideas, to the notion of John as a socially and historically determined piece of work which he believes calls for a social analysis of the text.

[25]Meeks suggests that the term is appropriate ("The Man from Heaven," 70) and Moody Smith claims a near consensus on the issue when he states, "...it can probably be agreed that on any reading of the Gospel and Epistles there appears a sectarian consciousness, a sense of exclusiveness, a sharp delineation of the community from the world" ("Johannine Christianity: Some Reflections on its Character and Delineation," *NTS* 21 [1976]: 222–48). Fernando Segovia argues the point on the basis on love/hate language in the farewell discourse ("The Love and

school,[26] or some other distinctive form of organization?[27] Research on
the similarities between the sectarian Qumran material and the Johannine
tradition has been an important element in this conversation.[28] Beyond
this question, there have been even more focused redaction critical
studies that look for evidence of the various conflicts and splits that
occurred within the community.[29]

Despite the scholarly energy devoted to this topic, the conception
of a community behind the Fourth Gospel as a presupposition for its
interpretation is not without its critics. A number of scholars have
become suspicious of basing Gospel interpretation on reconstructed
histories for which there is little evidence. As Mark Stibbe comments,

> The problem with redaction criticism of the Fourth Gospel...is that it
> has inferred far too much from very little evidence. The evidence
> which we have for the so-called Johannine community (itself a rather
> vague description) is internal to the Gospel.[30]

Hatred of Jesus and Johannine Sectarianism," *CBQ* 43 (1981): 258–272). Cf. also
Rensberger, *Johannine Faith*, 26–29, 135–144. Brown offers an opposing view,
arguing that if one takes the term "sect" in a purely religious sense, the Johannine
community would have had to be alienated from most other Christians in order to be
considered sectarian, which he does not think was the case (*Community*, 14–17).

[26]This is the conclusion of Alan Culpepper's dissertation (*Johannine School*).
However, he does not rule out the description of the community as also a sect.
According to Culpepper, the Johannine school may have been part of a group that
had sectarian characteristics (259).

[27]Although, as discussed above, the difference between John and the Synoptics
was noted since patristic times, Ernst Käsemann seems to be the first to argue that
the Gospel's uniqueness is an indication of a Christian community whose views
diverged from "orthodox" Christology. According to him, behind the Fourth
Gospel is a conventicle exhibiting a näive docetism in its conception of Jesus (*The
Testament of Jesus: A Study of the Gospel in Light of Chapter 17* (Philadelphia:
Fortress, 1968).

[28]Cf. James Charlesworth and Raymond Brown, eds., *John and the Dead Sea
Scrolls* (New York: Crossroad, 1990) and Charlesworth, "Reinterpreting John:
How the Dead Sea Scrolls Have Revolutionized Our Understanding of the Gospel
of John," *BRev* 9 (1993): 18–25.

[29]E.g., D. Bruce Woll, *Johannine Christianity in Conflict: Authority, Rank, and
Succession in the First Farewell Discourse* (SBLDS 60; Chico, CA: Scholars Press,
1981); John Painter, "Christology and the History of the Johannine Community in
the Prologue of the Fourth Gospel," *NTS* 30 (1984): 460–474; L. Schenke, "Das
Johanneische Schisma und die Zwölf," *NTS* 38 (1992): 105–121.

[30]Mark W. G. Stibbe, *John as Storyteller: Narrative Criticism and the Fourth
Gospel* (Cambridge: Cambridge University Press, 1992). Note that Stibbe is not
dismissing socio-historical approaches, however. He proposes that a more useful

Along the same line, Thomas Brodie argues with regard to the New Testament writings in general,

> It may seem at first that the Gospels and epistles provide ample material for writing a social history, but that is debatable. If a text is primarily theological or rhetorical, then it is not easy to use it as a basis for reconstructing social conditions. The present-day endeavor to write the social history of the early church is a variation on the nineteenth century endeavor to write a life of Jesus, and it may end the same way—with a realization that the key documents are not adequate for the task.[31]

Similarly, Frederik Wisse presents a sharp critique of the notion that "early Christian writings are virtually unique among literary texts in that they bear the transparent imprint of the historical situation of a community." In Wisse's view, to assume that early Christian authors encoded this situation in their writings for the convenience of latter-day historians is "wishful thinking."[32] While Wisse may go too far in dismissing the socio-historical location of the Gospel texts, his critique is a worthwhile reminder that in the mind of the interpreter, historical reconstructions are often prone to slide from hypothesis to reality. In such cases, what began as a reconstruction becomes data to be interpreted, resulting in a circularity that can make very little progress towards understanding the text. A good example of this procedure can be seen in the standard treatment of women's roles in the Gospel. Most of the studies on women in the Fourth Gospel have presupposed the existence of a particular Johannine community that lies behind the depiction of women in the text. As the review below will show, interpretation of women's roles in the Gospel all too easily becomes interpretation of women's roles in a reconstructed community.

---

approach is illustrated by Wayne Meeks ("The Man From Heaven") whose method "starts with a literary analysis before it proceeds to sociological explanation or community reconstruction. It does not depend upon allegorizing John's story of Jesus into a history of John's community" (62). For his part, Stibbe goes on to construct a theory of composition for John's Gospel which is just as hypothetical as the histories that he criticizes. Cf. Culpepper's review of Stibbe's work in *JBL* (1994): 734.

[31]Thomas L. Brodie, *The Gospel According to John: A Literary and Theological Commentary* (New York: Oxford University Press, 1993) 6.

[32]Frederik Wisse, "Historical Method and the Johannine Community," *ARC* 20 (1992): 35–42, esp. 39–40.

RESEARCH ON WOMEN IN THE FOURTH GOSPEL

The first article that explicitly addressed the topic of women in the Fourth Gospel came from Raymond Brown.[33] The purpose of the article, as Brown explains, is to address the contemporary question of the ordination of women in the Roman Catholic church. To this end, he investigates the general picture of women presented in John's Gospel. In keeping with his basic understanding of Gospels, Brown takes for granted that such an investigation will tell us something about the role of women in John's own community.[34]

Brown promises to discuss all of the narratives in the Gospel dealing with women, except for 7:53–8:11 since it is a later non-Johannine insertion. However, he gives no specific attention to Mary's anointing of Jesus (12:3–7) and the other narratives are treated only briefly given the limits of the article. In fact, he does not engage in a thorough exegetical study of each narrative, but instead discusses the women in relation to two main characteristics: apostolic function and intimate discipleship.

According to Brown, the Fourth Evangelist assigns women a "quasi-apostolic" role in the Gospel. For example, the Samaritan woman is "led to the brink of perceiving that Jesus is the Christ" and then proceeds to share that perception with others. He notes that it is because of the woman's word (*dia ton logon*) that the villagers believe, a missionary function that Jesus associates with the disciples (cf. 17:20). Moreover, 4:37–38 makes clear that while the disciples are sent by Jesus to reap the harvest, others, specifically the Samaritan woman, had sown the seed. The narrative suggests that female disciples also were important figures in church founding.[35]

For Brown, Mary Magdalene provides an even better example of a "quasi-apostle" in the Fourth Gospel. She is depicted as the one to whom Jesus first appears, despite the fact that Peter and the Beloved Disciple also investigate the empty tomb. Additionally, Jesus sends Mary to tell "his brothers" of his ascension to the Father. Mary's proclamation, "I have seen the Lord" is, according to Brown, "the standard apostolic announcement of the Resurrection." Thus Mary

---

[33]Raymond E. Brown, "Roles of Women in the Fourth Gospel" *TS* 36 (1975): 688–699. The article also appears as an appendix to *The Community of the Beloved Disciple*. Further page references will be to the journal article.

[34]Brown, "Roles of Women," 689, nt. 4.

[35]Brown, "Roles of Women," 691–692.

Magdalene becomes in Western Church tradition "the apostle to the apostles" (*apostola apostolorum*). Apparently for Brown, that her mission is not to the whole world makes her a "quasi" apostle in the Fourth Gospel.

The second category that Brown uses to discuss the role of women is that of intimate discipleship with Jesus. As he puts it, "discipleship is the primary Christian category for John," and in various ways the Gospel makes clear that women are included in this category. Mary and Martha are described as women "loved" by Jesus. Only the Beloved Disciple (the "disciple par excellence" as Brown calls him) and Lazarus share this honor with the two women.[36] Similarly, in chapter 20, Mary Magdalene is called by name, something that Jesus claimed would happen to those who are "his own" (cf. 10:3–5). That this phrase is a designation for his disciples is confirmed by its use at the beginning of the last supper (13:1). From this, Brown concludes that the Fourth Evangelist places women in the same category of relationship to Jesus as the Twelve. Finally, Brown argues, chapter 2:1–11 and 19:25–27 reflect Jesus' reinterpretation of his relationship with his mother in terms of discipleship. Indeed, the scene at the foot of the cross suggests that the mother of Jesus, along with the Beloved Disciple, is an ideal model for Jesus' "own."[37]

In sum, according to Brown, John's open attitude toward women testifies to the community's acceptance of the equality of men and women "in the fold of the Good Shepherd." He states, "This seems to have been a community where in the things that really matter in the following of Christ there was no difference between male and female...." Furthermore, he suggests that Martha's role in place of Peter as the confessor of Christ (11:27) may be a hint from John that "ecclesiastical authority is not the sole criterion for judging importance in the following of Jesus."[38] Thus, in a qualified way, Brown finds biblical support for a

---

[36]As Brown points out, this fact has led some to believe that Lazarus should be understood as the Beloved Disciple. For reviews of this argument see Brown, xcv.

[37]Brown, "Roles of Women," 694–695.

[38]Brown is quick to make the point that the presence of leading figures like Martha and Mary Magdalene is in no way meant to denigrate Peter (693). He is not the first to suggest that the presence of women in the text brings into question the authority of the apostles for the Fourth Gospel. Ernst Käsemann notes, "The relationship to the Lord determines the whole picture of the Johannine church to such an extent that the differences between individuals recede, and even the apostles represent only the historical beginnings of the community. Perhaps the most

more tolerant and inclusive attitude toward women's activity in the contemporary Catholic church. His comments on the role of women in John's community are suggestive about women's significance within the church community, but the unofficial, or "quasi" official nature of these roles is always maintained.[39]

In 1979, Eugene D. Stockton undertook another study on the significance of women in the Fourth Gospel.[40] Stockton approaches the question differently than Brown, focusing more on the typological significance of the characters rather than their historical relevance. In so doing, he joins a long line of traditional scholarship that treats the Johannine characters as types (see the discussion on Johannine characters below). Stockton argues that the Johannine circle is composed of four types of characters: the disciple, the minister (i.e., John the Baptist), the woman, and Jesus. As he understands it, "the women in the gospel play a consistent role relative to Jesus and the believer: mother, witness, support/supplier of faith."[41] To prove this he begins with a source critical analysis of chapter 11 in which he isolates two distinct stories—a Mary version and a Martha version. In its original form, he contends, the point of the Martha story is that "Martha supplied the faith for her dead brother to be raised to life." The Mary version highlighted her "role in a miracle whose outcome was to show Jesus' glory and to bring many to faith...."[42]

Following these observations, Stockton looks briefly at each of the other stories about women in the Gospel, showing in each case how the woman's role is directed to believers or disciples. In this regard, the

---

interesting feature in this connection is the role in the Gospel of John of women who are presented quite emphatically, like Mary Magdalene, as witnesses of the Easter event, or like the Samaritan woman, as servants in the ministry of the proclamation of the Word" (*The Testament of Jesus*, 31).

[39]This can be seen most explicitly in a footnote addressing the issue of women's ordination in the Catholic church. Brown states, "It may be useful to remind ourselves that it remains more important to be baptized than to be ordained, more important to be a Christian than to be a priest, bishop, or pope" ("Roles of Women," 694, nt. 16). This reminder from Brown, himself an ordained priest, also illumines his statement about "things that really matter in the following of Christ." From his position of authority, he can easily downplay the significance of that authority. Nevertheless, coming in 1975 and from a Catholic biblical scholar, Brown's study of women in John was no doubt an advance for Catholic women.

[40]Eugene D. Stockton, "The Fourth Gospel and the Woman," in *Essays in Faith and Culture*, ed. Neil Brown (Catholic Institute of Sydney, 1979) 132–144.

[41]Stockton, "The Fourth Gospel and the Woman," 134.

[42]Stockton, "The Fourth Gospel and the Woman," 140.

Samaritan woman, Mary Magdalene, and Mary of Bethany in 12:1–8 all play the role of witness to Jesus, while the mother of Jesus and Mary at the raising of Lazarus play a key role in a miracle that brings others to faith. As mentioned above, Martha supplies the faith necessary to resurrect her brother.[43] As a conclusion to his article, Stockton notes that the names used for all of the women in the Gospel—either Martha or Mary—are, by popular etymology, practical equivalents to "Lady." For this reason, along with their consistent roles, Stockton posits that the women in the Gospel are all types of the Church.[44]

In his brief study, Stockton makes several significant observations about individual women characters in the Gospel. On the whole, however, his move to allegorize all the women as types of the church is not particularly helpful. The interpretation seems dictated more by his theological position and by traditional readings of the symbolic nature of the mother of Jesus than by the actual narrative.

More closely related to Brown's article on women in the Fourth Gospel is a 1982 study by Sandra M. Schneiders. Even more explicitly than Brown, Schneiders takes up the question of what John's Gospel offers to the contemporary debate on women's ecclesiastical roles.[45] Schneiders' starting point is a claim that the sex of believers is not an issue in the New Testament. Rather, "everything in the New Testament which is addressed to human beings is addressed to them as actual or potential believers, regardless of age, sex, family connections, ethnic background, nationality, race, political affiliations, economic conditions, or social status."[46] This claim is important to Schneiders because she does not want her work to be viewed as a search for scriptural warrant to expand the role of women in the contemporary church. The need for such a warrant would suggest that the Church's restriction of the roles of women was the result of a careful study of scripture, rather than mere cultural accommodation. In short, according to Schneiders, research into women's roles in the New Testament need not be restricted to a "spurious apologetic effort to ground the equality of women in the

---

[43]Stockton, "The Fourth Gospel and the Woman," 141–143.

[44]Stockton, "The Fourth Gospel and the Woman," 143–144.

[45]Sandra M. Schneiders, "Women in the Fourth Gospel and the Role of Women in the Contemporary Church," *BTB* 12 (1982): 35–45.

[46]Schneiders, "Women in the Fourth Gospel," 35. Schneiders notes that the disciplinary injunctions of the epistles are an exception (e.g., 1 Cor. 11:3–16; 14:34–35; 1 Tim 2:8–15).

Church," but may instead be motivated by the desire to balance years of male-dominated exegesis.[47]

In describing the approach that she will take to the biblical text Schneiders distinguishes her method from a strictly historical one. For Schneiders, the Gospels are primarily reflections of the faith of the early Christian communities; thus she emphasizes their religious nature rather than their use as historical documents. Drawing on the hermeneutical theories of Gadamer and Ricoeur,[48] Schneiders contends that every text overflows with a surplus of meaning beyond what its author explicitly intended. This means that what can be observed and interpreted about the roles of women in the Fourth Gospel may be valid even if the Evangelist was not conscious of the possibility of a particular interpretation. However, this does not mean that any interpretation is valid. Instead, according to Schneiders,

> the process of validation consists in seeking the continuity of interpretation with the direction of the author's intention and its coherence with the totality of the New Testament message as embodied in the lived faith of the community, rather than in verifying that the interpretation coincides by identity with the explicit intention of the author.[49]

It is clear from her careful discussion that Schneiders is sensitive to the problems of historical interpretation, especially concerning its usefulness for the contemporary debate on women and the Church. For this reason, it is surprising that her exegetical work on the Fourth Gospel is filled with historical claims about women in the community behind the Fourth Gospel. For example, the disciples' unvoiced question in 4:27

---

[47]Schneiders, "Women in the Fourth Gospel," 35–36. Schneiders' point is well taken given the view of at least one critic. An article by S. J. Nortjé, "The Role of Women in the Fourth Gospel," *Neot* 20 (1986): 21–28, seems to be an attack against feminist theology, "a phenomenon seeking to secure itself in Scripture passages" (21). Nortjé's conclusion about the woman of the Fourth Gospel is that she is instrumental in the ministry of Jesus as a *woman* and "never as a woman with a chip on her shoulder." Women in John are "positioned in a 'higher femininity' and not in an individualistic feminism" (27). Given the hostility that Nortjé projects in this article, one might ask who, in fact, has a chip on her shoulder? Nevertheless, her adamancy about the essential womanhood portrayed in the Gospel is a position that needs to be taken seriously in a study of how gender is constructed within the text.

[48]Schneiders cites Paul Ricoeur, *Interpretation Theory: Discourse and Surplus of Meaning* (Fort Worth: Texas Christian University Press, 1976) and H. G. Gadamer, *Truth and Method* (New York: Seabury, 1975).

[49]Schneiders, "Women in the Fourth Gospel," 37.

makes sense to Schneiders only if there was a controversy within the community about women's roles. The detail is no doubt aimed at "those traditionalist male Christians in the Johannine community who found the independence and apostolic initiative of Christian women shocking."[50] Likewise, Martha appears with Jesus in chapter 11 as the representative of the believing community responding to the word of Jesus with a full confession of Christian faith. According to Schneiders, this role is difficult to understand unless women historically functioned as leaders in John's community. Similarly, when Mary of Bethany is seemingly deliberately presented as a disciple "in the strict sense of the word," i.e., as one who studies at the feet of her teacher, it is probably because "women in [the Evangelist's] community were active members of the school who devoted themselves to sacred study and discussion."[51]

Thus, despite her opening caveat about authorial intention and the usefulness of historical assessments, Schneiders appears in line with Brown in both her method and interpretation. It is true that at points she avoids making her interpretation dependent upon speculations about the Johannine community.[52] Nevertheless, she draws heavily on Brown's work throughout and seems in basic agreement with his view of women's roles in the Johannine community. The main difference in her work is that she does not qualify women's authoritative positions, as Brown does. For example, she speaks of the Samaritan woman's apostleship as fully effective and points out that the apostleship of Mary Magdalene "is equal in every respect to Peter's and Paul's" (not "quasi").[53]

In general terms, Schneiders makes the following helpful observations: 1) women are presented positively and in intimate relationship with Jesus; 2) women are not one dimensional, or stereotypical, but strikingly individual characters; 3) women play unconventional roles that are defined apart from their relationship to men

---

[50]Schneiders, "Women in the Fourth Gospel,"40.

[51]Schneiders, "Women in the Fourth Gospel,"42. Schneiders is here drawing on the work of Culpepper, *The Johannine School.*

[52]See, for example, the turn that is made following a discussion of leaders in John's community, "But whatever role women held in the Johannine community, the Gospel text as it stands presents Jesus as addressing the foundational question to a woman [11:25–26] and the woman as making...the Christian confession" ("Women in the Fourth Gospel," 41).

[53]Schneiders, "Women in the Fourth Gospel," 40 and 44, respectively.

(except for the mother of Jesus and Mary of Clopas). To summarize her study of individual characters, Schneiders argues,

> ...women officially represent the community in the expression of its faith (Martha), its acceptance of salvation (Mary Magdalene), and its role as witness to the Gospel (Samaritan Woman, Mary Magdalene). Two women in John hold the place occupied by Peter in the Synoptics: Martha as confessor of faith and Mary Magdalene as recipient of the Easter protophany and the commission as apostle to the Church. Women were disciples in the strict sense of the word as students of the word of Jesus (Mary of Bethany) in the Johannine School.[54]

As early voices in the conversation, Brown, Stockton, and Schneiders have made valuable contributions to the discussion of women in John and to the contemporary debate of women's roles in the church.[55] While many earlier studies discussed aspects of individual women characters,[56] these scholars called attention to the role of women in general in John's Gospel.[57] It was not until the female characters were looked at together that their importance in the Gospel as women began to emerge. Indeed, although Schneiders claims that the New Testament is not interested in the question of gender, the evidence she lays out for John's Gospel suggests otherwise.

---

[54]Schneiders, "Women in the Fourth Gospel," 44.

[55]That this question is still open to discussion is seen by the appearance of a more recent article that is, in essence, a restatement of Brown and Schneiders, though from a different denominational perspective. Karen Heidebrecht Thiessen ("Jesus and Women in the Gospel of John," *Direction* 19 [1990]: 53–64) states that while there is agreement that women are called to minister, there is still debate on the nature of ministry and forms of expression appropriate for women.

[56]Research on the significance of individual women characters, such as the mother of Jesus or Mary Magdalene is too extensive to be included here. Where relevant, such work will be reviewed in the course of the investigation.

[57]For the sake of chronology, we should mention the work of Stephen Dollar, "The Significance of Women in the Fourth Gospel," (Unpublished Th.D. diss. New Orleans Baptist Theological Seminary, 1983). Dollar's first chapter reviews the position of women in the first century. The second discusses John's portrayal of women in the public ministry of Jesus, and the third, his portrayal of women in the passion and resurrection ministry of Jesus. These last two chapters consist of one or two pages of exegetical comments on the passages concerning women (mainly summaries of the text) followed by several pages briefly discussing the significance of these passages. Dollar concludes that women are given a prominent role in the Gospel as agents of potential, perception, and proclamation. As a whole, his work is quite cursory and in need of further development.

A third scholar whose work on women on John is in line with Brown and Schneiders is Elisabeth Schüssler Fiorenza. Her discussion of the topic comes in the final section of her well-known feminist reconstruction of Christian origins.[58] Under the subheading "women as paradigms of true discipleship" she discusses the women characters in the Gospel of Mark and in the Gospel of John. Her work, too, is based on an assumed Johannine community. She defines it as an "alternative" community, characterized by relationships of equality—a community of friends in which special leadership roles (e.g., the twelve) are de-emphasized.[59] In this setting, the five women in John's Gospel serve as "paradigms of women's apostolic discipleship as well as their leadership in the Johannine communities."[60] Thus, like Brown and Schneiders, Schüssler Fiorenza relies on the Johannine community for understanding the presence of women characters in the Fourth Gospel.

With regard to the present investigation, this kind of work is limited in several respects. First, as discussed above, despite the assumptions of form and redaction criticism, the transition from Gospel narrative to historical community may not always be as smooth as these scholars presume.[61] Texts *may* be realistic reflections of a particular community but there is no certainty of that, particularly when dealing with ancient texts.[62] Secondly, regardless of whether one accepts a historical reconstruction of the Johannine community, this approach does not take up the thematic importance of women for the Gospel. For instance, the question of what the portrayal of women in relation to

---

[58]Elisabeth Schüssler Fiorenza, *In Memory of Her: A Feminist Theological Reconstruction of Christian Origins* (New York: Crossroad, 1987) 323–334.

[59]Schüssler Fiorenza, *In Memory*, 324. This is similar to Brown's theory of the nature of leadership in the Johannine church.

[60]Schüssler Fiorenza, *In Memory*, 333.

[61]Turid Karlsen Seim offers the same critique, stating of Brown and Schneiders that both "tend to relate some individual features of the text too easily to an estimated socio-historical situation of congregational life" ("Roles of Women in the Gospel of John," in *Aspects on the Johannine Literature*, ConB 18, ed. Lars Hartman and Birger Olsson (Uppsala, 1987] 57 nt. 4),

[62]Elizabeth Clark demonstrates the possibility of incongruity between religious text and social reality in her study of Jerome, Chrysostom and Augustine, whose various writings on the topics of women and marriage do not coincide with the social relationships these men actually had with women ("Theory and Practice in Late Ancient Asceticism: Jerome, Chrysostom, and Augustine," *JFSR* 5 [1989]: 25–46).

Jesus suggests about the Gospel's Christology or theology is not addressed.

Nevertheless, at one point Schüssler Fiorenza's treatment of the subject does move in the direction that this study will take. As she begins her discussion of individual women she recognizes that aside from merely including individual women in the Gospel the Fourth Evangelist places them at crucial points of plot development and confrontation. In her words, it is, "astonishing that the evangelist gives women such a prominent place in the narrative."[63] Although Schüssler Fiorenza does not develop this observation beyond its possible historical significance, for the purpose of this study it is a crucial point and one that needs to be analyzed much more closely for its significance to the Gospel narrative as a whole.

In an article that appeared in 1986, John Rena also addresses the topic of women in the Gospel of John.[64] He begins with two guiding questions, "How does John present important female characters?" and "Why does he describe them as he does?" As in Schüssler Fiorenza's observation, these questions show an interest in the narrative role of women in the Gospel, though Rena makes clear that his study is dependent on Brown's reconstructive work.[65] He intends to build upon Brown's reconstruction and attempts to locate each of the women within one of the groups that comprised the Johannine community according to Brown. As he puts it, "...the women represent ethnic, social, historical and theological issues or groups in the Johannine community. They help the Johannine Christian think of the past, present and future in symbolic but relevant ways."[66]

However, Rena demonstrates ambiguity about which group each of these characters represents. He begins with a degree of certainty about the mother of Jesus—she represents a group of non-apostolic Jewish Christians within the community who have come to adequate faith, a group which Rena believes should be added to Brown's reconstruction. Beyond this character, however, questions arise as to what each woman represents. For instance, Martha and Mary may represent the same group of Jewish Christians with adequate faith, but they may also model

---

[63] Schüssler Fiorenza, *In Memory*, 326.
[64] John Rena, "Women in the Gospel of John," *Église et Théologie* 17 (1986): 131–147.
[65] Rena, "Women in the Gospel of John," 131, nt. 2.
[66] Rena, "Women in the Gospel of John," 146.

the opposite—Jewish Christians with *inadequate* faith, who need greater spiritual maturity.[67] Similarly, Mary Magdalene might represent this latter group, or she may reflect an "apostolic Christian" group; Rena is uncertain as to which group she represents.[68] His confusion is understandable given the method he has chosen, and should serve as warning about the limitations of an approach to the topic that depends on an abstracted community.

Rena concludes with the following general observations. First, women have no single role in the Gospel. Second, their roles are important. Third, there is no distinction between discipleship opportunities of men and women. "In the Johannine narrative, listening, learning, believing and confessing are equal rights and equal responsibilities."[69] Fourth, John uses women as part of subtle polemic against anything that threatens the Lordship of Christ. Fifth, they are used as symbolic figures. The fourth observation is especially significant since it begins to question the function of female representation within the narrative of John. Along with this point, Rena poses the question, is the prominence of women an effort to control the influence of the Twelve? He then asks more broadly, "is John worried about authority figures?"[70] Similarly, in his attempt to grasp the symbolic significance of the individual characters within the Gospel, Rena moves toward a larger question than simply their function for the Johannine community. Finally, Rena's article is of note in that it does consider all of the important women in the Gospel, excluding only the women in 7:53–8:11 on the basis of this pericope's late addition to the text.

Another more recent review of women in the Gospel appears as an appendix to Robert Kysar's revised edition of *John: The Maverick Gospel.*[71] Kysar points out the significance of the women in relation to the structure of the Gospel—scenes with women occur in crucial places at the beginning, middle and end of the Gospel (chapters 2, 4, 11, 12, 19, 20). He understands this structure to create a subliminal message for the reader that women were disciples, equal to the male disciples and

---

[67]Rena, "Women in the Gospel of John," 137, 143.

[68]Rena, "Women in the Gospel of John," 145, nt. 38.

[69]Rena, "Women in the Gospel of John," 146.

[70]Rena, "Women in the Gospel of John," 146. The idea is similar to Käsemann's in its downplaying of the apostolic role by the Evangelist and to Brown's notion of a critique on ecclesiastical authorities.

[71]Robert Kysar, *John: the Maverick Gospel,* rev. ed. (Louisville: Westminster/ John Knox Press, 1993).

central to Jesus' story. As such they join with male disciples as models of faith for the reader.[72] The conclusions Kysar draws from these observations echo those of Schüssler Fiorenza. The Gospel's attitude toward women reflects "an egalitarian community in which both genders occupy prominent places and in which the gifts of both are valued."[73]

Kysar also addresses the issue of the dominant male image for God presented in the Gospel. He concludes, again with Schüssler Fiorenza, that the function of the "Father" title for God is actually to "loose the grip" of patriarchal authority wielded over women and children. "There is but one authority, and that is God. There is but one father who claims absolute obedience, and this is God...By imaging God as Father, the authority of males is subverted."[74] There are problems with this solution—it is not clear that the deification of patriarchal authority would necessarily be an improvement for women and children. Nevertheless, Kysar correctly perceives that the issue of patriarchal language in the Gospel should be raised alongside an examination of the function of women in the text.

Another recent work that addresses the role of women in the Gospel is Martin Scott's *Sophia and the Johannine Jesus*.[75] Although Scott's main interest is Christology, his secondary concern with the women characters of the Gospel makes his work pertinent here. In his investigation, Scott intends, 1) to examine the relationship between Sophia and the Jesus of the Fourth Gospel, and 2) to investigate what effect, if any, the use of a female figure as a basis for christological reflection had on the way women were portrayed in the Gospel.

The bulk of his study is concentrated on the first aim, but since the presentation of Jesus is not my primary interest, I will give this part of Scott's discussion only brief attention. After an introductory chapter, Scott traces the development of Sophia within Jewish literature, concluding that as a female expression of God she reached her pinnacle in the Wisdom of Solomon, only to be "contained" within the bounds of Torah by Jesus ben Sira. He then rehearses the relationship between Logos and Sophia in the Prologue, and Jesus and Sophia in the rest of

---

[72]Kysar, *Maverick Gospel*, 148–149.

[73]Kysar, *Maverick Gospel*, 153.

[74]Kysar, *Maverick Gospel*, 153–154. Cf. Schüssler Fiorenza, *In Memory*, 150–151.

[75]Martin Scott, *Sophia and the Johannine Jesus*, JSNT Supp 71 (Sheffield: JSOT Press, 1992).

the Gospel.[76] His conclusion is that not only was the tradition of Sophia influential for John's Christology (a common view); it was dominant. According to Scott, John's Christology is a thoroughgoing Sophia Christology so that "Jesus Christ is none other than Jesus Sophia incarnate."[77]

In his last chapter, Scott takes up the question of the role of women in the Gospel. Significantly, he attempts to answer a question that had remained at the level of observation in previous studies, namely, why is it that key moments of revelation occur during Jesus' encounters with women? By tracing the influence of the Sophia tradition on the Gospel (specifically in 2:1-11; 4:1-42; 11:1-44; 12:1-8; 19:25-27; 20:1-18), Scott argues that women in John are depicted as representative disciples of Sophia, or, citing Proverbs 9:3, "handmaidens of Sophia." Just as the influence of Sophia has overwhelmingly shaped the depiction of Jesus, according to Scott,

> ...(the) discipleship pattern presented through the role of women owes much of its origins to the same Sophia tradition. ...(T)he influence of Sophia language... permeates the *whole* presentation of the women as disciples of Jesus Sophia throughout the Gospel.[78]

Scott further suggests that the depiction of women in dialogue with Jesus reflects the femininity of Jesus Sophia. He asserts, "Here something of a balance is maintained between the maleness of Jesus and the femaleness of so many of the main Gospel figures."[79] Finally, Scott also draws the usual historical conclusions about women in the Gospel—they must have had leadership roles within the Johannine community.

---

[76]Here, Scott is highly dependent on Brown and James Dunn (his dissertation director) who have both studied Jewish Wisdom themes in the Fourth Gospel. Cf. Brown, *The Gospel According to John* (AB 29, 29A; New York: Doubleday) cxxii–cxxv. J. D. G. Dunn, *Christology in the Making: An Inquiry into the Origins of the Doctrine of the Incarnation*, 2d ed. (London: SCM Press, 1989) 163–212; "Let John Be John: A Gospel for Its Time," *Das Evangelium und die Evangelien* , WUNT 28, ed. P. Stuhlmacher (Tübingen: J. C. B. Mohr, 1983) 303–39, esp. 330ff.

[77]Scott, *Sophia*, 170. Along with this claim, Scott argues that the Fourth Evangelist was conscious of a gender problem in the association of female Sophia with male Jesus. The author's solution was to employ the masculine Logos, a term which had already been closely related to Sophia by Philo, as a substitute for Sophia.

[78]Scott, *Sophia*, 237.

[79]Scott, *Sophia*, 250.

Scott's work is thought provoking in a number of ways, but particularly on the point of the Evangelist's awareness of gender categories, both in relation to Jesus and to the women characters of the Gospel. Scott is willing to consider the possibility that women are significant in the Gospel precisely because they are women. In other words, it is not their sameness, or equality with men that is noted, but their status as women. Furthermore, while I am less convinced by Scott's insistence on the pervasive influence of the Sophia tradition, I am convinced that his attempt to understand the Gospel's portrayal of women in relationship to Jesus and to Johannine Christology is on the right track. I will argue in the next chapter that the best way to understand Johannine characterization is in close relationship to other systems of meaning (e.g., Christology) in the Gospel.

However, for the purpose of the present study Scott's work is limited in certain respects. First, because it is primarily a Christological investigation, the question of women is secondary, discussed only in the final chapter. In essence, once Scott has identified Johannine Christology as thoroughly influenced by Sophia, his work with the question of women characters functions merely as a complement to that point. Also, he does not treat the male characters in relation to Jesus, leaving his thesis with unanswered questions. If women characters represent handmaidens of Sophia, what do male characters represent? Similarly, if women in the Gospel reflect the femininity of Jesus, do male characters reflect his masculinity? Moreover, if Jesus is intended to represent a female figure so thoroughly, why would the Evangelist seemingly emphasize the maleness of Jesus with such a heavy use of Father/Son language?[80] Finally, if one is not convinced by Scott's argument about women as disciples of Sophia, what remains is once again a theory concerning women in the Johannine community, rather than an interpretation of their role in the narrative. In short, while Scott presents some tantalizing ideas about female characters and Johannine Christology, in the end his thesis does not go far enough in explaining how the gender identity of Johannine characters, both women and men, relates to the broader scheme of the Gospel narrative.

---

[80]Recognizing that the preponderance of Father/Son imagery creates a problem for his thesis, Scott suggests that "the answer probably lies in the insistence of early Christian tradition upon Jesus' use of *Abba*-language to talk to God, particularly in prayer" (*Sophia*, 144). But why when the author has supposedly gone to such lengths to present a radically different picture of Jesus than has been given thus far, would s/he be compelled to adhere to, even enhance, this tradition?

The last two articles to be reviewed in this section represent the beginning of a move away from studying women in John from a strictly socio-historical perspective. The first is an article by Turid Karlsen Seim, which in several ways is the most relevant article to date for this investigation.[81] Like Schneiders, Seim cautions against the limitations of a strictly apologetic or utilitarian approach to the topic. In her words, "There is more to women's perspectives than just focusing on particular women in a fragmentary way, isolating the individual women found in the text and making 'a list' of them." Instead, her goal is to focus on the "internal role pattern" of the text itself and to "outline some significant female features in the picture."[82] As far as possible in her brief article, she seeks a coherent view of the roles and functions of women in the Gospel. With this as her aim, Seim leaves behind, for the most part, the concern for the Johannine community. As she puts it, "...within the limitations of this article I am hesitant to infer from text to socio-historical background. This means that I do not presuppose that the roles of women as described in the text correspond to or mirror without reservation a practical function in a specific historical situation."[83]

Even more significantly, Seim raises a question that correctly challenges the traditional reading of women characters in the Gospel. Once the observation about John's inclusive presentation of women has been made, there remains the question "as to whether the women are mainly indisputable and representative examples of discipleship as such, or whether the specific point that they are women is explicitly reflected in the text."[84] To put it another way, Seim asks, "May it be that asking for the roles of women genuinely coincides with an explicit interest of the Gospel of John itself, visible on its textual surface?"[85] For Seim, the

---

[81]Turid Karlsen Seim, "Roles of Women in the Gospel of John," in *Aspects on the Johannine Literature*, ConB 18, ed. Lars Hartman and Birger Olsson (Uppsala, 1987).

[82]Seim, "Roles of Women," 56. The comment is a critique against certain "Women in the Bible" compilations. Seim cites Leonard Swidler, *Biblical Affirmations of Women* (Philadelphia: Westminster, 1979) as a typical example.

[83]Some tentative conclusions are drawn, however, as seen in the following proposition concerning chapter 20:1–18. "Provided that a prominent position in the resurrection story may be connected with an authoritative and prominent position in the Christian community, [citing Hengel] this apportionment among Mary of Magdala, Peter and the beloved disciple could imply an egalitarian interest in the leadership of the Johannine community" (67).

[84]Seim, "Roles of Women," 58–59.

[85]Seim, "Roles of Women," 57.

answer is yes. She argues convincingly that there are indications within the text that gender itself is significant for the Fourth Gospel. In this way, she suggests that gender difference more than gender equality is an issue in the text.

First, she points out that the women in John are not found in passing, but rather, appear in extremely rich material which consists of "large, literary and theologically complicated passages to be reckoned among the highlights of the Gospel."[86] Moreover, the women actors share a singleness of purpose in the way they are presented—all act intentionally and decisively. From the comment made in 4:27, "they were astonished that he was speaking with a woman," Seim surmises that the "sexual" aspect of women is important to the Gospel. In this verse, the controversy between Jews and Samaritans is left behind and instead gender becomes the essential point of difference and scandal. Finally, Seim points out the predominance of the address *gunai* in the scenes with women (2:4; 4:21; 19:26; 20:13; 15). There is no corresponding address to men; they are either addressed by name (11:43 and 14:9) or not at all. Even if the term is simply a typical form of address and no more, its use with respect to the mother of Jesus has long troubled commentators. The common understanding of the use of this term in chapters 2 is that it indicates the distance between Jesus and his mother. Jesus is always self-determined in accordance with the will of God, not by the demands of his human relationships. This may be the case, but Seim rightly argues that the use of *gunai* throughout the Gospel also shows an emphasis on femaleness in the passages with women characters.[87]

Thus, Seim makes an important contribution and advance over much of the work that preceded her. Like Scott, she recognizes the possibility that gender, and particularly gender difference, is an explicit concern in the Gospel. Yet for the purposes of her article, she limits herself to description rather than explanation, so that, while she convincingly demonstrates the importance of gender in John, she does not yet attempt to explain it. Additionally, in her brief individual analyses, Seim does not make clear what is important about women *qua* women for the narrative. Instead, she tends to focus on precisely that aspect from which she initially seemed to distance herself in her study, i.e., women as examples of discipleship without regard to their gender.

---

[86]Seim, "Roles of Women," 57.
[87]Seim, "Roles of Women," 59–60.

So, for example, Martha is seen as the representative of the christological confession and faith of the community, and Mary of Bethany is defined as the prototype of the practice of discipleship.[88] Thus, while her article is a helpful beginning point, more work is required to understand fully the narrative significance of these women characters.

Finally, an article by Martinus C. de Boer should be mentioned at this point since to a certain degree it is a response to Seim, though he does not explicitly address her work until his concluding section.[89] Unlike the works reviewed thus far, de Boer attempts a three-fold analysis that includes narratological, historical and theological aspects. He believes that each of these approaches contributes to the other two, and that no single approach can fully answer the questions brought to the text without the benefit of the other two. De Boer's work also differs in its specificity—he discusses women in John in the context of a study on "the problem" of John 4:27.

De Boer's analysis of this verse begins with a discussion of how it fits within the narrative of chapter four. He argues that prior to 4:27, the main emphasis of the story had been the relationship between Jews and Samaritans. It is the woman's ethnic identity that is emphasized, not her gender. Indeed, according to de Boer, from all initial appearances it seems that the character just "happens to be a woman."[90] He goes on to posit that from a "narratological angle" (putting aside the remote possibility that the evangelist is a "proto-feminist") the character is portrayed as female because of the law of verisimilitude. In other words, men did not normally come to wells to draw water in first century Palestine so that a male character in this setting would make the narrative unrealistic. The story needs to be set at a well, according to de Boer, so that Jesus can readily talk about water.

Given this explanation of the presence of a woman in the story, de Boer goes on to argue that 4:27 is a narratological aporia. "It stands out from the narrative flow of this story and disrupts it. Regarded from a narrative-critical point of view, it is entirely dispensable. In fact, without it John 4 would be more narratively cohesive and thematically

---

[88]Seim, "Roles of Women," 73.

[89]Martinus C. de Boer, "John 4:27—Women (and Men) in the Gospel and the Community of John," in *Women in the Biblical Tradition*, Studies in Women and Religion 31, ed. George J. Brooke (Lewiston: The Edwin Mellen Press, 1992) 208–230.

[90]de Boer, "John 4:27," 215.

coherent."[91] For de Boer, it is only to this point that a narrative analysis of this text can take the critic, i.e., it can only show why verse 27 should not have been included, not why it has been. To answer that question, de Boer feels it is necessary to move to an historical analysis.

At this level of analysis, de Boer engages in a brief redaction history of chapter four. First, he notes that prior to this chapter, Jesus has talked only to men, except for the "understandable exception of his mother at a wedding feast."[92] Furthermore, his named disciples are all male, and in the Last Discourse his named conversation partners are male. In addition, all of the characters who are miraculously healed or resuscitated by Jesus are male (cf. 4:46–54; 5:1–9; 9:1–7; 11:1–44). To de Boer this suggests that the Johannine Jesus tradition, attested and primarily preserved in the narrative portions of the Gospel, was thoroughly androcentric.[93] He concludes that the attention given to women characters occurred at a later stage in the tradition in which "unprominent women have been given prominence."[94] This development occurred, according to de Boer, after the expulsion of Johannine Christian Jews from the synagogue.

Based upon his redaction analysis, de Boer surmises that 4:27 is not a relic of the Jesus tradition but a modification of that tradition. As he states, "The 'disciples' in 4:27...represent not disciples of the historical Jesus, but the disciples of the post-Easter Johannine community."[95] It was added to a story about the mission of a woman Samaritan to a Samaritan city at a time when the relation between men and women disciples had become an issue. In sum, the verse reflects

---

[91]de Boer, "John 4:27," 219. From the perspective of most narrative critical work on the New Testament, such a statement might seem odd. Typically, a literary critic may point out places of tension or gaps within the narrative, the presence of which has a certain effect on the reader. However, a verse would not be labeled as dispensable. Indeed, this sort of conclusion is more in keeping with redaction-critical assessments of a Gospel text. This overlap is understandable given de Boer's view that the lines between narrative criticism and historical criticism are not clearly drawn and that narrative critical observations can actually be used in the service of historical critical work (cf. "Narrative Criticism, Historical Criticism, and the Gospel of John," *JSNT* 47 [1992]: 35–48).

[92]de Boer, "John 4:27," 224.

[93]For de Boer these narrative sections include John the Baptist's testimony, the coming of the first disciples, the miracle stories, the Last Supper, the arrest and trial narrative, and the resurrection appearances (224).

[94]de Boer, "John 4:27," 225.

[95]de Boer, "John 4:27," 226.

"the growing and developing faith of Johannine Christianity away from an androcentric understanding of discipleship and mission to one emphasizing and recognizing the equality of women to men in Christian life and practice."[96] With this statement it becomes clear that despite de Boer's promising attempt at a narrative analysis, he ultimately relies on the reconstructed Johannine community to answer the question of the importance of women in the Fourth Gospel.

Nevertheless, de Boer closes with a highly significant statement in the theological postscript to his essay. Discussing Seim's assessment of the importance of the "sexual aspect" of Johannine women, de Boer observes that for Seim's claim to be convincing, more attention needs to be given to the portrayal of male characters in the Fourth Gospel. In effect, de Boer is calling for the introduction of gender to the discussion of Johannine characterization. De Boer has his own ideas about what such a discussion would uncover. He contends that the women characters of the Gospel are given attention only to show that their identity as *women* characters is insignificant.[97] He thereby rejects that notion that gender differentiation is a crucial component in narrative. He may be correct, but in order for de Boer's claim to be convincing both men's and women's roles need to be carefully analyzed, as de Boer himself suggests.

On this point, one should also note the statement by Jane Kopas, in her brief theological reflection on the women in John.[98] She points out the number of times that the Gospel conveys a definite lack of understanding in the conversations that Jesus has with men (e.g., 3:1–15; 13:6–10, 36–38; 14:8–11; 20:24–25). Though she states that Jesus' encounters with women are "neither indictments of men as men nor glorification of some kind of mystique of women," she also notes, "...there are enough examples of lack of comprehension of the person's relationship to God among the men who follow [Jesus] to make his encounters with women all the more amazing."[99] Given de Boer's call for attention to the male characters in the Gospel, Kopas's passing observation is particularly intriguing.

As can be seen from the above review, previous studies on women in the Fourth Gospel have gone a long way in laying the

---

[96]de Boer, "John 4:27," 228.

[97]de Boer, "John 4:27," 230–231.

[98]Jane Kopas, "Jesus and Women: John's Gospel," *TToday* 41 (1984): 201–205.

[99]Kopas, "Jesus and Women," 201–202.

groundwork for a more in-depth study on the subject. Apart from the significant individual contributions, the cumulative effect of these works makes it apparent that women characters are of fundamental importance in the Gospel. Yet, these studies have also been limited in large part to an assessment of the role of women in the Johannine community, to the degree that the characters of the Gospel are frequently read as representatives of some real women behind the text. Moreover, "equality" becomes a key word in these interpretations, notwithstanding the complete lack of attention devoted to the presentation of the male characters with whom the women are deemed to be equal.

As I pointed out in the introduction, speculating about men and women's equal roles in the Johannine community no doubt serves an important function for contemporary women seeking affirmation for their ecclesial roles. However, letting these speculative conclusions suffice for interpretation of women's roles in the Gospel narrative is problematic. Such an approach does not go far enough in understanding how the women characters contribute to the Gospel itself. What role do they play in the story, in the drama of salvation that is the Gospel of John? On this point, Jeffrey Staley aptly observes, "The role of women in the Fourth Gospel—its relationship to the Johannine portrayal of salvation and its implications for feminist theology—has not yet been adequately investigated from a narrative critical perspective...."[100]

In light of this, the present study will approach the question of the women in John from a literary perspective. Whether there were women leaders in a so-called Johannine community (something we likely will never know), it is certainly true that women characters play a major role in the narrative of the Fourth Gospel. One of my primary concerns will be to understand this role, especially in relation to the role that male characters play in the Gospel. Analyzing both will require an understanding of literary critical categories, especially that of characterization. Fortunately, progress has already been made in understanding the literary aspects of the Gospel, including characters and characterization. I turn now to a review of that work.

LITERARY CRITICISM AND THE GOSPEL OF JOHN

A growing awareness of the limits of historical criticism, combined with an increased recognition of the relevance of literary style

---

[100] Jeffrey Staley, "The Structure of John's Prologue: Its Implications for the Gospel's Narrative Structure," *CBQ* 48 (1986): 261–262, nt. 55

and technique for biblical interpretation has led to the development of a literary critical approach to the Bible. With respect to Gospel studies, the tools and knowledge gained from narratologists have proved especially useful, to the degree that the term "narrative criticism" has emerged as a programmatic label for literary criticism of the Gospels.[101] Broadly speaking, narrative criticism looks to the structures and literary devices within the text and their impact upon the reader to derive an interpretation.[102]

Though narrative criticism as it is currently practiced in Gospel studies is a recent development, recognition of the Fourth Gospel's literary qualities is not. A recently published anthology by Mark Stibbe makes clear that the literary aspects of the Gospel have long been noted.[103] As early as 1911, British scholar F. R. M. Hitchcock called for a more literary reading of John, which he intended as evidence for the Gospel's apostolic authorship. As such, his work was undertaken in opposition to the partition theories that were popular in Germany in the early part of the century.[104] Yet also in Germany, some voices were highlighting the Gospel's literary qualities. For instance, a 1923 essay by Hans Windisch compares John's narrative style, governed by dramatic sensibilities, with the Synoptic "pericope-compositions."[105] In America,

---

[101] The label is unique to the field of biblical studies. According to Stephen Moore, although Norman Petersen had used the term occasionally in earlier studies, David Rhoads is responsible for first using it in a consistent and definitive way, beginning with his article "Narrative Criticism and the Gospel of Mark," *JAAR* 50 (1982): 411–34 (see *Literary Criticism and the Gospels: The Theoretical Challenge* [New Haven/London: Yale University Press, 1989] 7). The degree to which this term has become standard is reflected in the 1990 volume by Mark Allan Powell, *What is Narrative Criticism?* (Minneapolis: Fortress Press, 1990).

[102]For general discussions of literary criticism and the New Testament see William A. Beardslee, *Literary Criticism of the New Testament* (Philadelphia: Fortress, 1969); Norman Petersen, *Literary Criticism for New Testament Critics* (Philadelphia: Fortress, 1978); Moore, *Literary Criticism*; and Powell, *What is Narrative Criticism?*

[103]Mark W. G. Stibbe, ed. *The Gospel of John as Literature: An Anthology of Twentieth Century Perspectives* (Leiden: E.J. Brill, 1993).

[104]F. R. M. Hitchcock, *A Fresh Study of the Fourth Gospel* (London: SPCK, 1911). Cf. also "Is the Fourth Gospel a Drama?" *Theology* 7 (1923): 307–17; reprinted in Stibbe, *John as Literature*,15–24.

[105]Hans Windisch, "Der Johanneische Erzählungsstil," *Eucharisterion: Studien zur Religion und Literature des Alten und Neuen Testaments, Festschrift für H. Gunkel* , 2 vols. (Göttingen: Vandenhoeck and Ruprecht, 1923) 174–213. Translated and reprinted in Stibbe, *The Gospel of John*, 23–64. Since Hitchcock and Windisch the idea of the Gospel as "drama" has been discussed numerous times. Cf.

the literary characteristics of the Fourth Gospel caught the attention of James Muilenburg. In his words, the "dramatic element obtrudes itself so obviously" in the Fourth Gospel that "the chief end of analysis should be perception of the literary unity in which one gains a sense of form, a central purpose, and if possible, the occasion which inspired the narrative."[106]

To be sure, this early attention to the literary character and unity of the Gospel of John was in the minority compared to the rest of Johannine scholarship at this time. Indeed, following the publication of Bultmann's commentary and the interest in source and redaction criticism it generated, attention to the literary aspects of John diminished.[107] It was not until the new literary criticism of the Bible emerged in the late 1960's and the 1970's that interest in the Gospel's literary features resumed. One of the earliest studies during this time was a 1970 dissertation by David Wead, which explored devices employed by the Fourth Evangelist such as point of view, double meanings, irony and metaphor.[108] Similarly, a 1973 essay by G. W. MacRae studied the use of irony, specifically in relation to Johannine theology.[109]

Other important work generated in the early 1970's was not explicitly designated "literary critical" but nevertheless drew on literary observations. For instance, Martyn's *History and Theology in the Fourth Gospel*, though primarily interested in identifying the historical situation of the Johannine community, gives detailed attention to the

---

C. Bowen, "The Fourth Gospel as Dramatic Material," *JBL* 49 (1930): 292–305; C. M. Connick, "The Dramatic Character of the Fourth Gospel," *JBL* 67 (1948): 159–169; E. K. Keck, "The Drama of the Fourth Gospel," *ExpTim* 65 (1953): 173–176; E. L. Pierce, "The Fourth Gospel as Drama," *RelLi* 29 (1960): 453–455; N. Flanagan, "The Gospel of John as Drama," *BibT* 19 (1981): 264–270; L. Schenke, *Das Johannesevangelium: Einführung-Text-dramatische Gestalt*, Urban-Taschenbücher 446 (Stuttgart: Kohlhamner, 1992).

[106]James Muilenburg, "Literary Form in the Fourth Gospel," *JBL 51* (1932): 42. Reprinted in Stibbe, 65–76.

[107]Stibbe, *John as Literature*, 6–7.

[108]David W. Wead, *Literary Devices in John's Gospel*, Theologischen Dissertationen 4 (Basel: Friedrich Reinhart Kommissionsverlag, 1970). Cf. also, "Johannine Irony as a Key to the Author-Audience Relationship in John's Gospel," in *AAR Biblical Literature: 1974*, Complied by Fred O. Francis (Missoula: Scholars Press, 1974) 33–50.

[109]G. W. MacRae, "Theology and Irony in the Fourth Gospel," in *The Word in the World: Essays in honour of F. K. Moriarty*, ed. F. J. Clifford and G. W. MacRae (Cambridge, MA: Weston College, 1973) 83–96.

Gospel's dramatic conventions.[110] Wayne Meeks's highly influential study on the ascent/descent motif in the Gospel involves an analysis of the way symbolic language functions in the text, and includes a discussion of the characterization of Jesus and Nicodemus.[111] In this way, although Meeks comes to sociological conclusions, his thesis emerges out of literary critical observations.

In a similar manner, the work of Marinus de Jonge should also be mentioned. In 1977, de Jonge gathered eight essays, which he had written during the previous decade, under the title, *Jesus: Stranger From Heaven and Son of God*.[112] While de Jonge does not claim a literary critical approach, his presuppositions are aligned with the literary method that would be more fully developed in the 1980's and 1990's. In the preface to his collection he writes,

> Behind these studies lies the assumption that the Fourth Gospel is a meaningful whole, highly complicated in structure with many paradoxes and many tensions in thought and syntax, but yet asking to be taken seriously as a (more or less finished) literary product in which consistent lines of thought can be detected....(M)uch emphasis is laid on the composition and structure of the Fourth Gospel as a whole, and the separate narratives and discourses are treated as literary units within the framework of the Gospel. Great caution is exercised in drawing conclusions regarding earlier stages of redaction, sources or for that matter, the historical circumstances reflected in the Gospel....[113]

Thus, as with the early literary observations of Hitchcock and Windisch, emphasis is once more placed on the unity of the text, rather than on its fragmentation. Yet there is a fundamental difference between the earlier and more recent literary critical work. Hitchcock's interest in preserving the unity of the text was motivated by a primary concern to prove its apostolic authorship. In contrast, the literary critical work that

---

[110]Martyn, *History and Theology*, 24–36.

[111]Meeks, "The Son of Man" *JBL* 91 (1972): 44-72.

[112]Marinus de Jonge, *Jesus: Stranger from Heaven and Son of God* (Missoula: Scholars Press, 1977).

[113]*Jesus*, vii–viii. de Jonge sees his method as a "consistently redaction-critical approach," i.e., one that is highly skeptical of source critical theories. That he is moving beyond a purely redaction-critical approach is reflected in the fact that he treats "both supposedly redactional and supposedly traditional elements...as integral parts of a new literary entity, which has to be studied on its own, because it functioned as a whole among people who did not take its prehistory into account" (197–198).

emerged in the 70's was influenced by New Criticism, a movement in secular literary studies whose focus was explicitly away from the author. It is the influence of this movement, along with work in structuralism and narratology that is reflected in the most recent literary critical work on the New Testament.

R. Alan Culpepper was the first to undertake a thoroughgoing analysis of the Gospel based on the recent developments in literary theory.[114] In describing the basic principles of literary criticism in contrast to historical criticism, Culpepper evokes the frequently used metaphor of the text as "mirror" rather than text as "window."[115] For the historical critic, the Gospel has been used as a window through which the critic can catch "glimpses" of the history of the Johannine community. From this perspective, meaning lies behind or outside of the text itself. Literary criticism, on the other hand, attempts to read the text as a "mirror." That is to say that meaning is found in what is reflected back from the text to the reader in the experience of reading the text as a whole. The metaphor of mirror further suggests that the primary purpose of the Gospel narrative is to reflect back to the readers the world created by the text that challenges their perception of the "real" world.[116] In short, this method of interpretation emphasizes the text as it stands, rather than its sources or historical background. The key here is emphasis. A literary approach is not inherently or necessarily ahistorical.

---

[114]R. Alan Culpepper, *The Anatomy of the Fourth Gospel: A Study in Literary Design* (Philadelphia: Fortress, 1983). Culpepper's work will be discussed more fully below.

[115]The images are drawn from Murray Krieger, *A Window to Criticism: Shakespeare's Sonnets and Modern Poetics* (Princeton, NJ: Princeton University Press, 1964). Cf. also Petersen, *Literary Criticism,* 24–28; Powell, *What is Narrative Criticism?* 8; Elizabeth Struthers Malbon, "Texts and Contexts: Interpreting the Disciples in Mark," *Semeia* 62 (1993): 82.

[116]Culpepper, *Anatomy,* 4–5. The idea of "text as mirror" has drawn criticism from both ends of the interpretive spectrum. In the introductory essay to his edited volume, *The Interpretation of John* (Philadelphia: Fortress Press, 1986), John Ashton regards the simile as infelicitous, "except for readers whose only purpose in looking at the text is to see their own image staring back at them" (15). Similarly, Stephen Moore (" 'Mirror, Mirror...' Lacanian Reflections on Malbon's Mark," *Semeia* 62 [1993]: 165–171) states, "When the interpreter looks to the text as a mirror, she also necessarily sees herself. As such, the more unity and coherence she is able to find in the text, the more gratifying and reassuring will be the reflection she receives back from it" (168). As a decontructionist, the desire for unity in a text is even more problematic for Moore than the dissecting tendencies of historical criticism (cf. *Literary Criticism and the Gospels*).

Its focus and questions are different from those of historical criticism, but it does not categorically deny the historical realities of the Gospel text. Instead, Culpepper, along with other biblical literary critics, argues that the literary approach should be a first step, and that "once an effort has been made to understand the narrative character of the gospels, some rapprochement with the traditional, historical issues will be necessary."[117]

With *Anatomy*, Culpepper concentrates on the first step. He sets out to understand the Gospel as a narrative text, "what it is, and how it works."[118] In developing his approach, he draws on a wide range of literary critics, though his primary theoretical model is derived from Seymour Chatman.[119] To that end, he analyzes the point of view of the Johannine narrator, the Gospel's narrative time, as well as its plot, characters, implicit commentary (i.e., misunderstanding, irony, and symbolism) and its implied reader. As the title suggests, Culpepper's work is limited for the most part to naming and describing the various narrative parts of the Gospel of John. Nevertheless, his accomplishment is significant in that he is able to show that a narrative analysis cannot only be sustained throughout the Gospel, but also opens the way to new understandings of the text.

Indeed, since Culpepper's work, there have been several studies that have successfully used literary categories to analyze the Fourth Gospel. Paul Duke has built on *Anatomy* by focusing on the function of a single literary device in John, that of irony.[120] Gail O'Day has worked with irony in the Fourth Gospel as well, demonstrating how, as part of the narrative form of John, it is integral to the mode the Gospel uses to convey its theology.[121] Also in conversation with Culpepper, is Jeffrey Staley, though he draws on reader response criticism rather than

---

[117]Culpepper, *Anatomy*, 11. Likewise, Malbon makes clear that she believes that it is necessary to view the text as both window and mirror for the interpretive task to be fully carried out ("Texts and Contexts," 82, nt. 3).

[118]Culpepper, *Anatomy*, 5.

[119]Seymour Chatman, *Story and Discourse: Narrative Structure in Fiction and Film* (Ithaca: Cornell University Press, 1978). Cf. Culpepper, *Anatomy*, 6. Other literary critics frequently cited by Culpepper include Genette Gerard, Wolfgang Iser, Robert Scholes and Robert Kellogg, Northrop Frye and Wayne Booth.

[120]Paul Duke, *Irony in the Fourth Gospel* (Atlanta: John Knox Press, 1985).

[121]Gail R. O'Day, *Revelation in the Fourth Gospel: Narrative Mode and Theological Claim* (Philadelphia: Fortress Press, 1986).

narratology for his critical method.[122] More recently, Mark Stibbe has produced what he describes as an integrative work on the Fourth Gospel, which seeks to combine literary, sociological and historical approaches in an analysis of John 18–19.[123] What all four of these studies demonstrate is the fruitful yield that can be produced through literary approaches to the Fourth Gospel. A literary critical perspective will inform the present study, with particular attention to characterization. The significant work that has already been done in this area will undergird my own analysis of Johannine characters. In what follows, I will review only those studies that focus on Johannine characterization in general. Theoretical discussions of biblical characterization will be taken up in the next chapter and studies of individual Johannine characters will be reserved for chapter three.

PERSPECTIVES ON THE JOHANNINE CHARACTER

The unique quality of Fourth Gospel characters appears to have been noted from very early in the history of interpretation. For example, though it is likely that most pre-critical readings of the Fourth Gospel understood its characters as historical figures, there is evidence as early as the third century that they were also perceived symbolically.[124] For instance, Origen's method of interpretation allowed room for both a literal and a symbolic reading of the text, including the characters in the narrative. So for example, in the case of the mother of Jesus, he already gives indication of perceiving her as the spiritual mother of all believers.[125] Similarly, from Ephraem the Syrian and Ambrose come

---

[122]Jeffrey Lloyd Staley, *The Print's First Kiss: A Rhetorical Investigation of the Implied Reader in the Fourth Gospel*, SBLDS 82 (Atlanta: Scholars Press, 1988).

[123]Stibbe, *John as Storyteller: Narrative Criticism and the Fourth Gospel* (Cambridge: Cambridge University Press, 1992).

[124]Cf. Raymond Collins, "The Representative Figures of the Fourth Gospel," *Downside Review* 94 (1976): 26–46; 95 (1976): 118–32. Reprinted in *These Things Have Been Written: Studies on the Fourth Gospel.* Louvain Theological & Pastoral Monographs 2 (Grand Rapids: Eerdmans, 1991) 1–45. One should note that the two views are not mutually exclusive. It is possible to regard the characters as historical figures whom the author, in order to drive home a point, has presented in a particular way.

[125]In Origen's words, no one can understand the Gospel of John, "who has not leaned on Jesus' breast nor received Mary from Jesus to be his mother also" (*Commentary on the Gospel According to John*, Books 1–10 [Washington DC: Catholic University Press of America, 1989] 1.23). Cited in Collins, "Mary in the Fourth Gospel," 107–108.

interpretations of Mary as symbolic of the Church.[126] According to Collins, this type of symbolic interpretation persisted in the scholasticism of the Middle Ages, for example, in the writings of Ruppert of Deutz.[127] Much later, in the twentieth century, Bultmann put forth his own highly symbolic interpretations of such figures as the Beloved Disciple and Peter.[128]

More recently, Raymond Collins has taken up the symbolic aspect of the Johannine characters in a different way. In "The Representative Figures of the Fourth Gospel," Collins explores the nature of the Gospel's individual characters and what they suggest about the background and history of the text.[129] Indeed, Collins believes that the individualism of the Gospel is the key to its interpretation because it provides "a basic insight into the meaning of the Gospel, the tradition that lay behind it, and the purpose for which it was compiled."[130]

According to Collins, the Evangelist drew on traditional homiletic Johannine material in which various individuals appear as illustrative types. In his words, "The evangelist and final redactor would have compiled these several units of traditional Johannine homiletic material into his Gospel where they remain as types which can serve to support the basic theme of his Gospel."[131] Thus what now appears in John's Gospel are representative figures who stand for a particular trait or characteristic, especially in relation to Jesus. Collins reviews fifteen of these figures who "appear to have been definitely type-cast by the

---

[126] Cf. Collins, "Mary in the Fourth Gospel," 107-108.

[127] Collins, "Representative Figures," 2.

[128] Bultmann contends that the Beloved Disciple represents Gentile Christendom, while Peter, as well as Jesus' mother, stand for Jewish Christendom (484–485, 685).

[129] See nt. 124 above.

[130] Collins, "Representative Figures," 4. Collins is here responding to an earlier article by C. F. D. Moule ("The Individualism of the Fourth Gospel," NovT 5 [1962]: 171–190). Moule notes that the Fourth Gospel is full of encounters between Jesus alone with an individual or with small groups and that "throughout the Fourth Gospel, it is the individual who is in question" (182). His thesis is that this individualism determines the Gospel's realized eschatology. Collins suggests that the importance of the Gospel's individualism lies elsewhere, as indicated by the quotation above.

[131] Collins, "Representative Figures," 6. For the fullest development of the homiletic provenance theory see Barnabus Lindars, Behind the Fourth Gospel (London: SPCK, 1971) 43–60 and The Gospel of John (New Century Bible; London: Oliphants, 1972) 51–54. Brown also views oral preaching and teaching as a decisive stage in the organization of Johannine traditions into the Gospel form (xxxiv-xxxv). Similarly, cf. Schnackenburg, 1.73.

evangelist so that he might teach his readers about salvific faith and thereby enkindle and confirm that faith within them."[132]

Although Collins' interest in the subject is historical in nature, his focus on the individual characters in the Gospel contributes much to our understanding of Johannine characterization in general. Most critics of the Gospel now agree that many of its characters have a representative role, serving as examples of the various ways one might respond to Jesus. Among these is Culpepper, who, following Collins, has done the most extensive work to date on Johannine characterization.[133]

Similar to Collins, Culpepper finds that the characters "represent a continuum of responses to Jesus which exemplify misunderstandings the reader may share and responses one might make to the depiction of Jesus in the Gospel."[134] He summarizes these responses as follows: rejection (the Jews), acceptance without open commitment (Joseph of Arimathea, Nicodemus), acceptance of Jesus as a worker of signs and wonders (disciples who cease to follow Jesus, lame man), belief in Jesus' words (Samaritan woman, royal official, blind man), commitment in spite of misunderstandings (disciples), paradigmatic discipleship (Beloved Disciple), and defection (Judas).[135]

What is new in Culpepper's discussion is his attention to character as a literary element. In other words, unlike Collins, he is not interested in what the characters reveal about the history of the text. Instead, he wants to know how they function in the narrative. For this reason, he looks to contemporary literary theory to help understand Fourth Gospel characterization.[136] While he begins with observations

---

[132]Collins, "Representative Figures," 8. In this sense, Collins understands the importance of the reader in relation to the text, though because he is more focused on the intention of the Evangelist, one would not view his work as reader response theory. Examples of Collins's brief character studies include John the Baptist, representing the confessing Christian who bears witness to Jesus; Nicodemus, who, as the leading man among "the Jews" represents unbelief; Mary Magdalene, representing the believer who has faith in Jesus as the ascending one, but only because of the revelation of Jesus himself; and the Beloved disciple, who "typifies the disciple of Jesus *par excellence*."

[133]The fifth chapter of *Anatomy* is devoted to the characters of the Fourth Gospel (99–148).

[134]Culpepper, *Anatomy*, 104.

[135]Culpepper, *Anatomy*, 146–148.

[136]In doing so, Culpepper recognizes that some might question the legitimacy of applying theories designed for fictional characters in novels to the people described in an historical writing composed from oral traditions. His response is that he is interested in

from E. M. Forster's classic work on the novel,[137] his later discussion of three types of characters—protagonist, intermediate characters and background characters—is most pertinent for my interests. Drawing on W. J. Harvey, Culpepper explains that protagonists are the central characters and

> vehicles by which all the most interesting questions are raised; they evoke our beliefs, sympathies, revulsions; they incarnate the moral vision of the world inherent in the total novel. In a sense they are what the novel exists for; it exists to reveal them.[138]

If we consider Jesus as the protagonist of the Fourth Gospel, this statement demonstrates just how appropriate contemporary theory can be in relation to the Gospel. Even more important, though, is Culpepper's discussion of the function of the intermediate characters in the Gospel, or "ficelles," as he refers to them.[139]

Ficelles are "typical characters easily recognizable by the readers." While more developed than background figures, they exist primarily to serve some function in the narrative. They often reveal the protagonist, "and may carry a great deal of representative or symbolic value." Seeing the minor characters in this way, Culpepper contends, helps one to understand the "literary architecture of the gospel." He goes on to say,

> Progressively, in one episode after another, the author sketches his vision of the world, but in the process the vision "decomposes and splits into various attributes which then form the structure of

---

characterization as the art and techniques by which an author fashions a convincing portrait of a person within a more or less unified piece of writing. Even if one is disposed to see real, historical persons behind every character in John...the question of how the author chose to portray the person still arises. With what techniques or devices has he made a living person live on paper, and how is this 'person' related to the rest of narrative? (*Anatomy*, 105).

[137]Culpepper discusses three ideas from Forster's *Aspects of the Novel* (New York: Penguin Books, 1962). He cites Forster's well-known distinction between flat and round characters, his observation about the transparency of characters that distinguishes them from real people, and his distinction between "life by values," in which life is dictated by crisis moments and "life by time," in which life is controlled more by chronological succession (*Anatomy*, 102–103). Especially the first two points will be taken up in the theoretical discussion in chapter two.

[138]W. J. Harvey, *Character and the Novel* (Ithaca, NY: Cornell University Press, 1966; London: Chatto & Windus, 1965) 56. Quoted in Culpepper, 103–104.

[139]The term is borrowed from Harvey, *Character and the Novel*, 58, 62–68, who in turn attributes it to Henry James.

disparate characters." Instead of isolated units, the reader finds that the characters are profoundly related.[140]

This observation about the relationship between the Gospel characters, despite their narrative isolation from one another, is crucial to the theory of characterization that will form the basis for my own approach. The next chapter will develop this relational aspect of character more fully, drawing especially on the work of Baruch Hochman.

In a more recent study, Craig Koester also explores the nature of character in the Gospel of John.[141] Since he approaches the subject within the framework of the Gospel's symbolism, it is not surprising that he also discusses the characters in terms of their representative or symbolic role in the Gospel. Unlike Culpepper, however, Koester relies on an understanding of character portrayal in antiquity to understand the Evangelist's use of character rather than on contemporary literary theories.[142] For instance, Koester notes that the *dramatis personae* in Greek tragedies were understood by the audience to be real people, but they nevertheless functioned as types as well. Their responses to a given situation conveyed some general truth to the audience. Koester suggests that the same is also true of the Gospel of John. Individual characters are presented as types and their various responses to Jesus serve as character indicators. In addition, Johannine characters often communicate a general truth about a group of people or about the human condition.[143] Thus, Koester lends his voice in support of the representative understanding of Johannine characters, albeit from another theoretical perspective.

At the same time, Koester maintains that Johannine characters are portrayed as individuals with unique traits. He observes, "Their

---

[140]Culpepper, *Anatomy*, 104. The quotation is from Harvey, *Character in the Novel*, 124.

[141]Craig R. Koester, *Symbolism in the Fourth Gospel: Meaning, Mystery, Community* (Minneapolis: Fortress, 1995) 32–39.

[142]Note that Culpepper's discussion is not without reference to ancient modes of characterization. He begins with a brief review of Aristotle's discussion of character (101). Later he cites the distinction made by Robert Scholes and Robert Kellogg between the flat, static heroes of ancient Greek narrative and the evolving characters of the Old Testament (cf. *The Nature of Narrative* [New York: Oxford University Press, 1966] 123). In Culpepper's view "the Gospel of John draws from both Greek and Hebrew models of character development, but most of its characters appear to represent particular ethical types" (103).

[143]Koester, *Symbolism*, 36–37.

representative roles do not negate their individuality but actually develop out their most distinctive traits.[144] With this observation, Koester points to the fact that Johannine characters may function for the reader in more than one way. They may indeed play a representative role, standing for a particular response to Jesus from a particular group of people. But their characterization may also allow them to emerge as individuals in the mind of the reader, with some degree of autonomy in the narrative. This dual aspect of some of the Johannine characters will be discussed further in the next chapter.

CONCLUSION

As can be seen from the above review, previous studies on women in the Fourth Gospel and on Johannine characterization have gone a long way in laying the groundwork for a more in-depth study on the subject. Studies on women in the Gospel have made significant individual contributions, but perhaps more importantly, the cumulative effect of these works makes it apparent that women characters are of fundamental significance in the Gospel. Studies on Johannine characterization have also been fruitful, suggesting ways in which the Gospel's characters play a crucial role in communicating its meaning. The goal of the present study is to bring together both of these areas of investigation, pushing beyond them in a number of ways.

First, as has been discussed, the studies on women have been limited in large part to an assessment of their role in a reconstructed Johannine community, to the degree that at times the characters of the Gospel are read only as representatives of some real figures behind the text. It would seem that in an effort to correct the long-standing assumption that John is a "spiritual gospel,"[145] historical critics have swung too far in the direction of once more reading John as an accurate account of a historical situation. Granted, the Gospel is no longer viewed as the story of the historical Jesus, but the certainty that is now granted the historical Johannine community may be just as problematic. Regarding the study of female characters, this approach has focused more on their role in the community than on their significance to the narrative of the Gospel. In light of this, the present study will engage in a literary approach to the text.

---

[144]Koester, *Symbolism*, 35.

[145]So designated by Clement of Alexandria, according to Eusebius, *Ecclesiastical History*, VI.14.7

For the purposes of this study, employing a literary approach will mean that answers concerning the role of women in the Gospel will be sought internally. In other words, whether there were women leaders in a so-called Johannine community, it is certainly true that women characters play a major role in the narrative of the Fourth Gospel. A literary critique that includes gender as a category of analysis may provide an answer as to the nature of their significance.

This brings me to a second way in which this dissertation will move beyond earlier studies. As might be expected, given the topic, the previous studies have focused almost exclusively on women characters. While rightly highlighting the importance of women characters, these studies have made little attempt to understand their significance in relation to male characters in the Gospel. It is not until this full perspective is taken into account that the role of female (and male) characters in the narrative can be fully grasped. For this reason it will be necessary to introduce gender as an analytic category. This category will be defined more fully in the next chapter, but suffice it to say at this point that gender analysis does not simply equal the study of women. Instead, the term gender signifies, among other things, the relational aspect of the categories "male" and "female." As an analytic category, gender calls for the recognition and interpretation of this relationship.

Finally, for the purposes of this study, gender will come into discussion specifically within the framework of a study of Johannine characterization. The consideration of character brings me to an additional way that this study will move beyond previous studies. Earlier studies on Johannine characterization have in large part restricted analysis to determining what each character "represents" in the Gospel. As we have seen, this has been answered in terms of various responses to Jesus, and/or in terms of recognizable roles in the Johannine community. I suggest this approach is too limiting; Johannine characters are not only representative figures, but also characters in their own right, contributing in multiple ways to the Gospel narrative. In chapter two, I offer a more nuanced consideration of Johannine characters, one that is more in keeping with their presentation and function in the Gospel, and one that readily enables the incorporation of gender as an analytic category.

Chapter Two
Character, Gender, and the Fourth Gospel

INTRODUCTION

Before I am able to analyze the presentation of women and men in the Gospel, it is necessary to explore what theory of character and characterization best suits the Fourth Gospel. As we have seen, previous discussions of characterization in the Fourth Gospel have stressed the typical nature of Johannine characters. According to Culpepper, apart from Jesus, Johannine characters are primarily functional. They illustrate a particular way of responding to Jesus, and in so doing serve a specific purpose in the narrative. However, if one takes seriously the way readers respond to these characters, this conclusion is presents problems. For one thing, there is not always agreement as to what these characters are intended to represent, or even whether a particular character should be viewed positively or negatively. As our discussion in chapter three will demonstrate, characters such as Nicodemus, Peter and Martha have been seen in varying degrees as faithful followers of Jesus or as hopelessly misguided. This range of interpretation does not coincide well with the standard view of a flat character. Given this, we would do well to revisit the question of Fourth Gospel characterization, seeking a better explanation for how to understand character in the Gospel. In doing so, we must work through two major issues: the debate over the mimetic versus functional understanding of character and E. M. Forster's classification of characters as either flat or round. Following this discussion, it will also be necessary to consider techniques of characterization that are particular to biblical texts. Recognition of these techniques will strengthen the analysis of Johannine characters and characterization.

CHARACTERIZATION IN CONTEMPORARY LITERARY THEORY AND THE FOURTH GOSPEL

Johannine Characters: Mimetic or Functional?

The classic debate concerning literary characters is whether they are best understood as mimetic representations or as plot functionaries.[1] The older mimetic view, associated primarily with the Romantics of the nineteenth century, saw characters as more or less autonomous beings who possessed motives, values, and personality, all of which were open to analysis by the critic. As Hochman puts it, "Enchanted with the impression of life that certain characters in literature gave, the Romantics and post-Romantics often spoke of these figures as though they had really lived, and critics felt free to discuss dimensions of the character's experience that went well beyond the boundaries of the works in which they appeared."[2] In short, characters were treated like real people. This is not to say that characters were thought to correspond to actual people outside of the text, but rather, in the imagination of the reader, characters took on a life of their own. In this sense, characters existed apart from the text that generated them.

In the history of literary criticism, this mimetic understanding of character came under attack from several opponents, including the British Modernists, the American New Critics, the Russian Formalists and the French structuralists. For the Modernists and New Critics, meaning resided in the formal aspects of the work, in particular in the imagery of the text. This meant that forays into biographical details or psychological analyses of characters, not to mention of the author of the text, was considered an absurd undertaking. As Hochman puts it, these critics "recoiled from the tendency to confuse literature and life—to

---

[1]The dichotomy is discussed by Chatman (*Story and Discourse*, 109–119) and picked up by Baruch Hochman, *Character in Literature*, (Ithaca: Cornell University Press, 1985) 13–27, (cf. also Culpepper, *Anatomy*, 101–102). There are of course, other ways of thinking about character that do not fit neatly on one or the other side of this polarity. For example, in a more nuanced way, Rawdon Wilson, ("The Bright Chimera: Character as a Literary Term," *Critical Inquiry* 7 [1979] 750) presents four distinct views of character: "(1)...characters are products of the author's mind—memories, encapsulations of his experience or else (one might say) split-off slivers of his mind or self; (2)...characters are functions of the text in which they appear—embodiments of the theme and idea—to be considered much as tokens, pieces or counters in a game; (3)... characters are entirely artificial constructs to be analyzed in terms of the compositional techniques that have gone into their making; (4) ...characters are, for the purposes of critical reading, to be considered *as if* they were actual persons, and the emphasis in criticism...is to discuss the response they engender in an intelligent reader."

[2]Hochman, *Character in Literature*, 16.

contaminate the pristine quality of the literary artifact with the muck and moil of life."[3]

The Russian formalists and French structuralists were similarly ill disposed toward treating characters as anything close to mimetic figures.[4] They developed a deliberately mechanistic view of literature that focused on the structure and function of a literary work. Content was a concern only insofar as it was understood as a literary device through which a particular effect was achieved. Similarly, character was understood as a device that carried forth the action of the story; it was thus subordinated to plot. Moreover, this view of character again suggested that contemplating characters in and of themselves was a misguided endeavor.[5]

If we consider Johannine characters in terms of this debate, the distinction between mimetic and functional characters leads to confusion. First, previous understandings of Johannine characters do not fit neatly into either category. As we have seen, characters in the Fourth Gospel have been interpreted as representative, but "representative" in the Johannine context means something other than either mimetic or functional. The point of Collins's and Culpepper's discussion is not that Johannine characters are "lifelike" but that they represent various responses to Jesus. Culpepper quite pointedly argues that one cannot consider Johannine characters as autonomous beings to any extent. He suggests that given the limited presentation of most Johannine characters "one is almost forced to consider the characters in terms of their commission, plot functions, and representational value."[6] Clearly, for Culpepper, the representative nature of Johannine characters suggests that they are more functional than mimetic.

If we think of the trend to view Johannine women characters as representing "real" women in the Johannine community, one might wonder whether this suggests a mimetic understanding of character. However, this move toward a historical background is again something

---

[3]Hochman, *Character in Literature*, 17. The most well known representatives of these movements include Ezra Pound, T. S. Elliot, Cleanth Brooks, W. K. Wimsatt and Monroe Beardsley.

[4]Representatives include Roman Jakobsen, Vladimir Propp, Tzvetan Todorov, Roland Barthes, Algirdas Greimas, and Claude Bremond.

[5]Cf. Hochman, *Character in Literature*, 21. Cf. also William H. Shepherd, Jr. *The Narrative Function of the Holy Spirit as a Character in Luke-Acts* (SBLDS 147; Atlanta: Scholars Press, 1994) 51–67.

[6]Culpepper, *Anatomy*, 102, my emphasis.

different from a mimetic view of character. A mimetic view does not contend that a character represents a real person, but that literary characters evoke responses in readers as if they were real people. In other words, there is no sense of looking behind characters for the real people they represent, the characters themselves appear real.

If we consider Johannine characters apart from the traditional "representative" interpretation, the mimetic versus functional debate remains problematic. It soon becomes clear that taken alone neither alternative adequately describes the characters in the narrative; nor is it enough to define some characters as functional and others as mimetic.[7] To be sure, there are certain Johannine characters who appear to function solely for the advancement of the plot. John the Baptist is one such character—his one and only purpose in the Gospel is to point to Jesus. The fact that some form of witnessing appears eleven times in reference to him is striking evidence of this notion (1:7–8, 15, 19, 32; 3:26; 5:32–33). Moreover, the Gospel contains no physical description of the Baptist, as in Mark 1:6, and no account of Jesus' baptism, as in the Synoptics (Mk 1:9; Mt 3:13f; Lk 3:21).[8] As a witness, John never even speaks directly with Jesus, only about him.[9]

In keeping with John's function as witness is his gradual diminution and eventual disappearance as a character.[10] His introduction as a witness sent from God includes a negation—οὐκ ἦν ἐκεῖνος τὸ φῶς (1:6). Additionally, as witness, John's first words emphasize Jesus' rank—Jesus was "before" (πρῶτος) him (1:15). The verb used to describe John's speech (κέκραγεν) points ahead to his self-identification as simply a voice crying in the desert (1:23). Likewise, John's positive identification of Jesus as the Lamb of God and the Son of God (1:29–34) is prefaced by the negation of his own identity. He is neither the

---

[7]This is David Galef's approach. He categorizes minor characters as either structural types, which perform an active job in the unfolding of the narrative, or mimetic types, which come under the heading of verisimilitude. He also acknowledges that overlaps are possible and that "a skilled author combines types" (*The Supporting Cast: A Study of Flat and Minor Characters* [University Park, PA: Pennsylvania State University Press, 1993] 16).

[8]In this regard, note that the title "John the Baptist" never appears in the Fourth Gospel as it does in Mark 6:14 and Mt 14:2. Moreover, in the Fourth Gospel, there is no mention of a baptism for the repentance of sins. John's baptizing activity is defined strictly in terms relating directly to Jesus—he baptizes in order that Jesus may be revealed to Israel (1:31).

[9]Ernst Haenchen, *A Commentary on the Gospel of John* (Hermeneia, 2 vols.; Philadelphia: Fortress, 1984) 152. German original, *Das Johannesevangelium* (Tübingen: Mohr, 1980).

[10]There is no mention of John's execution in the Fourth Gospel, although there is one reference to his arrest (3:22). Instead, the last two references to John occur in the past tense and are attestations by other characters confirming the truth of his testimony (5:33–35; 10:41).

Christ, nor Elijah, nor the prophet, but only a voice (1:20–23).[11] Later, John makes his relationship to Jesus even more clear, "it is necessary for that one to increase, but me to decrease" (3:30). Thus, one could argue that in the Fourth Gospel, John is the quintessential plot functionary; he contributes to the plot as witness to Jesus, but apart from this role he would be nothing. As far as his character is concerned, the functionalist theory seems to fit very well.

However, if we consider another Johannine character who also testifies to others about Jesus, the situation is not so clear. Like John, the Samaritan woman functions in the narrative as a witness, one who leads her Samaritan villagers to Jesus. Unlike John however, she is not even given a proper name beyond the designation γυνὴ ἐκ τῆς Σαμαρείας. One might justifiably conclude that she, too, exists only to advance the plot. Yet, in the course of the narrative, this woman becomes a very "real" character. She takes on a personality with identifiable traits (e.g., boldness and curiosity), and an unpredictable quality that makes her come alive in a way that John the Baptist never does. Like a more rounded character she is capable of surprising the reader with her responses to Jesus.[12] Thus, she has a certain mimetic aspect in additional to her functional quality.

The example of the Samaritan woman suggests that in the Fourth Gospel, the mimetic and the functional views of character may not be mutually exclusive. Indeed, to account fully for the presentation of Johannine characters, we need a theory of character that includes aspects of both theories. Fortunately, some literary critics have seen the inadequacy of the mimetic/functional dichotomy and have sought a theory of characters and characterization somewhere in-between.

Seymour Chatman's understanding of character, for example, draws on the strengths of both the mimetic and the functional views, resulting in what he calls an "open structuralist theory."[13] First, he argues that treating characters as mere plot functionaries is too limiting. It fails to recognize that readers are interested in more than just a

---

[11]C. K. Barrett, *The Gospel According to St. John*, 2d ed. (Philadelphia: Westminster Press, 1978) 173. Along these lines, Thomas L. Brodie notes that even in John's dialogue one hears the "faint evoking of a process of self-emptying." In responding to the priests and Levites, John moves from "I am not the Christ," to "I am not," to the monosyllabic "no" (*The Gospel According to John* [New York/Oxford: Oxford University Press, 1993] 150).

[12]See below for a discussion of flat and round characters.

[13]Seymour Chatman, *Story and Discourse: Narrative Structure in Fiction and Film* (Ithaca: Cornell University Press, 1978).

character's role, at times appreciating character traits for their own sake. Therefore, Chatman believes that characters should be regarded as autonomous beings who are "subject to further speculations and enrichment, visions and revisions" on the part of the reader—hence the "open" element in his theory.[14] Applied to the Fourth Gospel, the Samaritan woman, for example, has been celebrated for her courage and tenacity, quite apart from the fact that she advances the plot in her role as witness.

On the other side, the "structuralist" element in Chatman's theory keeps this interpretive activity within the bounds of the narrative.[15] A reader perceives "what a character is like" through information gleaned from the narrative itself. Chatman argues that a character is actually a paradigm of traits, where trait is understood as "a relatively stable or abiding personal quality" that unfolds in the course of a narrative.[16] At a given encounter with a character in the narrative, the reader has available the entire set of traits that has been established for that character thus far. The reader sorts through the paradigm, either locating the trait that accounts for the character's action, or adding another trait to the list.

Structurally speaking, it is this paradigm that enables a character to take on an existence apart from its immediate context. In metaphorical terms, Chatman sees the paradigm of traits as a "vertical assemblage intersecting the syntagmatic chain of events that comprise the plot."[17] In this formulation, character is not subordinate to plot, but resides in a separate dimension. This explains how a reader is able to remember a character, even when the text or language that generated it has long been forgotten.[18]

Chatman's commitment to a sense of openness, coupled with his strong sense of narrative structure, make his theory particularly appealing. He embraces the idea that characters often seem "real" to the

---

[14]Chatman, *Story and Discourse*, 119.

[15]Chatman's narrative structure consists of two main components, story (=content) and discourse (=expression), hence the title of his work. Characters, along with setting, are termed "existents." Coupled with "events," they comprise the basic elements of story. For a diagram of the entire structure see *Story and Discourse*, 26.

[16]Chatman, *Story and Discourse*, 126.

[17]Chatman, *Story and Discourse*, 127.

[18]In this sense, Culpepper is only partially correct when indicates that Chatman champions the mimetic approach to character. While it is certainly true that Chatman advocates a view of characters as autonomous beings, he does so within a structuralist understanding of the narrative (cf. *Anatomy*, 102).

reader, and understands the reader's inevitable exercise of speculation and inference about a character as a legitimate interpretive activity. At the same time, his insistence that this speculation is based on a text-generated paradigm of traits grounds this activity and holds it accountable to the text. To illustrate this paradigmatic view with a Johannine character, Martha could justifiably be perceived as a forthright, bold, and faithful woman, since these traits can be inferred from her conversation with Jesus (11:17–27). Imagined in this way, she may become "real" for the reader.[19] However, to go beyond the picture that these traits suggest and to speculate as to the precise nature and length of her relationship with Jesus, for instance, would be going too far. Baruch Hochman puts it this way,

> ...the degree of fidelity of reader to text in the apprehension of character varies widely with the reader. There is always, in reading as in life, the permanent option of loosing oneself from the present data and losing oneself in fantasy about the characters one harbors in one's head....But this mode of response clearly violates the traditional conception of responsible reading.[20]

In sum, Chatman's theory of character is helpful in understanding why even the relatively undeveloped characters in the Fourth Gospel may take on autonomous qualities. As readers, we respond to them much as we would to people in real life.

Baruch Hochman also offers an alternative to the mimetic/functional dichotomy and adds to the conversation an aspect of characterization that will prove especially helpful in analyzing Johannine characters. Hochman follows Chatman closely in the notion that characters should be thought of as autonomous beings. He argues even more strongly that the cues by which we apprehend character are the same in literature and real life; therefore, the same interpretive skills serve us in both domains. In Hochman's words, "we necessarily read Homo Fictus [character in literature] in terms of Homo Sapiens [people in life]."[21]

Also like Chatman, Hochman takes seriously the effect of the narrative structure on the presentation of character. He maintains that, in

---

[19]Indeed, in the imagination of some Christians, it was apparently these traits that led to the Medieval artistic portrayal of Martha as a dragon slayer. Cf. Elisabeth Moltmann-Wendal, *The Women Around Jesus* (New York: Crossroad, 1988) 39–48.

[20]Baruch Hochman, *Character in Literature*, (Ithaca: Cornell University Press, 1985) 41–42.

[21]Hochman, *Character in Literature*, 86.

spite of the similarity between Homo Fictus and Homo Sapiens, there is a distinction between the two. He points out that while we conceive of people in life and characters in literature in identical ways (thus explaining why characters often seem so lifelike), there is a structural organization to literature that is usually absent in real life. It is this point that interests me most for my analysis of the Gospel of John. In speaking of this structural organization, Hochman means more than simply the formal structure of a text, though he includes this element as well. He refers to the structures of substantive meanings which exist at many levels, from the text's underlying organizing fantasy to its thematic articulation. Although characters may be viewed independently, they must still be seen as part of the structure that generates and contains them.[22] Regarding the characters of the Fourth Gospel, this suggests that they must be viewed as more than a single trait, or even a paradigm of traits (Chatman's answer to the mimetic/functional dichotomy). Hochman's ideas suggest that a character analysis must take account of the character's place within the entire network of relationships that comprise the narrative.

Hochman also makes clear that this network includes relationships with other characters. He writes,

> Because characters subsist within a complicated, stable phantasmagoria, within a given literary work each character tends to enter into mutually stabilizing and mutually illuminating relationships with all of the other characters in the work and with the elements that both generate and illuminate the characters.[23]

For Hochman, these relationships reflect the notion that characters, as opposed to people in life, intrinsically mean something. That is to say, they are part of a larger configuration of meaning that the work as a whole articulates. For this reason, Hochman contends, "characters are rendered palpable not only by what we know of them in themselves and from their interactions with others but also by the play of analogous structures, in both the action and the allusive texture of the work."[24]

Hochman also takes account of the text's formal structure, and sees a relationship between characters here as well. In his words,

---

[22]Hochman, *Character in Literature*, 66–68.
[23]Hochman, *Character in Literature*, 65.
[24]Hochman, *Character in Literature*, 65.

> ...the organization of the whole text creates a space...within which the character subsists. Characters who stand at the center of a work...are ordinarily flanked by lesser characters, of lesser complexity, dynamism, and wholeness. Such flanking characters usually serve compositional as well as thematic purposes....[25]

Hochman's ideas suggest that character analysis must go beyond a mere listing of traits for each individual. Rather, it must take account of each individual's place within the entire network of relationships that comprise the narrative. Thus, while a particular character may emerge as a "real" person with a well-developed personality, he or she does so only in relationship to other characters, and only within the confines of the narrative structure.

If we think again of the Samaritan woman, it is only through her relationship to the character of Jesus that she is able to emerge as an autonomous character. Her questions and responses to him are what make her come alive. Moreover, it is only by perceiving this woman in relation to John the Baptist, as well as to other characters (e.g., Nicodemus) that the full extent of her autonomy becomes apparent. These relationships do not exist at the surface level of the text; the woman never John the Baptist or Nicodemus in the course of the narrative. Rather, their relationship exists at a deeper level, through the central character and central theme of the Gospel, Jesus. That is to say that as both character and thematic concept, Jesus is the linchpin that holds all the characters in the Gospel in relation both to himself and to one another. These relationships constitute a crucial aspect of the narrative since they are what define the characters and ultimately what brings meaning to the Gospel as a whole.

Together, the work of Chatman and Hochman raises a host of questions that will enrich our understanding of Johannine characterization. Rather than simply labeling the characters as functional or mimetic, we must ask in what ways do these characters relate to other structures or systems of meanings in the Gospel narrative? In particular for my interests, do certain patterns emerge in the ways in which men and women are linked to each other and to other elements in the narrative, for example, the Gospel's soteriology, its Christology, and its dualistic world view? What insights into the difference in presentation

---

[25]Hochman, *Character in Literature*, 68.

between women and men might be seen in and through these relationships?

Johannine Characters: Round or Flat?

There remains another aspect of characterization that needs to be addressed since it has become a standard part of any discussion of characterization, namely Forster's well known classification of characters as either round or flat. According to Forster, round characters are more complex, more fully developed characters who, like people in real life, are capable of surprising us. In contrast, flat characters are less developed and more predictable; they are caricatures that embody a single idea or quality.[26] Given this definition, the representative view of Johannine characters expressed by Collins and Culpepper would seemingly put these characters in the flat category. Indeed Culpepper emphasizes that the minor characters of the gospel, by which he means characters other than Jesus, are usually conveyed as "the personification of a single trait"—a sure sign of flatness. If this is true, one might ask whether engaging in an in-depth study of minor characters in the Gospel will be a productive undertaking.

There are a number of possible responses to this question. First one might adopt the position of Hochman and a number of other contemporary critics and reject the flat/round dichotomy as highly reductive.[27] Second, one might argue that even a flat character may gain dimension, at times appearing to curve towards the round.[28] Third, one could argue that the representative characters in John's Gospel are not

---

[26]E. M. Forster, *Aspects of the Novel* (New York: Penguin Books, 1962) 73, 81.

[27]Hochman proposes in place of the dichotomy an elaborate series of eight spectrums that provide a more nuanced way of discussing individual characters (*Character in Literature* [Ithaca/London: Cornell University Press, 1985] 44). They are as follows:

Stylization	<—>	Naturalism
Coherence	<—>	Incoherence
Wholeness	<—>	Fragmentariness
Literalness	<—>	Symbolism
Complexity	<—>	Simplicity
Transparency	<—>	Opacity
Dynamism	<—>	Staticism
Closure	<—>	Openness

Cf. also Shlomith Rimmon-Kennan, *Narrative Fiction: Contemporary Poetics* [Methuen & Co. Ltd, 1983] 40–41; Thomas Docherty, *Reading (Absent) Character: Toward a Theory of Characterization in Fiction* (Oxford: Clarendon Press, 1983) 47–48.

[28]As is frequently noted, Forster leaves room for this option. He gives the example of Jane Austen's Lady Bertram as a flat character who momentarily appears round (*Aspects*, 112-113).

necessarily flat—that some do show signs of growth and unpredictability, and in this way, individuality. This certainly seems true of characters such as the Samaritan woman and the man born blind. This third position is the one I will adopt in this study. I contend that along with whatever functional role a character may play, he or she may also take on an aspect of autonomy, a mimetic quality. Along this line, it may be that biblical characters are mistakenly dismissed as flat and underdeveloped because biblical techniques of characterization differ from that of the modern novel. This is the view of Robert Alter and other biblical critics whose work will be discussed below.

In sum, what has been gained from revisiting the question of characters in Fourth Gospel? First, I have suggested that opting for an either/or approach to the questions of mimetic versus functional understandings of character may not be helpful for the Fourth Gospel. Instead, both Chatman and Hochman offer ways to think about character that move beyond this dichotomy. Chatman's "open structuralist" approach leaves room for the imaginative response of the reader, but also stays closely wedded to the text with his conception of a paradigm of traits. Hochman is especially useful in pointing to the relational nature of characters in a narrative, i.e., characters are best understood when analyzed in relation to other characters as well as to other systems of meaning that make up a narrative. Finally, a comment from David Galef provides a helpful reminder of the essential role of minor characters in adding depth and movement to the narrative. Indeed, his remarks seem almost to have been formulated with the Fourth Gospel in mind, if we understand characters other than Jesus to be minor characters.

> What is gained through the depiction of flat and minor characters? Oddly enough, depth; a contrasting, shifting background against which the major figures play out the drama of their lives. Why study such minor figures? Though the bold stroke of a protagonist may show the author's genius, or evocative style reveal his way with words, the analysis of minor figures will inevitably reveal the painstaking construction of the work; how the author intends to get from alpha to omega, or what contrast he has in mind, or what thematic principles he is stressing.[29]

---

[29]Galef, *The Supporting Cast*, 22.

BIBLICAL TECHNIQUES OF CHARACTERIZATION AND THE FOURTH
GOSPEL

Despite their usefulness in thinking about character theory, contemporary theorists like Chatman, Hochman and Galef all draw on characters in the modern novel as illustrations. Though their work theoretically applies to characters in the Bible,[30] it is also true that techniques of characterization in the Bible differ from those used in the modern novel. Generally, the biblical text gives little attention to a character's physical appearance or psychological profile. The reader is only rarely given access to a character's thoughts and inner motives. Instead, the biblical authors rely on other more subtle means to bring forth the personality of their characters.

Much of the scholarship on biblical techniques of characterization is situated in the broader framework of a poetics of biblical narrative developed by Hebrew Bible scholars such as Robert Alter,[31] Adele Berlin,[32] Meir Sternberg,[33] Shimon Bar-Efrat,[34] David Gunn and Danna Nolan Fewell.[35] While their emphases differ, their common goal is to illustrate the narrative sophistication of the Hebrew Bible. Their work can readily be extended to the Fourth Gospel, not only because it is a biblical narrative, but more importantly because its techniques of characterization are similar to those displayed by the Hebrew Bible.[36]

---

[30]To the question of bringing anachronistic notions of character to bear on ancient texts, Hochman responds that we have no alternative but to construct images of character in terms of our own knowledge or experience. Furthermore, he contends that the patterns of behavior projected in texts such as Homer and the Bible, lend themselves to interpretation along lines shaped within the novelistic mold (*Character in Literature*, 54–57).

[31]Robert Alter, *The Art of Biblical Narrative* (New York: Basic, 1981).

[32]Adele Berlin, *Poetics and Interpretation of Biblical Narrative* (Bible and Literature 9; Sheffield: Almond Press, 1983).

[33]Meir Sternberg, *The Poetics of Biblical Narrative: Ideological Literature and the Drama of Reading* (Bloomington: Indiana University Press, 1985).

[34]Shimon Bar-Efrat, *Narrative Art in the Bible* (Bible and Literature Series 17; Sheffield: Almond Press, 1989).

[35]David M. Gunn and Danna Nolan Fewell, *Narrative in the Hebrew Bible* (Oxford: Oxford University Press, 1993).

Robert Funk has formulated a poetics of narrative with respect to the New Testament, but unlike those mentioned above, he relies heavily on structuralism and linguistics, with Vladimir Propp as an influential figure. His highly technical work might be called more accurately a grammar of Gospel narrative (*The Poetics of Biblical Narrative* [Sonoma, CA: Polebridge Press, 1988]).

[36]In his discussion of Johannine characterization, Culpepper states that the Fourth Gospel draws from both Greek and Hebrew models of character development (*Anatomy*, 56). Jeffrey Staley picks up on the importance of the "Hebrew model" for John's Gospel, arguing that the use of repetition, direct discourse and narration in John's sabbath healing stories parallels Hebrew poetics

This is not to say that the Johannine characters are of the same sort as those we find in the Hebrew Bible. Moses, Saul or David, for example, are certainly more fully developed characters than Nicodemus, or even Jesus. What is similar are the means of characterization, i.e., the ways in which the characters are brought forth in the narrative.

With respect to recognizing the narrative sophistication of the Bible in general, and biblical techniques of characterization in particular, the work of Robert Alter has been seminal. Alter understands his work to be a practical investigation of the distinctive ways in which the biblical story is told.[37] In terms of characterization, he suggests that the biblical writers "worked out a set of new and surprisingly supple techniques for the imaginative representation of human individuality," techniques which he describes under the heading "the art of reticence."[38] By this Alter means that while the Bible is quite reticent in its presentation of individuals—often lacking descriptions of outward appearance or inward motivation—it nevertheless forms strikingly vivid characters. Indeed, Alter argues that it is precisely this reticence that produces "both sharply defined surfaces and a sense of ambiguous depths in character." In other words, when it comes to characterization the biblical narrative is often "selectively silent in a purposeful way."[39]

According to Alter, every reliable third-person narrative, including the Bible, has available the following scale of means for conveying information about a character:

- statements by the narrator about attitudes and intentions of the character
- inward speech
- direct speech by the character
- one character's comments on another
- report of appearance, gesture, posture, costume
- report of action

At the top of the scale, the reader has certainty that the information given is an accurate account of the character's nature. The lower end—

("Stumbling in the Dark, Reaching for the Light: Reading Character in John 5 and 9," *Semeia* 53 [1991]: 56). These techniques are not limited to John's healing stories; the importance of the Hebrew model of character development extends to other parts of the Gospel as well.

[37] Alter, *Art of Biblical Narrative*, 178.

[38] Alter, *Art of Biblical Narrative*, 115.

[39] Alter, *Art of Biblical Narrative*, 115.

reports of action or appearance—leaves the reader in the realm of inference as to what this information reveals about the character. With the middle categories, there is relative certainty, but the reader still must weigh the comments made by or about the character against other information.[40] Alter's scale suggests that the means used for presenting characters is highly significant to the reader's perception of them. Characters who are presented in a way that leaves them open to inference and speculation come across as more complex, ambiguous and intriguing. Thus, the fact that a character is not presented in full-blown fashion by the narrator does not necessarily mean that he or she is undeveloped or insignificant.

Along with Alter's scale of means for characterization, one should include a technique that is discussed by Adele Berlin, especially since it clearly overlaps the theoretical discussion above. First, Berlin speaks of character contrast as an important means of characterization, contrast which can occur in three ways: 1) contrast with another character 2) contrast with an earlier action of the same character 3) contrast with the expected norm.[41] Attending to these types of contrast is in keeping with an understanding of character as part of the larger system of meaning articulated by the narrative. Examining the way character contrast operates in the Fourth Gospel will be crucial to this study.

Alter concludes his study with a summary of the types of narrative elements to which one should pay particular attention when reading the Bible.[42] He groups them under four general rubrics: words, actions, dialogue, and narration. Although all of these elements are important for a literary analysis of the Bible, dialogue is particularly significant for the Fourth Gospel, since so many of its characters engage in conversations with the protagonist, Jesus. Especially pertinent is Alter's suggestion to take note of characters who ostensibly answer one another without truly responding to what the other person has said. Likewise, he calls attention to occasions when the dialogue breaks off sharply, withholding the rejoinder that might be expected from one of the two speakers.[43]

---

[40]Alter, *Art of Biblical Narrative*, 116–117. Alter's scale has been used for analysis by several New Testament critics. Cf. John Darr, *On Character Building: The Reader and the Rhetoric of Characterization in Luke-Acts* (Louisville: Westminster, 1992) 44–45; Marianne Meye Thompson, "God's Voice You Have Never Heard, God's Form You Have Never Seen: The Characterization of God in the Gospel of John," *Semeia* 63 (1993): 177–204; Stibbe, *John as Storyteller*, 25.

[41]Berlin, *Poetics and Interpretation*, 40.

[42]Alter, *Art of Biblical Narrative*, 178–185.

[43]Alter, *Art of Biblical Narrative*, 182–183.

Finally, David McCracken's approach to biblical characterization places special emphasis on both the relational and dialogic aspects of character formation.[44] Quoting Mikhail Bakhtin, he writes, "Life by its very nature is dialogic. To live means to participate in dialogue: to ask questions, to heed, to respond, to agree, and so forth."[45] McCracken goes on to claim, "This statement...is also true with regard to the life of biblical characters: it is relational and occurs in the between."[46] He borrows the psychological term "interdividual" to express this relational nature of character. While I will not adopt his terminology, McCracken's general point is well taken. Biblical writers rely heavily on conversational exchanges to indicate what sort of characters populate the Bible's pages. This is especially true in the case of the Gospel of John.

By focusing on these major techniques of characterization—dialogue, narration and character contrast—I suggest that insight into ways individual men and women are portrayed in the Gospel will become evident. By considering the ways these characters relate to other systems of meaning in the Gospel, insight into the difference (or lack thereof) between men and women characters may also be gained. Thus, as we work through the text we must ask, how are the male and female characters constructed and what does this tell us about their respective roles in the Gospel? To do this, we must bring to the surface another aspect of their identities, namely their gender. Because gender is a relatively new category to both biblical studies and literary criticism, it will be necessary to define and describe how gender will be used in this analysis.

GENDER AS AN ANALYTIC CATEGORY OF LITERARY CRITICISM

Although my approach in this dissertation will be primarily informed by the preceding discussion of characterization, my goal is to do more than describe the characters in the Fourth Gospel. My main concern is to explore and clarify in what ways the Gospel's presentation of female and male characters differ. Thus, in this study, gender will be

---

[44]David McCracken, "Character in the Boundary: Bakhtin's Interdividuality in Biblical Narratives," *Semeia* 63 (1993): 29–42.

[45]"Character in the Boundary," 33. From Mikhail Bakhtin, *Problems of Dostoevsky's Poetics* (Minneapolis: University of Minneapolis Press, 1984) 293.

[46]"Character in the Boundary," 33.

introduced as a category of analysis within the framework of Johannine characterization.

To this end, it may be helpful to begin with a more general discussion of the term gender in relation to biblical studies, since not long ago the word would have come up only in discussions of grammatical issues. Since the advent of feminist biblical criticism and its interdisciplinary approach to the text, gender is becoming an increasingly important category for analyzing the Bible. Feminist biblical scholars are beginning to use the fruits of gender studies in a multitude of areas such as anthropology, sociology, history, linguistics, semiotics, psychoanalysis, and literary criticism to understand better the ways in which the Bible, like any other text, is "gender inflected."[47]

Given this wide variety of approaches, it is important to clarify my own use of the term gender. First, generally speaking, I stand with the majority of feminist critics who understand gender as a term that signifies "the social, cultural and psychological constructs imposed upon biological sexual difference."[48]   While this idea will not be at the forefront of my study, it is one of my presuppositions. It may well be that there are biological influences that play into the construction of human identity as male and female. Nevertheless, I am skeptical about the possibility of being able to speak of such differences outside the realm of an already constructed cultural discourse of gender

---

[47]This range of perspectives can be seen even within the more narrow field of Gospel studies. The following examples include sociological approaches (Love and Wire), literary critical perspectives (Anderson) and also a redaction critical study employing gender as a critical category (Seim). Stuart Love, "Women's Roles in Certain Second Testament Passages: A Macrosociological View," *BTB* 17 (1987): 50-59; "The Household: A Major Social Component for Gender Analysis in the Gospel of Matthew," *BTB* 23 (1993): 21–31; Antoinette C. Wire, "Gender Roles in a Scribal Community," in *The Social History of the Matthean Community: Cross Disciplinary Approaches* (Minneapolis: Augsburg/Fortress) 87–121; Janice Capel Anderson, "Matthew: Gender and Reading," *Semeia* 28 (1983): 3-27; "Mary's Difference: Gender and Patriarchy in the Birth Narratives," *JR* 67 (1987): 183–202; Turid Karlsen Seim, *The Double Message: Patterns of Gender in Luke-Acts* (Nashville: Abingdon Press, 1994). The list could be greatly expanded if work on the Hebrew Bible was also taken into account. Cf. e.g., Peggy L. Day, ed. *Gender and Difference in Ancient Israel* (Minneapolis: Fortress, 1989); David Gunn and Danna Fewell, *Gender, Power and Promise: The Subject of the Bible's First Story* (Nashville: Abingdon Press, 1993); Athalya Brenner and Fokkelien van Dijk-Hemmes, *On Gendering Texts: Female and Male Voices in the Hebrew Bible* (Leiden: E. J. Brill, 1993).

[48]Elaine Showalter, "Feminism and Literature" in *Literary Theory Today*, ed. Peter Collier and Helga Geyer-Ryan (New York: Cornell University Press, 1990) 196–197. Cf. also Joan W. Scott, "Gender: A Useful Category of Historical Analysis," *The American Historical Review* 91 (1986): 1053–1075. Reprinted in *Gender and the Politics of History* (New York: Columbia University Press, 1988). Scott writes, "In its most recent usage, 'gender' seems to have first appeared among American feminists who wanted to insist on the fundamentally social quality of distinctions based on sex" (1054).

differentiation. In any case, whatever conclusions may be drawn concerning the portrayal of male and female characters in the Gospel in this study, they are not to be understood as a statement about the essential or sexually determined aspects of men and women.

Second, and more specifically for the purpose of this study, I use gender to introduce a relational aspect to the study of men and women in the Gospel. In doing so, I am drawing on a particular use of the term as it first emerged in feminist discourse. As Joan Scott notes, feminist scholars who were concerned that women's studies scholarship focused too narrowly and separately on women used gender to introduce a relational notion into analytic vocabulary. As she puts it, "According to this view, women and men were defined in terms of one another, and no understanding of either could be achieved by entirely separate study."[49] In the same sense, Elaine Showalter explains that one goal of gender theory is "to introduce comparative studies of women and men into [a] specific disciplinary field."[50]

In disciplines such as history or the social sciences a comparative approach would involve the analysis of the roles of real men and women in particular periods and social locations.[51] In literary studies, introducing gender as a category of analysis involves considerations of the gender identity of the author and the reader, along with observations of gender configurations and symbolism within the text itself. In Showalter's words, "gender theory explores the ideological inscription and the literary effects of the sex/gender system."[52]

Concerning my literary investigation of the Fourth Gospel, emphasis will be on the presentation and function of gendered characters in the narrative. Since the identity of the Gospel's author is unknown, it is impossible to discuss the effects of his or her gender identity on the Gospel's writing with any certainty.[53] As for the reader, which in the case of this investigation is a woman, it is likely that effects of gender

---

[49]Scott, "Gender: A Useful Category of Historical Analysis," 1054.

[50]Showalter, "Feminism and Literature," 197. Cf. also Jill K. Conway, Susan C. Bourque, Joan W. Scott ("Introduction: The Concept of Gender," *Dædalus* [Fall 1987]: XXIX) who write "the study of gender is a way of understanding women not as an isolated aspect of society but as an integral part of it."

[51]For an outstanding example of this work, cf. Joan Wallach Scott, *Gender and the Politics of History* (New York: Columbia University Press, 1988).

[52]Showalter, "Feminism and Literature," 197.

[53]One should note, however, that studies of Johannine women characters have led both Schüssler Fiorenza (*In Memory of Her*, 333), Scott (*Sophia*, 239–242) and Kysar, (*Maverick Gospel*, 153–154) to speculate about the possibility of a woman author behind the Gospel.

identity will become evident in the course of the study. For example, part of my analysis will involve the careful scrutiny of past interpretive assumptions about both women and men in the Gospel. That is to say, I approach this history of interpretation and to some extent the Gospel with a hermeneutic of suspicion.[54] My overriding concern, however, is to compare and contrast the presentation of men and women characters in the Gospel and to see how they are interwoven with other systems of meaning in the Gospel.

Thus, for the purposes of this study answers to questions regarding the significance of gender categories will be sought internally, through a literary analysis of characters. At this point, the importance of a relational theory of character becomes even more evident. Not only is such a theory helpful in explaining the way in which characters contribute to the creation of meaning in a narrative; it is also well suited to incorporating gender as a critical category of analysis. Using the work of Hochman, I have argued that there is no way to understand characters in isolation from the text that generates them, and especially in isolation from one another. The introduction of the relational aspect of gender reinforces this claim. Gender identity becomes an aspect of character to be studied and analyzed in relation to other gendered characters; it is not a given. Indeed, another assumption of this study is that the author gave deliberate attention to gender identity as part of the creative process of character construction.

There are several reasons for making this assumption. The clearest evidence is found in the disciples' unvoiced question in 4:27. They are astonished that Jesus is talking to a woman, but reluctant to ask him why he is doing so. One gets the strong impression that the author is well aware of the gender dynamics in the narrative. Other aspects of the Gospel suggest that this consciousness regarding gender is not limited to this scene, but extends to the larger narrative as well. Jesus' repeated use of the vocative γύναι in his encounters with women lends additional

---

[54]For a thorough discussion of feminist biblical hermeneutics see Carolyn Osiek, "The Feminist and the Bible: Hermeneutical Alternatives," *RelIntel* 6 (1989): 96–109. Reprinted in *Feminist Perspectives on Biblical Scholarship.* ed. Adela Yarbro Collins (Chico, CA: Scholars Press, 1985): 93–105, K. D. Sakenfeld, "Feminist Biblical Interpretation," *Princeton Seminary Bulletin* 3 (1988): 179–196; Sandra M. Schneiders, "Feminist Ideological Criticism and Biblical Hermeneutics," *BTB* 19 (1989): 3–10; Mary Ann Tolbert, "Defining the Problem: The Bible and Feminist Hermeneutics," *Semeia* 28 (1983): 113–126; Elaine Wainwright, "In Search of the Lost Coin: Toward a Feminist Biblical Hermeneutic," *Pacifica* 2 (1989): 135–150.

support (2:4; 4:21; 19:26; 20:15; cf. also 8:10).[55] Finally, it appears that in a number of places the author has deliberately contrasted male and female characters, e.g., Nicodemus with the Samaritan woman and Mary of Bethany with Judas.[56] Taken together, these aspects of the narrative are enough to suggest that gender identity should be viewed as an intentional aspect of Johannine characterization.[57]

It remains to explain how the introduction of gender will be incorporated into my analysis of Johannine characters. In large part, this will be determined by the presentation of the characters themselves. In some cases, consideration of gender identity will be immediately relevant to the narrative analysis of the scene. This will be the case with the Samaritan woman, and also with the mother of Jesus and Mary Magdalene. In these instances, analyzing the characters will include a focused look on how their identities as women are directly related to the nature of their exchanges with Jesus. In other cases, however, explicit attention to gender may not be possible until an individual character can be placed in relation to others. This will be the situation primarily with the male characters, which suggests all the more that a relational approach to both gender and characterization is the only way to discover what significance gender categories may have in the Gospel. As the analysis continues, it will become increasingly possible to look for patterns of relationships between the various characters and between the characters and the presentation of the Gospel narrative as a whole.

Given all this, my procedure in the next chapter will be to study the characterization of a select group of male and female characters. Because I am interested in gender, I will concentrate only on individual characters, rather than character groups such as "the Jews" and "the disciples" since these arguably could include both men and women. Because a fundamental aspect of minor Johannine characters is their presentation in relation to Jesus, the main character, I will focus primarily on those scenes in which a character has a direct encounter with Jesus. Moreover, since dialogue is one of the most important means

---

[55]So Seim, "(T)he common use of *gunai*...shows a common emphasis on femaleness in these passages" ("Roles of Women," 60).

[56]These contrasts, as well as others between male and female characters, will clearly emerge in the course of the analysis.

[57]Recall also Martin Scott's argument that the author of the Gospel was conscious of discontinuity between the female figure of Sophia and the masculine Jesus. It is for this reason, Scott argues, that the author substitutes the masculine term Logos for Sophia (*Sophia*, 170. Cf. also O'Day, 519).

of characterization in the Gospel, scenes in which a character engages in conversation with Jesus will be particularly important. I do not intend to explore in depth the characterization of Jesus; my interest lies in the other Johannine characters. Nevertheless, the nature of the analysis will undoubtedly uncover aspects of the characterization of Jesus as well. As there are a relatively small number of women appearing in individual scenes in the Gospel (five women appearing in seven different scenes), it will be possible to include all of the women characters as part of the analysis; these are the mother of Jesus (2:1–12; 19:25–26), the Samaritan woman (4:7–26), Martha (11:17–27), Mary (11:28–33; 12:1–8) and Mary Magdalene (20:1–18).[58] With male characters, the question of whom to include is more difficult. Not only are there more of them, but their appearances are also more widely interspersed throughout the Gospel. Since my interest does not lie in minor characters *per se*, but in the significance of their gender identity it will not be necessary to include every male character. Instead, to keep a balanced presentation between men and women, I will concentrate on five male characters that have direct encounters with Jesus. These will include: Nicodemus (3:1–10), the man born blind (9:1–40), Peter (13:6–11, 21–26; 18:15–27; 20:1–10; 21:15–19), the Beloved Disciple (13:21–26; 19:25–27; 20:1–10; 21:20–24),[59] and Pilate (18:28–19:16a).

To stay within a narrative framework, I will for the most part discuss each scene chronologically. However, the process will also involve comparisons with other Gospel characters and with other places in the text where the same character appears. Therefore, though the focus will be on a series of particular encounters with Jesus, information from other parts of the Gospel will also be considered when necessary.

---

[58]Mary Magdalene is also mentioned in the list of women near the cross of Jesus (19:25).

[59]Although in general, the characters of Peter and the Beloved Disciple will be treated separately, in the case of the scene at the empty tomb (20:1–18) they will be discussed together, along with Mary Magdalene, since in this scene the presentation of these three characters is intricately interwoven.

Chapter Three
Men and Women in the Fourth Gospel

INTRODUCTION

As stated at the close of the previous chapter, this chapter will analyze in detail ten minor characters in the Gospel of John. The order of their presentation is based primarily on the order of their appearance in the narrative, with some exceptions. Peter and the Beloved Disciple appear in several places in the Gospel, often together, so that maintaining narrative sequence with these two characters is difficult. I have opted to place them last, along with the presentation of Mary Magdalene. To some extent, this is fitting, since these two male characters appear together in the Gospel's epilogue. Apart from this deviation, the characters fall neatly into an alternating pattern of women and men, which serves the discussion well.

In all the analyses, my focus will be on the presentation of individual characters in relation to Jesus and in comparison to each other. I will not, therefore, attempt a complete exegesis of every passage, but for the most part restrict my discussion to those critical issues that have a direct bearing on the interpretation of the Johannine characters.

THE MOTHER OF JESUS

Introduction

As a female character in the narrative, the mother of Jesus is distinct in a number of ways—most obviously in her relationship to Jesus. Her maternal role is a central aspect of her character, a point made especially evident in that she is never named in the Gospel. The narrator consistently refers to her only as "the mother of Jesus" or "his mother" so that, as Seim puts it, "her identity is always established by her relationship to Jesus."[1] In this way, she is similar to the anonymous beloved disciple of Jesus, whose designation also indicates his relationship to Jesus. Still, it is remarkable that the name Mary, so well known in the tradition, is never associated with Jesus' mother in the Fourth Gospel, even in a list that includes other woman's names (cf. 19:25). Brown notes that among contemporary Arabs, "the mother of X"

---

[1] Seim, "Roles of Women," 61.

is an honorable title for a woman who has borne a son.[2] If this is true in the Fourth Gospel, it adds to the impression that this character's maternal role is her defining characteristic. Also distinctive is the location of the two scenes in which the mother of Jesus appears, first, at the wedding in Cana (2:1–12) and later at the crucifixion (19:25–27).[3] This makes her the only character that is specifically identified at the beginning and the end of Jesus' earthly ministry and thus the only witness to both the first and final revelation of Jesus' glory.[4] Furthermore, as Adele Reinhartz notes, in neither of these scenes is the mother of Jesus confronted with the choice of accepting or rejecting Jesus, a point that distinguishes her from virtually all the characters in the Gospel except John the Baptist.[5]

Given the uniqueness of her character, one might wonder whether the mother of Jesus should be discussed in the same categories as the others. After all, a whole field of study has emerged devoted specifically to interpreting her position in the New Testament and in Christian theology. In this vein, Schneiders omits the mother of Jesus from her investigation of the roles of Johannine women arguing that

> [w]hatever role Mary is assigned in the Fourth Gospel, it is either unique to her or universal, in neither of which cases is it more significant for women than for men....The femaleness of the Mother of Jesus is both an historical fact and an integral part of the symbolism attached to her in the Fourth Gospel, but it is theologically irrelevant for the contemporary question of the role of women in the Church...[6]

While Schneiders's statement may be true for her understanding of what is at issue (and even that is debatable), examining the mother of Jesus precisely with her femaleness in mind is crucial for my interests. Only by considering her in relation to other women and men in the Gospel will it become clear whether her gender identity is of any account in the narrative.

---

[2]Raymond Brown, *The Gospel According to John* I-XII, Anchor Bible 29 (New York: Doubleday, 1970) 98.

[3]Apart from her appearance in chapters two and nineteen, the mother of Jesus is referred to one other time by Jesus' opponents (6:42).

[4]This observation is based on the Gospel's view of the death of Jesus as one and the same with his ascension and glorification (cf. 3:14; 17:2, 5; cf. also 11:4).

[5]Adele Reinhartz, "The Gospel of John," in *Searching the Scriptures,* Vol. 2 (ed. Elisabeth Schüssler Fiorenza; New York: Crossroad, 1994) 569.

[6]Schneiders, "Women in the Fourth Gospel," 37.

The Wedding at Cana (2:1–12)

The story of the wedding at Cana recounts the first miracle of the Gospel, marked in the narrative as the first of Jesus' signs (2:11). For this reason alone, Christology is a major focus of the story. The detailed way in which the miraculous act is described—the number, type and size of the jars, Jesus' step-by-step directions and their completion by the servants, the lengthy verification of the miracle by the chief steward—contributes to a sense of importance surrounding Jesus' act.

Given this, the opening to the account is surprising. We learn first that there was a wedding at Cana, and next that Jesus' mother was in attendance (2:1). She is introduced to the narrative prior to Jesus so that as the story begins, the focus is more on the mother than her son. As mentioned above, she is introduced not by name, but in terms of her relationship to Jesus. The only reference thus far to Jesus' parentage occurred in the Prologue, in which Jesus was presented as the only begotten son of the Father (1:18). Now we discover that Jesus has a mother as well. However, unlike 1:18, in which the relationship between father and son is further defined (ὢν εἰς τὸν κόλπον τοῦ πατρός), here the narrator provides no immediate insight into the nature of the mother/son relationship. Instead, we watch it unfold in dialogue and narrative action.

Following the introduction of the mother of Jesus, the narrative provides three comments that contribute to her characterization. Two of these are spoken by the mother of Jesus herself; the third is a response from Jesus. In addition to these comments, we have the events of the narrative that follow the exchange between Jesus and his mother. What can we discern from this brief presentation about the role of this character in the narrative?

First, the mother of Jesus is the first character in the passage to speak and thereby the character who sets the story in motion. Her words to Jesus are terse and to the point—οἶνον οὐκ ἔχουσιν (v. 3). There is no indication why she brings this matter to Jesus' attention and no explanation concerning what she wants him to do. We can only surmise from her comment that she expects her son to do something about the lack.

Second, her opening comment comes across as redundant in the context of the narrative; she virtually repeats what the narrator has just stated. In this repetition may lie a further clue to her characterization. The mother of Jesus is constructed as a uniquely knowledgeable character. Unlike any other character in the narrative, apart from Jesus, she shares insight with the narrator. She is the character who perceives the problem and makes it known to Jesus. In terms of the narrative, her initial statement introduces conflict to the story and thereby moves the plot forward. Thus, it would seem that plot advancement is one function of her character. However, one is still left to wonder why the mother of Jesus, in particular, is given this role.

With this, we come to Jesus' reply; a verse that has been described as one of the most difficult in the Fourth Gospel.[7] The problem is threefold, corresponding to the three parts of Jesus' reply. First, there is his sharp retort, τί ἐμοὶ καὶ σοί. The expression is a literal translation of the Hebrew expression מה לִּי וָלָךְ, which may be roughly rendered, "What's it to me and to you?" Even in English, the rudeness of the comment is readily discerned and its use in the Hebrew Bible attests to its sharpness. According to Collins, in all cases where the same formula appears, the one using it is faced with hostility or an unpleasant situation. As he puts it,

> when used in dialogue, *ti emoi kai soi* is an oratorical question occasioned by the untoward action of the other person in the scene. In those passages in which the *mah-li walak* appears as a response to a question, it is tantamount to a refusal.[8]

From this, it seems clear that Jesus understands his mother's comment as a request for him to act and that his answer is a harsh rebuff. If this is a clue to the mother/son relationship, one possible reading is that Jesus responds to his mother with the arrogant attitude of a son who cannot be bothered with her wishes.

This impression is made even stronger by the second problematic aspect of the verse, namely, Jesus' use of the term γύναι. Not wanting to sully the reputation of Jesus, interpreters have gone to great lengths to

---

[7]F. M. Braun, *La Mère des fidèles: Essai de théologie johannique* (Tournai-Paris, 1954) 49. Cited in Collins, "Mary in the Fourth Gospel," 118.

[8]Collins, "Mary in the Fourth Gospel," 118. Cf. 2 Sam 16:10; 19:22; 1 Kg 17:18; 2 Kg 3:13. Brown distinguishes between two shades of meaning in the Hebrew occurrences. The first implies hostility (e.g., Judg 11:12, 2 Chron 35:21) and the second implies simple disengagement (2 Kg 3:13; Hos 14:8). However, "there is always some refusal of an inopportune involvement, and a divergence between the views of the two persons concerned" (99). Based on this evidence, André Feuillet concludes that "it seems wrong to seek to exclude from Christ's reply any nuance of opposition to His Mother's implied request" (*Johannine Studies* [New York: Alba House, 1964] 18).

soften and explain this odd way of addressing one's mother. To this end, Brown and others have noted that γύναι was a normal and polite way of addressing women, attested in the New Testament and other Greek writings as well.[9] The fact remains that no one has yet adduced Semitic examples for the use of this term between a son and his mother.[10] It may not be disrespectful in other situations, but in this context its appearance is, at the very least, surprising. What is particularly notable is that Jesus does not adopt the same language as the narrator regarding his mother. Instead, he uses an address that calls attention to this character in a way other than focusing on her maternal role. The possible significance of this use of γύναι remains to be seen.

Finally, Jesus closes his response with the enigmatic explanation, "My hour has not yet come." The meaning of this phrase in the context of chapter two has long puzzled interpreters. Elsewhere in the Gospel, ὥρα serves as a reference to Jesus' final hour, i.e., his crucifixion/glorification (cf. 7:30; 8:20; 12:23, 27–28; 13:1; 16:32; 17:1). If this is also the case in chapter two, which is likely, Jesus is apparently informing his mother that it is too soon to act, his time for glory has not yet come.[11] Thus, Jesus has harshly denied his mother's

---

[9]In addition to the other Johannine references (Jn 4:21; 8:10; 20:13), Brown cites Mt 15:28 and Lk 13:12, but gives no example of other Greek writings. Bultmann notes that a disguised Odysseus addresses Penelope (Od. 19.221) with γύναι as Oedipus also addresses Jocasta (Soph. Oed.tyr. 642, 800, 1054). However, he also acknowledges that Jesus gives his mother a "rough refusal" (116, nt. 5). Beasley-Murray cites Josephus, *Ant.* 17:74, which depicts a situation in which a husband, Pheroras, addresses his beloved wife with γύναι (34). This example demonstrates that the title can be used with affection, though a spousal relationship is different than a maternal one. Adele Reinhartz also argues that the title does not connote discourtesy in the Fourth Gospel, though she defends her position in a different way. She points out that aside from the three female characters in John's Gospel—the mother of Jesus, the Samaritan woman, and Mary Magdalene—the only other use of the vocative mood is when Jesus prayerfully addresses God as "Father" (11:41; 12:28; 17:1, 5, 11, 24, 25). "Hence, the fact that Jesus addresses his mother as 'woman' does not belittle his relationship to her but rather recognizes its intimacy" ("The Gospel of John," 569). For additional attempts to soften the abrupt nature of Jesus' response, cf. Feuillet, *Johannine Studies*, 30–31, nt. 31.

[10]Schnackenburg notes that the examples of "woman" as a respectful form of address come from the Hellenistic world. In the Semitic world, he claims, the term is "unusual and astonishing" when used towards one's mother (1.328 and nt. 17). As Seim puts it, "It is...a fact that γύναι pure and simple is a rather cool way of addressing one's mother" ("Roles of Women" 60).

[11]Alternatively, Collins cites three commentators (C. M. Henze, M. N. Eyquem, and H. Leroy) who argue that in the case of 2:4, ὥρα refers to the hour in which

implied request and in doing so, seemingly put an end to any forward movement in the narrative.

The story does not end, however, because his mother, as the narrator again refers to her, speaks once more. This time she addresses the servants at the wedding with the command, "Do whatever he tells you" (2:5). Following the reply of Jesus, her words are striking. They express an unyielding certainty that her son will act, despite his obvious refusal. Moreover, this character again knows how the narrative is to proceed and forges ahead in spite of Jesus.[12] In this regard, both aspects of her characterization are reinforced—she is presented as a determined mother who functions in this role to advance the narrative. Upon issuing the command to the servants, her role in chapter two is complete and she fades from the narrative, except for the brief reference in 2:12. That she has accomplished her task is evident in the fact that Jesus goes on to instruct the servants, and soon supplies fine wine in abundance for the wedding feast.

This understanding of the functional role of Jesus' mother seems clear enough until we consider again the response of Jesus in 2:4. If we are to view her purely as a confident and determined mother, why does the Johannine Jesus, her own son, detract from that image and refer to her as "woman?" Moreover, what does his rough refusal suggest about how we are to view his mother? In other words, if characters are constructed in "mutually illuminating relationships," as Hochman argues, how does Jesus' response illumine his mother's presentation?

As mentioned above, one implication of Jesus' response is that it disrupts her characterization as "mother" by inserting the title "woman."

Jesus is to work a miracle ("Mary in the Fourth Gospel," 120). This seems a remote possibility given the use of hour in the rest of the Gospel. Also, it makes little sense for Jesus to claim that the hour in which he is to work a miracle is not yet here in a story in which he does, in fact, perform a miracle.

[12]This is not necessarily to claim that Jesus' mother had knowledge of his messiahship, either historically or in the world of the text, although this issue is frequently a central concern in the exegesis of this story (cf. Collins, "Mary in the Fourth Gospel," 121–122). The main question has been whether the mother of Jesus expected a miracle from him, which would indicate both her knowledge of Jesus' messianic identity and her faithfulness. Yet, as we have already mentioned, there is no indication of what exactly Jesus' mother expected. Moreover, her expectation of him would not necessarily indicate knowledge of his messiahship. Reinhartz puts it this way, "[A] more whimsical, less reverent reading might recognize in this mother a rather natural appreciation of the abilities of her offspring without necessarily implying faith in him as the Messiah and Son of God" ("Gospel of John," 569).

Furthermore, Jesus' reaction toward her does not fit neatly into preconceptions of a mother/son relationship, except in a negative sense. If we are to understand this female character only as a confident mother, then Jesus must be understood as a rude and condescending son.

However, it is doubtful that presenting a negative picture of Jesus is the primary purpose for this perplexing exchange between mother and son. For this reason, interpreters have rightly sought alternative explanations for Jesus' behavior. Since the entire narrative is obviously Christological in focus, solutions have rested on the fact that Jesus is not only his mother's son, but also Son of God. Notably, the move to explain Jesus' behavior on this basis adversely affects the way the mother of Jesus is viewed. For this reason, it is important to look at the most common interpretation of Jesus' response in 2:4 and its resulting problems.

The standard explanation for Jesus' portrayal in this passage links the first part of the response, "What is it to me and to you, woman?" with the last part of Jesus' response, "My hour has not yet come." Together, the theory suggests, the epithet and the rationale create a distance between the divine Jesus and his human mother—between the heavenly and the earthly. Moreover, this theory suggests that Jesus acts only in relation to his hour rather than on the basis of human requests, even those of his own mother. So, for example, Charles H. Giblin argues that Jesus responds negatively in order to establish a dominant personal concern about his hour. Additionally, Giblin contends, the response establishes "the distinctive genre of Johannine signs and works. It prepares the reader to understand that if Jesus does act...he will act in accordance with his own conscious purpose. He will not act precisely on the basis of human concern, human need or the like."[13]

Following this line of interpretation, many commentators then set up a contest between the will of the Father and the will of Jesus' mother. For example, Haenchen comments, "Jesus does not permit himself to be prompted to act by any human agent, even when that agent is his own mother. He is driven by the will of the Father alone."[14] Similarly, Fausto

---

[13] Charles H. Giblin, "Suggestion, Negative Response, and Positive Action in St. John's Portrayal of Jesus," *NTS* 26 (1980): 203. Similarly, cf. Bultmann, "Human ties and obligations in no way influence Jesus' actions" (116).

[14] Haenchen, 173. Similarly, Heikki Räisänen states, "Der Sohn tut den Willen dessen, der ihn gesandt hat, seines Vaters. Deshalb kann er bei der Erfüllung seiner Berufung keine Befehle von Menschen annehmen, nicht einmal von den nächsten Verwandten" (*Die Mutter Jesu im Neuen Testament* [Helsinki, 1969], 162).

Salvoni argues that Jesus has to establish his independence from his earthly mother because he has to obey his heavenly Father.[15] Likewise, Seim claims that "the mother must give way to the father (cf. 6:42) and his mother accepts this submitting her will to his...."[16] Rena suggests that the mother of Jesus may provide a negative example, "warning people not to tell God how to act."[17]

Although the basic point of this theory is that the heavenly Jesus is distancing himself from the demands of the earthly sphere, there are fascinating gender dynamics at play in it as well. By introducing the Father to this scene, a male/female opposition is also introduced so that, according to this interpretation, Jesus is defined through his allegiance and affinity with the male father and his rejection of the female mother. Taken together, the quotations above suggest that the mother of Jesus has the audacity to tell God how to act, but that, in the end, she is on the losing end of the contest. Jesus rejects her in favor of his father and she submits to both.

As common as this interpretation of Jesus' reply may be, it presents one serious difficulty; namely that Jesus does *not* ultimately refuse the request of his mother. On the contrary, Jesus goes on to make fine wine in abundance for the feast, an act that actually coincides with the will of his mother. Nor does Jesus' mother submit to him, rather she ignores his refusal altogether. In other words, no matter how rough a refusal Jesus gives to her, he nevertheless acts at his mother's instigation and resolves the problem that she calls to his attention.[18]

---

[15]Fausto Salvoni, "Nevertheless My Hour has not Yet Come (John 2:4)," *Restoration Quarterly* 7 (1963): 240.

[16]Seim, "Roles of Women," 62.

[17]Rena, "Women in the Gospel," 137.

[18]Salvoni's recognition of this point results in his translation of 2:4 as "*Nevertheless,* my hour is not yet come," (my emphasis) meaning "Because the hour of my death and glorification has not yet come, I can still accomplish your will." In other words, because Jesus' final hour has not arrived, he can still submit to his mother. After his hour, he will leave his earthly body and completely cut ties with his mother ("Nevertheless," 239–241). While I do not agree with the whole of Salvoni's argument, he at least admits that in performing his first sign Jesus is in fact doing his mother's will.

Less convincing is Feuillet, who argues that although Jesus performs the miracle after his initial rejection, he presents no inconsistency because his actions do not correspond to what was expected. In Feuillet's words, "...it is clear that this miracle is much more than a material favor for a bridal couple in need of wine. It is fundamentally something different from what Mary could ask or wish, even if one were to hold that she did ask Her Son for a miracle of the messianic order....At

In effect, the miracle that Jesus performs takes place through the mediation of his mother. Indeed, the mother of Jesus becomes a participant in the miracle by alerting the servants that they must do whatever he tells them to do. In this way, she, who is assumed to have the authority, ensures that the servants will not balk when Jesus gives his order. Throughout all of this, there is no mention of the Father or the Father's will, or even Jesus' will. Only the mother's knowledge and determination are evident in the text.[19]

For this reason, the way the narrative concludes is also relevant to the characterization of Mary. It is in fulfilling her request that Jesus performs the first of his signs and in so doing reveals his glory (2:11). Following this revelation, the narrator reports for the first time that Jesus' disciples believed in him (2:11). They thus become the first characters who can be identified as children of God according to the Prologue (1:12). One could ask then if the mother's will corresponds to the Father's will so that, rather than "pushing" Jesus before his time, her actions actually contribute to the doing of the Father's will.[20] If this is the case, her function as a character that advances the plot takes on greater significance. She does not move the narrative forward in a disinterested, mechanical way; her actions are in line with the fundamental theological purposes of the Gospel.

If we consider the end of the story in light of Jesus' initial rejection, it becomes clear that his comment, not his mother's request, is incongruent with the narrative. Jesus thinks his mother should have no involvement with him because his hour has not yet come; he is proved wrong on both counts. Precisely her involvement with him makes clear that the time is right for him to act. In this regard, of critical importance is the recognition that there is no indication of what brings Jesus to

---

Cana, human lack gives way in an unforeseen matter to abundance, indicated by the generous amount and extraordinarily good quality of the wine (II: 6–10)" (*Johannine Studies*, 32). Aside from the fact that the narrative gives no indication of precisely what Jesus' mother expected, the fact remains that Jesus does resolve the issue which his mother brings to him.

[19]Contra O'Grady, "In the relationship between Jesus and his mother, Jesus alone knows the will of God but Mary has faith and thus awaits what he will do" ("The Role of the Beloved Disciple," *BTB* 9 [1979]: 61). The point is that Mary does not wait for Jesus, but proceeds with instructions to the servants despite his refusal.

[20]Hendrikus Boers makes a similar point about the Samaritan woman in John 4 (*Neither on this Mountain Nor in Jerusalem: A Study of John 4* [SBL Monograph Series 35; Atlanta: Scholars Press, 1988], 165, 200).

perform the miracle—no mention of a change of mind, no word from the Father. The only narrative link between his refusal and the performance of the miracle is his mother's preparations. In other words, it is his mother, not Jesus, who is attuned to what is about to take place. The opposition in this story, then, is not between the divine will of Jesus' Father and the earthly will of his mother. Instead, his mother, representing what is expected of Jesus as part of his mission from the Father, stands in opposition to Jesus' refusal. It is her persistence, not Jesus' refusal, that carries the day and that results in the revelation of his glory. She is in line with the will of the Father, not against it.

This leads us to consider the importance of this character's designation as γύναι. If the "distance" theory does not adequately explain Jesus' rationale in 2:4, neither does it satisfy as the reason behind his choice of address. Mainly, it does not take into account the other appearances of γύναι in the Gospel. Jesus uses the term three other times in addressing women, again with his mother (19:26) and in his conversations with the Samaritan women (4:21) and Mary Magdalene (20:13). In this way, the term draws a connection between the mother of Jesus and other scenes in which women appear in the Gospel. The result is that along with her unique construction as Jesus' mother, a common link is drawn between this character and the other women characters in the narrative.

Along this line, Heikki Räisänen notes, "Das Wort gynai betont, dass Maria keine Sonderstellung einnimmt, sie wird den anderen Frauen des Evangeliums an die Seite gestellt."[21] This does not mean that the importance of the mother of Jesus is diminished, as Räisänen's comment seems to imply.[22] On the contrary, the women characters of the Gospel, including Jesus' mother, may together share a highly significant role as women in the Gospel drama. That the mother of Jesus is designated γύναι in chapter two, points ahead to the significant role that women will play with respect to the revelation of Jesus in the rest of the Gospel. Granted, from the narrator's perspective, she remains above all the mother of Jesus. But there is added to this identity the indication of a broader significance of women in the narrative. E. J. Kilmartin comments that the use of γύναι in chapter two "should arouse suspicion that we are in the presence of another example of Johannine symbolism

---

[21]Cf. Räisänen, *Die Mutter Jesu*, 162.

[22]His statement is made in the context of an argument against the symbolic significance of the mother of Jesus (*Die Mutter Jesu*, 160–162).

and should prepare for an important revelation."[23] Whereas Kilmartin is only considering the term with regard to the mother of Jesus, I suggest that his observation may extend to the other major female figures in the Gospel as well.

A further indication of the connection between the mother of Jesus and the other woman characters is seen in the recurring theme of Jesus' hour. The mention of this hour first occurs with Jesus' comment to his mother, "My hour has not yet come." As we have seen, interpreters have long focused on the negative implications of this verse. Jesus' mother does not understand; she is mistakenly trying to influence the divine will. As we have also seen, this interpretation does not accord with the outcome of the narrative. In fact, this woman understands better than Jesus himself that it is time to set the journey toward that hour in motion. As John van den Hengel observes, "...Mary prepares the scene where that will of God, this hour, can unfold....[T]he Cana story shows the mother of Jesus setting in motion the event of the first sign of Jesus."[24] In this respect, it is highly significant that the mother of Jesus will reappear in the narrative when the journey is complete, at the moment of the hour itself, and that she again will be designated as γύναι (19:26).

In this framework, the theme of Jesus' hour will recur in conjunction with other appearances of women in the Gospel. It will be most evident in the case of the Samaritan woman, to whom Jesus announces that "the hour is coming" (4:21b), and then immediately claims that it has arrived (4:23). In addition to this, Martha and Mary of Bethany, and Mary Magdalene will all be linked in some way to the hour of Jesus, a point to be explored further as we continue the investigation.

The Crucifixion Scene (19:25–27)

The other scene in which the mother of Jesus appears takes place at his crucifixion. She is listed as one among several women standing near the cross (19:25b).[25] Although women appear at the crucifixion in

---

[23]E. J. Kilmartin, "The Mother of Jesus was There (The Significance of Mary in Jn 2:3–5 and Jn 19:25–27)," *Sciences Ecclésiastique* 15 (1963): 214.

[24]John Van den Hengel, "Mary: Miriam of Nazareth or the Symbol of the 'Eternal Feminine,'" *Science et Esprit* 37 (1985): 329.

[25]The phrasing makes the number of women ambiguous—are two, three, or four women present? The tendency of recent scholarship, and one with which I concur, favors the last option, with two named and two unnamed women. In this way, the

all four of the Gospels, only the Fourth Gospel places them in proximity to Jesus before his death. In the synoptics, the women are mentioned after the death of Jesus and they watch from a distance (Mt 27:55–56; Mk 15:40–41; Lk 23:49).[26] In contrast, the Fourth Gospel places the women so near to the cross that Jesus can actually speak to one of them, his mother. As the narrative focuses upon her and the character standing beside her, the disciple whom Jesus loved, the other women fade from view.

In contrast to chapter two, Jesus is the first and only character to speak in this scene. His words consist of two short sentences spoken in turn to each of the characters before him. To his mother he says, γύναι, ἴδε ὁ υἱός σου and to the beloved disciple, ἴδε ἡ μήτηρ σου. Following this pronouncement, only the narrator responds with the report that "from that hour the disciple took her into his own home" (19:27b). This concludes both the brief scene and the role of the mother of Jesus in the narrative.

Despite its brevity, this scene has drawn enormous critical attention to both the mother of Jesus and the beloved disciple. Scholars have endlessly debated the literal or symbolic significance of the scene and the possible meanings invested in each figure. Those who adhere to a literal, or in some cases, historical interpretation, agree that the scene relates the fulfillment of Jesus' filial duty, namely, providing for the care of his mother after his death.[27] In contrast, those who argue for a symbolic interpretation vary widely in their readings and in their emphases on each character. In general, Catholics tend to highlight the importance of the mother of Jesus, whereas Protestant scholars often focus on the significance of the disciple.[28] Thus, the mother of Jesus has

---

four women are contrasted with the four soldiers of verse 23–24 (cf. Barrett, 551; Beasley-Murray, 358; O'Day, 831). It is quite unlikely that only two women are mentioned since then this would be the only place where Mary is mentioned by name and also identified in relation to Clopas, an identification that does not appear in the synoptic traditions.

[26]O'Day, 831.

[27]So Lindars, 579; Barrett, 350; Haenchen, 1.193; also Beasley-Murray, 350, though he also admits to the possibility of an added symbolic meaning. There is actually little in the Gospel to prepare us to understand the scene as an expression of Jesus' filial devotion, except the fact that his mother has been mentioned previously. Moreover, given Jesus' attitude toward his mother in chapter two, we hardly expect a tender scene at this moment.

[28]Cf. O'Day, 832. For a thorough review of various positions, cf. Raymond Collins, "Mary in the Fourth Gospel, A Decade of Johannine Studies," *Louvain*

been viewed as a representative of Jewish Christianity,[29] Judaism,[30] the people of God, the Church, or the new Eve,[31] those who seek salvation, including receptive Israelites,[32] remembering mother and carrier of tradition,[33] and the spiritual mother of all believers.[34] Alternatively, the beloved disciple is seen as the earthly successor to Jesus,[35] or as his adopted brother.[36] Still another reading sees in the episode the creation of the new family of God.[37] The number and diversity of these interpretations raises the suspicion that the mother of Jesus, and this scene in particular, has been heavily over-interpreted.[38]

Studies 3 (1970): 99–142. If one understands Jesus to be transferring his earthly authority to the disciple (a common interpretation), the role of Jesus' mother must still be taken into account. Why choose an adoption scene to pass on the mantle of authority? Note that in the Gospel of Matthew the establishment of Peter's authority is indicated much more explicitly with Jesus' statement in 16:18.

[29]Bultmann, 673.

[30]Eva Krafft, "Die Personen des Johannesevangeliums," *EvTheol* 16 (1956): 18–19.

[31]Brown, 107–109, 923–927. Feuillet, *Johannine Studies*, 285–288.

[32]Schnackenburg, 278–279. Similarly, Brodie, 174–175, 549–550, who sees Mary as representative of responsive Judaism. Slightly different is Rena, who sees her representing the redeemed segment of the Jewish Christian church who no longer have inadequate faith ("Women in the Gospel," 136–137).

[33]Joseph A. Grassi, "The Role of Jesus' Mother in John's Gospel: A Reappraisal," *CBQ* 48 (1986): 67–80.

[34]This has been the traditional position of the Catholic church, cf. Collins, "Mary in the Fourth Gospel," 132–136.

[35]So Snyder, "John 13:16 and the Anti-Petrinism of the Johannine Tradition," *Biblical Research* 16 (1971): 12–13. Also A. H. Maynard, "The Role of Peter in the Fourth Gospel," *NTS* (1984): 539.

[36]Räisänen, *Die Mutter Jesu*, 179–180.

[37]Seim, "Roles of Women," 62–65. O'Day, 832. The difficulties with the other interpretations and the mention of the disciple's home make this explanation of the passage the most plausible.

[38]So Räisänen, *Die Mutter Jesu*, 176–77, and C. H. Dodd, *The Interpretation of the Fourth Gospel* (Cambridge: Cambridge University Press, 1953, reprinted New York: Cambridge University Press, 1992), 428, nt. 2. The interpretation of the mother of Jesus as the New Eve serves as a good example. Recognizing that γύναι likely carries symbolic weight, scholars have combed the biblical text to find a background for the term. Most often, their efforts have focused on two texts, Genesis 2–3 and Revelation 12, neither of which can be linked with any certainty to the Fourth Gospel. Taken together these to references have been used as a basis for reading Mary as the New Eve, that is, Genesis 2:22–23 depicts the creation and naming of γυνή, who is later named the "mother of all living" (Gen 3:20); the two descriptions, "woman" and "mother," are related to the mother of Jesus who becomes a symbol of the New Eve, the spiritual mother of all believers. The

In this study, my interest is in what the scene contributes to the characterization of the mother of Jesus. In chapter two of the Gospel, this character's identity was grounded in her maternal role, a role that contributed to the advancement of the narrative. Even more significantly, we discovered that in this role she acted in complete accord with the will of Jesus' heavenly father. Additionally, the unusual identification of the mother of Jesus as "woman" pointed ahead to the roles of other woman in the Gospel, especially in relation to the theme of Jesus' coming hour. In light of all this, it is significant that the same aspects of her character reappear in chapter nineteen. Again, she is the mother of Jesus from the narrator's perspective, but designated "woman" by Jesus. Again, she is closely associated with the arrival of Jesus' hour. However, in this scene, the mother of Jesus does not speak at all, so that we must rely on her actions and the words of Jesus to understand her role.

With regard to her actions, her presence at the foot of the cross, as well as her designation as the mother of Jesus, are relevant. Once more her maternal role is emphasized, perhaps even more strongly than in chapter two, as she is present with her son at the time of his death. Also, as a mother, she adopts a new son, the beloved disciple. Given this emphasis, the fact that Jesus once again addresses her as γύναι is striking. The title is given more prominence by the lack of a parallel in Jesus' statement to the disciple. As was the case in chapter two, Jesus' use of γύναι presents difficulties. To be sure, in this case there is no hint of hostility towards his mother, but the formal title appears even more out of place in this most intimate of moments dealing specifically with familial relationships. In this respect, the distancing theory discussed above may be more applicable here. Jesus is separating

---

interpretation is further enhanced by reference to Revelation 12. This text features a vision of a woman (γυνή) clothed with the sun, who gives birth to a male child, the messiah (12:5, cf. Ps 2:9). The connection with the Fourth Gospel is seen in the fact that both texts identify the mother of the messiah as "woman." It also assumes that the Gospel and the Apocalypse are related through a common Johannine tradition or school.

In response to this line of interpretation, Seim is on the mark when she states, "...this network of interpretations appears as a jungle growth of exegetical conjectures and catchword combinations." She goes on to raise the methodological question, "how much or how little is needed of a clue in the text to mobilize comprehensive and complex mythological ideas as the horizon of thought revealing the hidden meaning of the text?" ("Roles of Women in the Gospel of John," 61).

himself from his earthly identity, including his relationship to his mother.[39]

It is not evident, however, that in becoming mother to the disciple, this character is no longer to be considered the mother of Jesus. The scene may be a way of ensuring her continued significance as Jesus' mother and her participatory role in Jesus' mission through her relationship to Jesus' earthly representative, the beloved disciple. Moreover, as was the case in chapter two, to explain Jesus' use of γύναι as a means of distancing himself from his mother, would not take into account Jesus' use of the title elsewhere. Let me suggest again that the main effect of the use of γύναι is to create a link with the other women in the narrative. In chapter two, use of this term pointed ahead to the other women in the text. In chapter nineteen this connection between women in the Gospel is reaffirmed, with the climactic presentation of Mary Magdalene yet to occur (20:1–18). Thus, as the mother of Jesus, she maintains her individual role in the text, but as woman, she participates with other Johannine women in the Gospel's drama of revelation.

In this regard, it is significant that both in chapters two and nineteen the occurrence of the title is followed by highly dramatic scenes. Chapter two presents the initial revelation of Jesus' glory and thereby the first step toward his final hour of glory. In chapter nineteen, the disciple takes Jesus' mother to his home (εἰς τὰ ἴδια) from that hour (ἀπ᾽ ἐκείνης τῆς ὥρας). The precise significance of this act is difficult to determine. A common interpretation is that the revelation of Jesus is perpetuated through the presence of his earthly representative, the beloved disciple.[40] As mentioned above, the same idea of continuity may apply to the role of Jesus' mother. In other words, from the point of view of the Gospel, the mother of Jesus is as crucial as the beloved disciple to the continuation of Jesus' ministry and mission on earth. Along this line, the most plausible interpretation of 19:25–27 is that it creates a new family of God on earth and this family makes possible the

---

[39]Although, as we have seen, the distancing theory has been a mainstay in the interpretation of chapter two, scholars have not extended the theory to chapter nineteen (though cf. Seim, "Roles of Women," 60). Instead, discussions of the appearance of the title in chapter nineteen have centered more on its possible symbolic significance (see nt. 39). Cf., however, Schnackenburg (278) and O'Day (832) who both point to the narrative link that the address creates between chapters two and nineteen.

[40]Schnackenburg, 3.279.

continuity of Jesus' mission. Not only does this reading make sense of the adoption motif, it recognizes the importance of both Jesus' mother and the disciple in the scene. Indeed, what can be stated with certainty is that Jesus accords special significance to both his mother and his disciple, so that efforts to elevate one or the other are misguided. It is more the case that through her relationship with the beloved disciple, the mother of Jesus contributes to the establishment of the family of God. As in chapter two, she is once more linked to the fundamental purpose of Jesus' mission (cf. 1:12).

Also significant in this regard is that immediately after this scene has taken place (μετὰ τοῦτο) Jesus knows all things are finished (19:28). It is unclear whether all things are fulfilled with this adoption event, or whether the event signals that everything had already been fulfilled. In either case, as Brown indicates, the episode represents "the completion of the work that the Father had given to Jesus to do...,"[41] and thus has great eschatological significance. In the Fourth Gospel, Jesus permits himself to die when his work is fulfilled—his death does not mark the culmination of his work, but rather the return to the Father after his work is complete. The point is clearly reiterated in his dying words and actions, τετέλεσται, καὶ κλίνας τὴν κεφαλὴν παρέδωκεν τὸ πνεῦμα (19:30). In this way it becomes clear that Jesus' mother is crucial to the completion of his mission, just as she was to its beginning. Her presence at the beginning and the end of Jesus' earthly ministry corresponds to his origin from and return to the Father. In this sense, is it not possible that the mother of Jesus, a female, functions as the earthly counterpart of Jesus' heavenly father, a male?

To summarize, the mother of Jesus undoubtedly has a key role to play in the Gospel of John. She is present at the beginning and the end of his earthly ministry as mother and as "woman." As a character in 2:1–12, she is presented as one who contributes actively to the will of the Father. At one level, she is the determined mother who shows utmost confidence in her son's ability. In her persistence in urging Jesus forward she is characterized as more attuned to Jesus' mission than he is himself. Contrary to posing the heavenly father and earthly mother in opposition to one another, the narrative presents a complete coordination of the will of the heavenly father and the encouragement of Jesus' earthly mother. Jesus thinks his hour has not yet come: she rightly knows that the time for revelation and the movement toward the hour

---

[41]Brown, 925–926.

has come. In chapter nineteen, her presence, along with the beloved disciple, enables the establishment of a new family of God, an act that is crucial for the completion of Jesus' hour. Finally, that she shares the designation "woman" with other female characters in the narrative points to the possibility that what they do will also be linked fundamentally to the mission of Jesus and the fulfillment of his hour. This notion will be explored further in the course of the investigation.

NICODEMUS (3:1–10, 7:50–52, 19:39–40)

Introduction

A look through the commentaries soon reveals that Nicodemus is an opaque rather than transparent character. Throughout the narrative, his inner motives remain concealed from the reader. As a result, he has been viewed both sympathetically, as a Jew who gradually comes to faith in Jesus,[42] and negatively, as one who does not, or cannot, receive Jesus' testimony and consequently does not become a child of God.[43]

---

[42]John Bligh is perhaps the most positive in his reading of Nicodemus. In his words, "Nicodemus came to Jesus, not to mock him, but to disclose his own spiritual weariness and his lack of courage and hope; and Jesus treated him with gentleness" ("Four Studies in St John, II: Nicodemus," *HeyJ* 8 [1967]: 48). Also positive in his evaluation of Nicodemus is Schnackenburg who states, "Nicodemus can hardly be considered as a 'typical' case of the unbelieving Jew." Nor does Nicodemus represent superficial faith since "he has thought much about Jesus and considers him a teacher to whom he can turn for light on serious matters." From Nicodemus' appearances in 7:30 and 19:39, Schnackenburg deduces his gradual progress to faith and eventual conversion to Christianity (1.364–365). In considering Nicodemus, both Bligh and Schnackenburg make clear their opinion that the Gospel character represents a real historical figure. Schneiders sees Nicodemus as a type of the true Israelite who progresses from a sign-based faith, to openly confessing Jesus ("Born Anew," *TToday* 44 [1987]: 191). Brodie speaks of Nicodemus' growing acceptance of Jesus (169). Haenchen sees Nicodemus as a forthright man, who comes to Jesus with the good news that he has disciples in Jerusalem, himself among them (205). Cf. also Beasley-Murray, 47. Brown explains, "Nicodemus' role is...to show how some who were attracted to Jesus did not immediately understand him. Presumably some never came to understand him...but some like Nicodemus did" (*Community of the Beloved Disciple*, 72, nt. 128.) Cf. also Charles H. Talbert, *Reading John: A Literary and Theological Commentary on the Fourth Gospel and the Johannine Epistles* (Crossroad: New York, 1992), 97–98.

[43]Cf. Marinus de Jonge, "Nicodemus and Jesus: Some Observations on Misunderstanding and Understanding in the Fourth Gospel," in *Jesus: Stranger from Heaven*, 29–47. First published in *BJRL* 53 (1971): 337–359. Bultmann contends that in this scene Nicodemus is not moved to faith, but only to a point of questioning (133). Krafft, who considers Nicodemus to represent an historical figure, argues that

Such diverse readings of Nicodemus reflect both the complexity and ambiguity of his character. Indeed, Jouette Bassler contends that "Nicodemus' primary characteristic is ambiguity."[44] To be sure, when Nicodemus is considered alone, apart from his relationship to other characters, he is nothing other than ambiguous. However, when considered in context, in relation to Jesus and to other characters, e.g., the Samaritan woman, Nicodemus takes on a decidedly negative quality.

This analysis will concentrate on Nicodemus' initial appearance in the Gospel in 3:1–10, although attention will also be given to Nicodemus' two other brief appearances. The passage in chapter three is Jesus' first extended discourse with another character in the Gospel. Although the pericope continues through verse 21, my focus will be on the first ten verses since these feature Nicodemus as an active participant. After verse 10, he drops from the scene and though Jesus (or possibly the narrator at vv. 16–21)[45] continues to speak, he shifts to plural pronouns, indicating a broader audience. For purposes of discussion, the passage will be broken down into four sections: The introduction of the character (3:1-2) the first exchange with Jesus (3:2–3); the second exchange with Jesus (3:4–8); and the third exchange with

---

while he is willing to acknowledge Jesus as a teacher and miracle worker, he will not relinquish his traditional Jewish dogma and accept him as the Messiah ("Die Personen des Johannesevangeliums," 18–32). Culpepper views Nicodemus as "a man ready to believe but incapable of doing so" (*Anatomy*, 136). Similarly, Jerome H. Neyrey ("John III—A Debate over Johannine Epistemology and Christology," *NovT* 23 [1981]: 120) argues that Nicodemus is incapable of true knowledge because he is not born ἄνωθεν. For Collins, Nicodemus is "truly a man of the Pharisees, a Jew who does not have an authentic faith in Jesus" ("Jesus' Conversation with Nicodemus," in *These Things Having Been Written*, [66]. First published in *BibT* 93 [1977]: 1409–1419). For additional listings of various views of Nicodemus, cf. Debbie Gibbons, "Nicodemus: Character Development, Irony and Repetition in the Fourth Gospel," in *Proceedings: Eastern Great Lakes and Midwest Biblical Societies* 11 (1991): 123, nt. 5.

[44]Jouette Bassler, "Mixed Signals: Nicodemus in the Fourth Gospel," *JBL* 108 (1989): 645. Cf. also Wayne Meeks who sees Nicodemus' ambiguity as "an important and deliberate part of the portrait of this obscure figure" ("The Man from Heaven in Johannine Sectarianism," *JBL* 91 [1972]: 54).

[45]The issue of whether Jesus' discourse continues in vv. 16–21, or the narrator inserts himself at this point has been a focus of critical debate (cf. Brown, 149). The ambiguity points to the fluidity between the language of the Johannine Jesus and the theology of the Fourth Evangelist which is evident throughout the Gospel. With respect to the characterization of Nicodemus, the issue is not crucial; whether or not Jesus is the intended speaker, verses 16–21 may function, in part, as commentary on Nicodemus.

Jesus (3:9–10). Note that the first two sections share verse two, which concludes the introductory description of Nicodemus and opens the conversation with Jesus.

Introduction of the Character (3:1–2)

Chapter three opens with direct reporting from the narrator, introducing a new character. As is typical in biblical narrative, no physical description of the character is included.[46] This does not preclude description of any kind, however. In fact, in one sentence the narrator conveys quite a lot of information.[47] We learn first that the character is an ἄνθρωπος ἐκ τῶν φαρισαίων. The phrase is notable since φαρισαῖος would have sufficed or τις ἐκ τῶν φαρισαίων. The use of ἄνθρωπος creates an echo of the preceding verse, in which ἄνθρωπος appears twice (2:25).t In this way, the reader is put on alert from the beginning of the conversation that Jesus knows the nature of this man. Additionally, the phrase calls attention to the character's gender by announcing before anything else that "there was a man...." It is true that ἄνθρωπος can be understood more generally as "person" without regard to gender. However, in this case the term may be intended to be gender specific, given the parallel introduction of the character in the next chapter. In effect, The phrase ἄνθρωπος ἐκ τῶν φαρισαίων points forward, already creating a contrast with the character that Jesus will encounter in chapter four—γυνὴ ἐκ τῆς Σαμαρείας (4:7). More will be said of this contrast in the discussion of the Samaritan woman. At this point, it is important to note that the parallel descriptions draw out two points of comparison, ἄνθρωπος / γυνὴ and φαρισαῖος /Σαμαρεῖτις.

Following the identification of this man from the Pharisees, the narrator goes on to provide his proper name—Nicodemus. The name itself tells little about him,[48] but the fact that he is given a name at all

---

[46]The possible exception to this is the mention of γέρων ὢν which occurs in the context of the dialogue (v. 4). There is no certainty as to whether this is intended as a personal reference or simply a general statement, though Barrett notes that γέρων would coincide with being an ἄρχων (208).

[47]Adele Berlin correctly observes, while detailed physical description may be lacking in the Bible, there is nevertheless a substantial range of information that is given through other descriptive terms. Such terms may be based on status, profession, gentilic designation, and distinctive physical features (*Poetics and Interpretation of Biblical Narrative*, 35–36).

[48]As is frequently noted, the name was popular among Greeks, and adopted by the Jews in transliterated form (cf. Barrett, 204; Bultmann, 133, nt. 3). Jewish

may be significant. Narrative theorists frequently highlight the name as the first step in characterization. William Gass states, "a character is first of all the noise of his name, and all the sounds and rhythms that proceed from him."[49] Similarly, in Sternberg's words, "to bear a name is to assume an identity: to become a singular existent, with an assured place in history and a future in the story."[50] Nicodemus does reappear two more times in the story (7:50–52, 19:39–40), and he does takes on an individual quality in the narrative.[51] In addition, the name serves quite literally as a locus for character indicators; in its initial appearance it is surrounded by epithets.[52] Nicodemus is both ἄνθρωπος ἐκ τῶν φαρισαίων and ἄρχων τῶν Ἰουδαίων.

What is the significance of these epithets in the construction of Nicodemus' character? Do they simply designate him as a representative figure of official Judaism?[53] The opening identification of Nicodemus as a Pharisee suggests that this aspect of his identity is especially relevant.

---

sources provide evidence for a certain Naqdimon ben Gorjon, living in Jerusalem in 70 C.E. and possibly a contemporary of Jesus (cf. Brown, 129–130, Barrett, 204). As with all the Johannine characters, the Evangelist's interest is not in historical detail but in the character's significance to the Gospel narrative.

[49]William Gass, *Fiction and the Figures of Life* (New York: Knopf, 1970), 49.

[50]Sternburg, *Poetics of Biblical Narrative*, 330–31. Both quotations are cited in David Galef, *The Supporting Cast,* 9.

[51]Cf. Schnackenburg (1.364) who notes that in spite of whatever representational function Nicodemus has, he retains some personal traits.

[52]As such, it visually illustrates Chatman's understanding that the name provides the locus around which the paradigm of traits is assembled. In his words, "[The proper name] is a kind of ultimate residence of personality, not a quality but a locus of qualities, the narrative-noun that is endowed with but never exhausted by the qualities, the narrative-adjectives" (*Story and Discourse*, 131). Note however, that Chatman understands "proper name" in the widest sense possible. For him, it can be any deictic mark, whether an actual name, a personal pronoun, an epithet, a demonstrative pronoun, or even a definite article (the man vs. a man). If this is the case, the name "Nicodemus" may be no more significant in terms of characterization than the phrase "Samaritan woman." Indeed, in the end, this anonymous woman is more fully developed than Nicodemus. For additional discussion, cf. David R. Beck. "The Narrative Function of Anonymity in Fourth Gospel Characterization," *Semeia* 63 (1993):143–158. He argues that in the Fourth Gospel, anonymity creates an indeterminacy that invites the reader to identify with the unnamed character, thus entering the narrative world and experiencing a crisis encounter with Jesus. For a different view see William W. Watty ("The Significance of Anonymity in the Fourth Gospel," *ExpTim* 90 [1979]: 209–212), who contends that anonymity in the Gospel is a corrective response to a heavy emphasis on the Petrine tradition in the early church.

[53]So Bultmann, 133; Barrett, 204.

Yet determining what his Pharisaic allegiance indicates about his character is not easy. The Pharisees, like Nicodemus, are not presented in a consistent fashion in the Gospel. While much of the evidence suggests a clear and open hostility towards Jesus, there are indications that some of the Pharisees are sympathetic toward him, Nicodemus among them.[54] It is necessary, therefore, to take up the question of the Pharisees in more detail, in the hope of clarifying what the epithet ἐκ τῶν φαρισαίων means for the character of Nicodemus.

Prior to 3:1, the Pharisees are mentioned only in 1:24, and there is textual confusion concerning this reference. Are the Pharisees the ones who are sent or are they doing the sending? Some manuscripts resolved the question by including an article before the participle. In this case, the sentence clearly means that the ones sent were from the Pharisees. However, the stronger witnesses omit the article leaving the phrase ambiguous.[55] It could mean that a new delegation made up of Pharisees was now questioning John, or that the Pharisees were the senders of the priests and Levites (cf. 1:19). The second translation is more problematic. Not only would it be historically inaccurate for Pharisees to have authority over priests and Levites; it is inconsistent with 1:19, which clearly identifies the senders as οἱ Ἰουδαῖοι.[56] Nevertheless, a similar inconsistency also appears in chapter nine. There, in the context of another official inquiry, the name for the interrogators shifts from the Pharisees (9:13, 13, 16), to the Jews (9:18, 22), and back to the Pharisees (9:40). Apparently, though οἱ Ἰουδαῖοι and οἱ φαρισαῖοι are two distinct groups elsewhere in the Gospel, in these two instances their identities are similar enough to allow their titles to be interchangeable.[57]

---

[54]Cf. J. S. King ("Nicodemus and the Pharisees," *ExpT* 98 [1986]: 45), who rejects the idea that the Pharisees are presented as consistently hostile to Jesus.

[55]Manuscripts containing no participle include Bodmer papyri, p⁶⁶ and p⁷⁵. Attestations for the participle include later editions of ℵ, A, and C.

[56]Brown suggests that the more difficult translation has the best chance of being correct. For a full discussion of the problem cf. Brown, 43–44.

[57]The alternating use of the terms points to the historical setting of the Fourth Gospel. At the time of the Gospel composition, following the fall of the Second Temple, the Pharisees were emerging as the dominant group within a formerly diversified Judaism. More problematic is the varied use of the term Ἰουδαῖος. In some instances it is used in a neutral sense and in others in an extremely polemic nature. The author's use of the term in its most negative sense (cf. especially chapter 8) is restricted to the Jewish authorities who reject Jesus. Cf. U. C. von Wahlde, "The Johannine 'Jews': A Critical Survey," *NTS* 28 (1982): 33–60; R. J. Bratcher, "'The Jews' in the Gospel of John," *The Bible Translator* 26 (1975): 401–409.

In other words, on both of these occasions the Pharisees, like the Jews, appear as men with power and authority who oversee the religious activity of the people. Moreover, in both instances, hostility towards Jesus is obvious, especially in chapter nine, where the Pharisees deny that he is from God (9:16).

Other occurrences of οἱ φαρισαῖοι also suggest that "Pharisee" is not simply an authoritative title, but a hostile designation with respect to Jesus. In 4:1, Jesus leaves Judea to avoid the Pharisees. They openly dispute with Jesus (8:13), and it is the Pharisees and chief priests who send assistants out to arrest him (7:32, 11:57, 18:3). Finally, it is on account of the Pharisees that many (even ἐκ τῶν ἀρχόντων) who believe in Jesus, do not confess it openly (12:42).

Yet, in addition to these negative associations, the narrative also leaves room for another kind of Pharisee, perhaps represented by Nicodemus. As the Pharisees question their officers about a failed attempt to arrest Jesus, Nicodemus speaks up (7:47-51). The text reinforces both the fact that Nicodemus had gone to Jesus earlier, and that he is one of the Pharisees (εἷς ὢν ἐξ αὐτῶν), possibly pointing toward his split loyalties. Nicodemus' words, an appeal to give Jesus a fair hearing as required by Jewish law, are met with scorn from his colleagues (7:52). The conversation ends at this point, with the question of Nicodemus' allegiance unanswered. But the fact that he intervenes on Jesus' behalf suggests that his identity as a Pharisee does not necessarily imply hostility toward Jesus.

Indeed, in chapter nine there is an indication of a division among the Pharisees, with one side representing a view similar to that of Nicodemus. While the healing of the blind man draws anger from some Pharisees, others ask how a sinful person can do such signs. On this point, the narrator reports, καὶ σχίσμα ἦν ἐν αὐτοῖς (9:16), showing clearly that at least at this point, the Pharisees do not constitute a unified group in relation to Jesus. The passage contains no reference to Nicodemus, but the question put forward by others in 9:16 recalls his opening statement to Jesus. Both interpret the signs that Jesus performs as an indication of God's favor (3:2). By 9:24 the authorities (not explicitly identified as the Pharisees) do express a unified view, stating, "We know that his man is a sinner." Finally, in 12:42, there is reference to authorities who believe in Jesus, but do not confess it "on account of the Pharisees," for fear that they would be put out of the synagogue.

To summarize, in general the title Pharisee does not bode well as a character indicator for Nicodemus, in terms of his view of Jesus. In many instances, the Pharisees are depicted as opponents and enemies of Jesus. At the same time, the title does not unequivocally determine Nicodemus' character in terms of his view of Jesus. Some more positive or at least neutral references to the Pharisees leave room for a tolerant or even sympathetic attitude towards Jesus on the part of Nicodemus.

Like the designation Pharisee, the epithet following the name Nicodemus, ἄρχων τῶν Ἰουδαίον, bears the same uncertain quality. First, there is the question of the title's meaning. As it stands, it appears nowhere else in the Gospel. Focusing on οἱ ἄρχοντες, Bultmann and others understand the title as a reference to the Sanhedrin.[58] While this may be the case, the term remains vague in the Gospel,[59] and there is no certainty that such a specific meaning is intended. The only place where the Sanhedrin is mentioned in the Fourth Gospel is 11:47 in which the chief priests and Pharisees call the Sanhedrin together. Notably, the scene contains no reference to οἱ ἄρχοντες (11:47–53). Moreover, given 12:42, the Pharisees seem to have greater authority and control than do the rulers.

Second, like the Pharisees in the Gospel, οἱ ἄρχοντες include both enemies and sympathizers of Jesus. In 7:25, the people of Jerusalem identify οἱ ἄρχοντες as those who are trying to kill Jesus. Later, in 7:48, the Pharisees scoff at the idea that they or any of the rulers have believed in Jesus. It therefore comes as a surprise to read in 12:42 that some of the authorities did believe in Jesus. Thus, as an indication of character ἄρχων τῶν Ἰουδαίων provides little more help than "Pharisee" does. It is true that the majority of evidence casts the Pharisees and leaders in a negative light. Yet, both titles also have a measure of ambiguity, so that ultimately they offer no decisive information regarding Nicodemus' relationship to Jesus. In this way, the epithets surrounding the name of Nicodemus contribute to his portrayal as a fundamentally ambiguous character.

Along this line, still one more ambiguous clue to Nicodemus' character concludes his introduction to the narrative and opens the way for his encounter with Jesus. The narrator reports an action—Nicodemus came to Jesus by night (νυκτός). Recalling Alter's scale, the report of

---

[58]Bultmann, 133, nt. 4. So also Haenchen, 1.199; Barrett, 204; Brown, 130; Schnackenburg, 1.365.

[59]Cf. de Jonge, "Nicodemus and Jesus," 43, nt. 2.

an action leaves the reader in the realm of inference with respect to its significance as a character indicator, and the lack of scholarly consensus on this detail confirms this notion. Much has been made of Nicodemus' nocturnal approach and what it may suggest about his character. Many understand it to be symbolic of the dark, evil realm out of which Nicodemus comes to Jesus, the light.[60] References to night elsewhere in the Gospel lend weight to this negative interpretation (9:4; 11:10; 13:30). On the other hand, that Nicodemus came to the light perhaps should be regarded as an indication of the integrity of his motives, given the comment in 3:21—those who do what is true come to the light.

Still another view interprets νύξ itself positively, either with reference to the rabbinical habit of studying Torah well into the night,[61] or to the desire for uninterrupted conversation.[62] Another possibility depends on the association of Nicodemus with Joseph of Arimathea (19:38–42). Nicodemus comes secretly, under cover of night, to avoid being seen by the Jews.[63] Though the fear of the Jews is not assigned to Nicodemus in chapter nineteen, that νύξ is repeated, highlights its importance as a character indicator.[64] Given the symbolic weight of day/night and light/dark in the Gospel, it is difficult to accept a positive or even neutral interpretation. Furthermore, the word may serve as another point of contrast between this scene and the scene at the well.

---

[60]E.g., Brown, 130. Also Schnackenburg (1.365), though he prefaces his opinion with the comment that the detail "allows of no sure conclusion about the character." Adele Reinhartz ("The Gospel of John," 570), understands the gratuitous detail to imply that "Nicodemus is 'in darkness,' an unbeliever." Slightly different is Brodie who claims that as a representative of human achievement and learning, "the enlightened Nicodemus is in the dark" (194).

[61]Cf. Str.-B II 420, cited by Bultmann (133, nt. 5). With the rabbinic reference in mind, Bultmann views the phrase as an illustration of Nicodemus' great zeal. Above all, however, he believes it adds to the air of mystery that pervades the passage. Barrett also cites 1 QS 6.7 (204). Haenchen, on the other hand, points out that the rabbinic reference does not fit with the situation in chapter three, i.e., Nicodemus and Jesus do not meet in the daylight and talk into the night (1.199).

[62]Beasley-Murray, 47.

[63]E.g., L. Martyn, for whom Nicodemus represents the secret believers who were members of the Gerousia (*History and Theology*, 87). Cf. also Rensberger, *Johannine Faith*, 37–41.

[64]Contra F. B. Cotterell, who argues from a syntactical perspective that because νυκτός is not fronted in 3:2, it signifies no more than a chronological marker ("The Nicodemus Conversation: A Fresh Appraisal," *ExpTim* 96 [1985]: 239).

Nicodemus speaks to Jesus while in the dark; the woman's encounter with Jesus takes place in daylight (ὥρα ἦν ὡς ἕκτη, 4:6).[65]

In sum, from the opening description, we discover that we know quite a bit, and yet not very much at all about Nicodemus. While Nicodemus bears titles that mark him as a man with power in the Jewish community, the titles reveal little about his personal convictions, especially with respect to the man he is about to meet. Indeed, they add to the presentation of Nicodemus as a complex figure, marked by "cross-currents of ambivalence."[66] Moreover, the added detail of Nicodemus coming by night does little to simplify his portrait; it only adds to the ambiguity. Coming "by night" implies secrecy at best, and at worst, symbolizes the darkness (σκότος) loved by οἱ ἄνθρωποι because their deeds were evil (3:19, cf. also 8:12; 11:10; 12:35, 46). Up to this point, Bassler's description of the character of Nicodemus as ambiguous remains to the point. If we are to get a clear picture of his character, we must rely on more than narrated description. We must look carefully at his words and at the response his words evoke in Jesus.

The First Exchange (3:2–3)

Following the introduction by the narrator, Nicodemus initiates a conversation with Jesus. In keeping with the description thus far, he opens with a statement that reinforces his authoritative status. His first sentence conveys that he speaks for a group (cf. the plural, οἴδαμεν) that knows about Jesus and about God (3:2). His words have an air of formality, suggesting that he is talking in an official stance. He assigns Jesus a title, ῥαββί, thereby echoing the disciples in 1:38.[67] He also calls Jesus διδάσκαλος and speaks of his origin ἀπὸ θεοῦ. Nicodemus bases this knowledge on his interpretive ability; he and the people whom he represents are able to read signs and know when God is present. Like the description of Nicodemus as ἄνθρωπος, the reference to signs also recalls 2:23–25. Nicodemus speaks as one who believes because of signs and as one whom Jesus does not trust. Thus, there is irony in the way that Nicodemus approaches Jesus. As Brodie notes, he "seems to feel that he can speak to Jesus with some assurance of the things of God. There is therefore in his approach a certain tone of confidence."[68]

---

[65]Reinhartz, "The Gospel of John," 573.
[66]Hochman, *Character in Literature*, 123.
[67]Brodie, 196.
[68]Brodie, 196.

In one sense, from the point of view of the narrative, Nicodemus may have reason to feel confident since his opening words are accurate. Certainly, Jesus' origin ἀπὸ θεοῦ is a central truth in the narrative (cf. 13:3; 16:30; also παρὰ θεοῦ 9:33, παρὰ πατρός, 1:14, 16:28; παρ᾽ αὐτου, 7:29). Likewise, Jesus himself affirms that διδάσκαλος is an appropriate way to address him (13:13f., cf. also 11:28; 20:16).[69] Finally, Nicodemus is correct in his assessment that God is with Jesus (ὁ θεὸς μετ᾽ αὐτοῦ). This, too, is a theme that recurs throughout the narrative (e.g., 8:29: 16:32). Therefore, as de Jonge points out, "the terminology used by Nicodemus is not wrong in itself."[70]

In sum, if Nicodemus' status as a Pharisee and ruler of the Jews leaves his relationship to Jesus in question, his opening words seem quite amicable. Haenchen calls them a profession of affection,[71] while de Jonge goes so far as to call them a confession of faith.[72] Recall, however, that while direct speech may present a clearer picture of the character, we are still in the middle of Alter's scale in which claims by the character must be weighed by the reader. In the case of Nicodemus (and most other characters in the Gospel), his words of confession must be weighed against the response of Jesus. To put it another way, a relational view of character suggests that the words of Nicodemus cannot be taken simply at face value—their meaning is not to be found in themselves alone, but also in the way in which Jesus responds to them.

However, this is not to say that Nicodemus is merely a foil for Jesus. As we have seen above, his character is presented with a complexity that suggests more than this. Moreover, to take Jesus' response into consideration does not mean one should completely abandon the sense of Nicodemus' words. For instance, it is often

---

[69]Cotterell downplays the fronted qualifying phrase, ἀπὸ θεοῦ, arguing that the use of διδάσκαλος rather than προφήτης (as in Mk 11:32) suggests a conservative estimate of the status of Jesus by Nicodemus ("Nicodemus Conversation," 239). Bassler, on the other hand, points out that precisely this phrase contains an insight that is missing from the disciples' professions of faith in 1:41, 45, 49: Jesus has come from God ("Mixed Signals," 637).

[70]de Jonge, "Nicodemus and Jesus," 40. What is wrong, according to de Jonge, is that Nicodemus does not use these terms within the proper framework, namely, within the knowledge that Jesus is ὁ ἄνωθεν ἐρχόμενος, ἀπὸ θεοῦ, παρὰ του θεοῦ, and above all ἐκ τοῦ θεοῦ.

[71]Haenchen, 1.205.

[72]de Jonge, "Nicodemus and Jesus," 37. Meeks also calls Nicodemus' opening statement "a declaration of faith" ("Man from Heaven," 54).

suggested on the basis of Jesus' response that Nicodemus' opening statement is actually a question. Bultmann, for instance, argues that Nicodemus comes to Jesus "with the one question which Judaism...has to put to Jesus, and must put to him. It is the question of salvation."[73] Similarly, Schnackenburg comments that "Jesus understands Nicodemus as being moved by the question which preoccupied all Jews: 'What must I do to share in the world to come?'"[74] Brown, also, suggests that Jesus treats Nicodemus' words as an implicit request about entrance into the kingdom of God.[75] The problem with all of these statements is that they leave the narrative behind. As we have seen, far from being a question, Nicodemus' words are a confident, even cocky, opening statement. To turn this statement into a question smoothes away the disjunction between his words and Jesus' response. Moreover, it destroys the narrative progression of Nicodemus' own comments, from confident statement to confused questions.[76] Recognizing the tension between Nicodemus' opening proposition and the rest of the conversation is critical for interpreting the nature of his relationship with Jesus.

With this in mind, we turn to the first words of Jesus in this conversation. If it were not for the warning of 2:23–25, one would expect Jesus to respond with words of affirmation or even revelation. But in keeping with the link between the characterization of Nicodemus and the end of chapter two, Jesus says nothing to acknowledge Nicodemus' praise, nor does he respond directly to his statement. Instead, he replies to the confident οἴδαμεν by shifting the conversation to an individual level, λέγω σοι, thereby either ignoring or negating Nicodemus' representational status. Likewise, Jesus counters Nicodemus' knowledge of God's presence, οὐδεὶς γὰρ δύναται ταῦτα τὰ σεμεῖα ποιεῖν ἃ σὺ ποιεῖς, ἐὰν μή ᾖ ὁ θεὸς μετ' αὐτοῦ, with his own knowledge about God, ἐὰν μή τις γεννηθῇ ἄνωθεν οὐ δύναται ἰδεῖν τὴν βασιλείαν τοῦ θεοῦ.[77] In this way, Nicodemus'

---

[73]Bultmann, 134–135.

[74]Schnackenburg, 1.366.

[75]Brown, 138.

[76]Cf. Neyrey, who states, "(I)t is a critical mistake to interpret Nicodemus as asking a question in v. 2; his subsequent questions are literary ploys which prove that he does not know what he claimed to know in v. 2" ("John III," 118, nt. 12).

[77]Neyrey notes that Nicodemus' statement introduces the rhetorical pattern which dominates the discourse. The pattern is then turned into an absolute claim by the Christians (represented by Jesus' response) ("John III," 119).

religious expertise, his ability to discern the presence of God, is subtly called into question.

Given this initial exchange, the observations of F. B. Cotterell are compelling.[78] Using discourse analysis, Cotterell notes that in rabbinic culture it was typical for the senior dialogue partner to initiate a conversation through a proposition-response pattern, in contrast to a question-answer pattern, which either partner could initiate. If this is the case, reading Nicodemus' opening words as a proposition rather than an implied question becomes especially significant. In both form and content, Nicodemus' opening statement is calculated to display his superiority to Jesus.

Similarly, in both form and content, Jesus' response contests this superior position. Cotterell points out that Nicodemus initially offers Jesus at least four substantive topics for conversation: the concept of Rabbi, the implication of Jesus' status as teacher, the significance of being ἀπο θεοῦ, and the significance and provenance of τὰ σεμεῖα Jesus takes up none of these.[79] Cotterell explains further, "In refusing to follow Nicodemus' lead, Jesus implicitly brings into question the fundamental principle on which the discourse has been founded; the priority of Nicodemus."[80] In other words, Jesus' non-response to Nicodemus' proposition undermines his status as a man of authority in the community. In this way, although Jesus does not openly reject or condemn Nicodemus, he calls into question his role as representative of the "we" of verse 2. Moreover, he provides a way to further determine the character of Nicodemus. In other words, with his response to Nicodemus, Jesus identifies the conditions under which one might justifiably speak about God—one must be born ἄνωθεν. It remains for Nicodemus, who has spoken so confidently about the ways of God, to demonstrate whether he is in this condition.

The Second Exchange (3:4–8)

Upon hearing Jesus' response, Nicodemus leaves behind his confident declarations about Jesus and God and begins to question Jesus

---

[78]While I do not follow Cotterell in reading the pericope "as a record of a historical encounter and an actual conversation," his use of discourse analysis yields significant insight into the text ("Nicodemus Conversation," 237).

[79]Cf. Neyrey, however, who argues that verse 2 is the topic statement of the third chapter containing the terms to be discussed: epistemology and Christology ("John III," 116).

[80]Cotterell, "Nicodemus Conversation," 239–240.

instead (v. 4). But what type of questions are they? In general, one may view Nicodemus' words as didactic tools employed by the author—he asks in order for Jesus to be able to expound on the topic. That Jesus does so in verses 5–8, without ever directly addressing Nicodemus' question, adds to the impression that Nicodemus is simply a functional character and thus completely expendable to the narrative. Even if this is the case, we must consider what it is about his character that lends itself to expendability. Additionally, we must account for why, if his character is so purely functional, he reappears twice more in the Gospel.

Most difficult to determine is the tone behind Nicodemus' inquiry. When he asks Jesus about the possibility of a person reentering his or her mother's womb is he mocking Jesus, or is he in a true state of perplexity? On the one hand, the absurdity of his statement suggests the former. Considering Jesus' words about being born again to be ridiculous, Nicodemus responds in kind.[81] On the other hand, the subsequent admonition by Jesus (μὴ θαυμάσῃς, v. 7) may suggest that Nicodemus is expressing genuine incredulity. Another possibility is that Nicodemus' exaggerated objection may simply reflect a style that was typical of rabbinic argumentation.[82] He accepts Jesus' offer of a different subject matter and pursues it in the form of rabbinic debate.

The interpretive options above illustrate that taken alone the character of Nicodemus is difficult to define with any certainty. It is only in the third exchange that it becomes clear to the reader how Nicodemus should be perceived. For now, what can be readily determined from his questions is that he misinterprets Jesus' statement as a literal reference to physical birth. For this reason, he invokes birth imagery himself, asking in graphic terms whether an adult can enter into the womb of his mother a second time (v. 4). Note that with this statement, issues of gender may come into play as the conversation takes up the contrast between two different types of birth. Jesus speaks of a heavenly, spiritual birth,[83] while Nicodemus thinks of an earthly, physical birth.

---

[81]Slightly different is Cotterell's reading. He views Nicodemus' response as "woodenly uncooperative," and suggests that he is demonstrating his pique at being superseded by Jesus ("Nicodemus Conversation," 240).

[82]Cf. Schnackenburg, who claims that in rabbinic scholastic exercises objections were stated as paradoxically as possible (1.367). Along this line, Bultmann points out that μὴ θαυμάσῃς appears frequently in rabbinic argumentation, suggesting that the phrase is more formulaic than descriptive (142, nt. 1).

[83]Whether one translates ἄνωθεν as "from above" or "again," a spiritual birth is implied, as Jesus makes clear in verse 6.

One might explore whether at a symbolic level, these two types of birth represent a male begetting and a female birth, but this is moving outside the bounds of a character analysis.[84]

Of course, this type of misunderstanding in itself is not enough to cast a negative light on Nicodemus, since misunderstandings of Jesus occur frequently in the Gospel, among Jesus' disciples as well as among his opponents (e.g. 6:52ff., 13:6–10). Indeed, in chapter four the Samaritan woman will exhibit a very similar type of misunderstanding regarding the phrase ὕδωρ ζῶν (4:10–11). However, in the case of Nicodemus, who has been introduced as a man of authority and has presented himself as knowledgeable, his questions appear particularly ignorant. In the end, Jesus confirms this impression; he responds quite differently to Nicodemus than he does to the Samaritan woman. Whereas in his conversation with the woman, Jesus takes a new tack to bring her to a point of understanding, here he virtually ignores Nicodemus' comment, merely restating his initial proposition and then elaborating on it. He neither answers Nicodemus' question, nor makes any effort to bring him along in the conversation.

In fact, Jesus' words do more to alienate Nicodemus than they do to help him understand. In place of the ambiguous ἄνωθεν, Jesus substitutes the equally puzzling phrase ἐξ ὕδατος καὶ πνεύματος, and instead of being able to see (ἰδεῖν) the kingdom, he speaks now of the ability to enter it (εἰσελθεῖν εἰς) (v. 5). Presumably, both changes are meant to explain further Jesus' first statement, but it will soon be clear that for Nicodemus they provide little help. Jesus then distinguishes the two types of birth under question—the earthly birth, to γεγεννημένον ἐκ τῆς σαρκὸς and the heavenly birth to γεγεννημένον ἐκ τοῦ πνεύματος. The distinction draws attention to Nicodemus' misunderstanding—he wrongly can think of only one earthly birth. In

---

[84]Raymond Brown argues that γεννηθῇ ἄνωθεν means, to be begotten from a male deity. According to him, while the passive form of the verb γεννάω can mean either "to be born," as of a feminine principle, or "to be begotten" as of a masculine principle, in this context, the masculine "begotten" is probably intended (cf. 1:12, also 1 John 3:9) (138). The seriousness of the matter for feminist interpretation is seen in how Brown goes on to explain the logic and "crude realism" of the passage.

> A man takes on flesh and enters the kingdom of the world because his father begets him; a man can enter the kingdom of God only when he is begotten by a heavenly Father. Life can come to a man only from his father; eternal life comes from the heavenly father through the Son whom he has empowered to give life (v 21).

addition, the contrast of the two types of births implies the existence of two types of people—the fleshly and the spiritual. When Jesus shifts from a singular to a plural pronoun, εἶπόν σοι δεῖ ὑμᾶς γεννηθῆαι ἄνωθεν, he decidedly includes Nicodemus in the class of people who still lack the spiritual birth necessary to see and enter the kingdom of God.

Jesus ends his elaboration with a play on words that once more confuses more than it clarifies (v. 8). The analogy of wind to spirit (both πνεῦμα) turns on the uncertainty of the origin or destination of both.[85] In this sense, the figure calls to mind a theme that runs throughout the Gospel, namely, the question of Jesus' origin and destination (e.g., 6:41–42; 7:27–29, 33–36; 14:5; 16:16–18). Though Jesus speaks in general terms here (οὕτως ἐστὶν πᾶς...), thus far he is the only character in the Gospel with whom the Spirit has been explicitly associated (cf. 1:32–33). Moreover, when Jesus resumes his explanation in verse 13, he speaks specifically of the Son of Man descending and ascending from heaven. Is Nicodemus to understand that the figure refers primarily to Jesus as an example of one who has been begotten by the Spirit, in other words, one who has been born ἄνωθεν?[86] If so, the point of the figure may be, "do not be amazed by the idea of being born from above, because the one whom you hear talking to you has been thus born, though you, in fact, can know nothing of his origin or destination." If this is correct, Jesus' words stand in direct contrast to Nicodemus' opening statement, in which he claimed to know all about Jesus' origin. In this way, rather than educating Nicodemus on the nature of salvation, as he will do with the Samaritan woman on the topic of worship, Jesus only highlights the ignorance of Nicodemus. This reality will be driven home in their final exchange.

The Third Exchange (3:9–12)

Nicodemus' final response vividly illustrates his complete lack of understanding. Jesus' words leave him confounded and nearly speechless. Despite Jesus' urging to the contrary, μὴ θαυμάσῃς, Nicodemus' last words in the conversation certainly convey

---

[85] Though Haenchen points out that the comparison is not appropriate because one can readily perceive from what direction the wind is coming and wither it goes (1.201).

[86] This also puts another light on Jesus' mention of flesh and spirit. In chapter one, both words occur in reference to Jesus (vv. 14, 32). Note, however, that the Word was not "born" of flesh (ἐγεννήθσεν) but "became" flesh (ἐγένετο).

astonishment (v. 9).[87] As a character, he has shifted from a man who, bolstered by his authoritative status, confidently and knowledgeably initiates a conversation, to one who can only stammer out a brief question. No longer confident about the who δυνάται ταῦτα σεμεῖα ποιεῖν, Nicodemus can only respond to the words of Jesus with—πῶς δύναται ταῦτα γενέσθαι.[88] In other words, from Nicodemus' perspective there is no revelation, only confusion. In this way, he contrasts sharply not only with several women characters of the Gospel, such as the Samaritan woman, Martha and Mary Magdalene, but also with the man born blind in chapter nine.[89]

Jesus' last direct words to Nicodemus point back to where the conversation began, with the granting of titles. This time, however, the title is issued by Jesus and couched in skepticism. He calls Nicodemus ὁ διδάσκαλος τοῦ Ἰσραήλ and in the same breath remarks on his lack of knowledge, ταῦτα οὐ γινώσκεις. This comment from Jesus completes the character construction of Nicodemus in this narrative. There can be little doubt that, despite his seemingly earnest approach, this character is to be viewed negatively. As Reinhartz comments, "Decisive is not Nicodemus' persistent misunderstanding of Jesus' words but rather the accusatory tone of Jesus' comments to Nicodemus. Rather than inviting him to believe, Jesus upbraids Nicodemus...."[90]

By verse 11, the conversation with Nicodemus is over. The dialogue becomes a monologue as Nicodemus drops from the scene. If there is any doubt as to Jesus' view of Nicodemus, verses 11–12 make it clear. Though these verses do not refer to Nicodemus specifically, the

---

[87]Haenchen, 1.201.

[88]Commenting on this lack of understanding, Meeks speaks of the passage as a "virtual *parody* of revelation discourse. What is 'revealed' is that Jesus is incomprehensible, even to the 'teacher of Israel' who holds an initially positive belief in him" ("Man from Heaven," 57). It may be more accurate to say that Nicodemus is a parody of those characters who come to belief in Jesus. While he is left behind in utter confusion, others are indeed brought to a point of revelation.

[89]Notably, the man born blind begins with an admission of not knowing about Jesus (9:12), moves to arguing that Jesus must be from God (9:33), and ends with his profession of faith in Jesus as the Son of Man (9:35–38).

[90]Reinhartz, "The Gospel of John," 570. In the same vein, Bassler points out, "Jesus responds differently to Nicodemus at their initial encounter than he does to Philip for example, or Thomas, who are affirmed and supported in spite of their theological bumbling (14:8–11; 20:24–29)" ("Mixed Signals," 643). One should note, however, that Philip and Thomas are also reprimanded by Jesus (cf. 14:9–10; 20:29).

move from the singular σοι in verse 11a to the plural ὑμιν in verses 11a–12 may point back to Nicodemus' οἴδαμεν in verse 2. Thus, Jesus speaks of the lack of belief of both Nicodemus and those associated with him. Once this point is made, as far as Jesus is concerned, Nicodemus becomes irrelevant and fades into the background. The reader may recall him at verses 19–20, however, where the dualism of light and dark are explicitly evoked. With respect to the way Jesus has interacted with this man, it seems unlikely that he is to be understood has one who came to the light. More probable, recalling his visit by night, is that Nicodemus is to be associated with darkness.

If chapter three were the only place in the Gospel where Nicodemus appears, his character would be less difficult to determine. Although he is introduced in an ambiguous way, by the end of this exchange, it is clear that he is to be viewed negatively. Moreover, we would be justified in seeing him primarily as a foil set up most immediately for the Samaritan woman, but also for the other characters who come to faith in Jesus. However, this is not Nicodemus' only appearance; he shows up briefly in two more Gospel scenes (7:50–52, 19:38–42).

Following chapter three, Nicodemus next appears in 7:50. As mentioned above, his introduction includes both a reference to his having gone to Jesus, recalling chapter three, and the fact that he is one of them. At first glance, both of these descriptions appear to be negative character indicators. Surprisingly, however, Nicodemus comes to the defense of Jesus, at least insofar as he attempts to secure a fair trial for him. Furthermore, he does so in spite of the rebuke he received earlier from Jesus. To be sure, his colleagues quickly put down Nicodemus, and he makes no further attempt to protect Jesus.[91] Neither of these factors completely diminishes the positive implications of his action, however. Moreover, as Bassler points out, the context of Nicodemus' comment

---

[91]Kraff maintains that Nicodemus' silence in the face of the objection from his colleagues implies that, while he reveres Jesus as an exemplary teacher, he is not willing to support him against traditional Jewish dogma ("Die Personen das Johannesevangeliums," 20). Similarly, David Rensberger points out that in speaking of Jewish law, Nicodemus refers to "our Law" and thereby remains confined to the realm of Pharisaic legal debate (*Johannine Faith,* 39). Bassler suggests that Nicodemus' primary concern is for correct legal procedure. She points out that "his words...unveil the hypocrisy of the Pharisees, who rebuke the crowd for their ignorance of the law (v. 49) yet fail to follow it themselves, but not necessarily the depth of Nicodemus's faith" ("Mixed Signals," 640).

further promotes a positive reading. The chief priests and Pharisees have just berated their officers with the sarcastic question, "Has any one of the authorities or of the Pharisees believed in him?" (7:48). Immediately following this, Bassler notes, "Nicodemus, who has been identified as both an authority and a Pharisee (3:1) and whose link with these groups is reaffirmed here (7:50), speaks out in Jesus' defense."[92] Still, his efforts are tentative at best and the question of his ultimate loyalty remains uncertain.

The next and last time Nicodemus is mentioned occurs after Jesus is crucified. Once more, his introduction is accompanied by a reference to chapter three; this time we are reminded that Nicodemus came to Jesus first by night (19:39; cf. 3:2). In this way, all three of his appearances are linked, suggesting that they are supposed to build on one another. In this scene, Nicodemus says nothing, but his actions speak of his continued interest in Jesus. He brings an extravagant amount of spices for embalming the body, and together with Joseph of Arimathea, a secret disciple of Jesus (cf. 19:38), he gives Jesus a proper Jewish burial (19:40). Although this action has been read in a negative sense,[93] that Nicodemus is present in this way at the end of Jesus' life indicates his continued loyalty of a sort to Jesus. However, he is never called a disciple, even a secret one, nor does he ever indicate his faith in Jesus in any way. In this regard, Pamment notes, "Nicodemus is the only individual character who fails to make a decision, remaining the good, but uncommitted observer who tries to prevent injustice."[94] Bassler may be even more on target when she points out that although Nicodemus is "characterized by intimations of Christian discipleship," he shows no real movement in the narrative. By the end of the Gospel, he remains ambiguously on the margin between belief and unbelief.[95] While Schneiders argues that Nicodemus evokes sympathy from the reader,[96] it

---

[92]Bassler, "Mixed Signals," 640.

[93]de Jonge writes, "...Joseph and Nicodemus are pictured as having come to a dead end; they regard the burial as definitive." They "have not been able to look further than the tomb in the garden" to see that through Jesus, a new era of God's dealings with humanity has begun (*Jesus*, 34). See also Meeks, who points to the "ludicrous" one hundred pounds of embalming spices as an indication that Nicodemus has not understood the "lifting up" of the Son of Man ("Man from Heaven," 55). So also Rensberger, *Johannine Faith*, 40–41.

[94]Margaret Pamment, "Focus in the Fourth Gospel," *ExpT* 97 (1985–86): 73.

[95]Bassler, "Mixed Signals," 646.

[96]Schneiders, "Born Anew," 191.

may be more accurate to see him as a pathetic character. From beginning to end, Nicodemus is genuinely interested in Jesus, but is never able to gather the courage and conviction to confess his belief openly. As for Jesus, who represents the point of view of the Gospel, he shows little more than disdain for Nicodemus in their only face to face encounter.

THE SAMARITAN WOMAN (4:4–42)

Introduction

The next meeting that Jesus has with an individual character comes soon after his exchange with Nicodemus. Chapter four depicts an extended conversation between Jesus and a woman—the first such occurrence in the narrative. Moreover, this particular scene draws more attention to the gender identity of its participants than any other in the Gospel. First, the setting of the story alerts the reader to the gender of its characters. This is not the first time in the Bible that a man and woman meet at a well—Isaac, Jacob and Moses all meet their future wives at a well (Gen 24:10–61; Gen 29:1–20; Exod 2:15b–21). That such encounters typically lead to a betrothal accents the male/female relationship between Jesus and the woman. The contrast is brought out further in the woman's opening comment to Jesus, in which she juxtaposes Jesus' identity as a male Jew with her own identity as a Samaritan woman (4:9). The gender issue comes most explicitly to the surface of the story in 4:27. At this point, through the astonished eyes of the disciples, the reader is compelled to look closely at the gendered identity of both characters—a man in deep conversation with a woman (4:27). Finally, throughout the scene one can detect several links to both 2:1–11 and 3:1–10 that further highlight the gender identity of Jesus and his conversation partner.

As frequently noted, the conversation with Nicodemus provides the most immediate and obvious text for comparison with chapter four.[97]

---

[97]Cf. Collins, "The story of Jesus' encounter with the woman of Samaria (4:1–42) creates a diptych with the story of Jesus' meeting with Nicodemus, the panels of which...depict the same theme in different tonality ("From John to the Beloved Disciple: An Essay on Johannine Characters," *Int* 49 [1995]: 363). Collins is here drawing on Herman Sevotte, *According to John: A Literary Reading of the Fourth Gospel* (London: Darton, Longman & Todd, 1994), 22. See also Mary Margaret Pazdan, "Nicodemus and the Samaritan Woman: Contrasting Models of Discipleship," *BTB* 17 (1987): 145–148, and Marla J. Selvidge, "Nicodemus and the Woman with Five Husbands," *Proceedings: Eastern Great Lakes Biblical Society* 2 (1982): 63–75.

Parallels between the two passages were already noted in the discussion of Nicodemus. At a general level, both pericopes feature Jesus engaged in a series of exchanges with another character. Additionally, the two encounters overlap thematically; both evoke images of water and the concept of spirit, though admittedly in different ways.[98] Finally, both Nicodemus and the Samaritan woman demonstrate various levels of misunderstanding with respect to these themes.

Yet, there are also fundamental differences between the two encounters. In contrast to the conversation with Nicodemus, it is Jesus who shows an initial interest in the woman; he is the one who initiates the dialogue (4:7). Furthermore, Nicodemus' three exchanges with Jesus are brief, serving as a preface to Jesus' monologue that runs from 3:11 through 3:21. The conversation with the Samaritan women is longer, consisting of seven comments by Jesus and six responses from the woman. As Reinhartz notes, this is one of the few places in the Gospel where a dialogue between Jesus and another character does not turn into a monologue by Jesus. Significantly, another place where this is true is in 11:1–44, a story that also features Jesus in conversation with a woman.[99] Moreover, as in chapter 11, the conversation with the Samaritan woman is woven into a longer narrative. The story begins in verse 4 and features several scene changes before its completion beyond the conversation between Jesus and the woman in verse 42.

Such general points of comparison and contrast invite a deeper comparison between the Samaritan woman and Nicodemus, and the way in which Jesus interacts with each of them. Key questions are as follows: In what way does the characterization of the woman differ from that of Nicodemus? Does her character resemble the mother of Jesus in any way or does she differ substantially from this other female character?

For purposes of discussion, the pericope will be divided into four sections. Verses 4–6 constitute the introduction. Following the introduction, the conversation proceeds in two rounds. The first round, verses 7–15, opens with a command by Jesus and deals with a topic evoked by this command, living water. The second round, verses 16–26,

---

[98]The reference to water in 3:5, which may refer either to baptism or to natural birth, is peripheral to the conversation with Nicodemus and is not developed in the course of the discourse. In contrast, the living water of 4:10–14 is central to the first half of Jesus' discussion with the woman in chapter four, and does not refer to baptism or birth, but to Jesus himself as the source of eternal life.

[99]Reinhartz, "The Gospel of John," (563, 599, nt. 23).

also opens with a command by Jesus,[100] but after that the woman introduces a new topic, proper worship. The last section, verses 27–42, details the results of the conversation. In this last section, special attention will be paid to verses 27–30 and verses 39–42 since these most directly concern the characterization of the woman.

Introduction to the Scene (4:4–6)

The narrative opens with a terse statement claiming that it was necessary (ἔδει) for Jesus to go through Samaria. This necessity may simply indicate a geographic reality.[101] However, given the theological freight which δεῖν carries in chapter three (vv. 7, 14, 30, cf. also 9:4) there is good reason to suspect that here, too, divine necessity is implied.[102] Verses 4–6 give a detailed introduction that sets the scene for the meeting between Jesus and the woman.[103] The location, time of day, and Jesus' physical condition are all included in the description. Location is given prominence, with Samaria mentioned twice (vv. 4–5) and the particular city Sychar identified, along with the patriarchal association of that city, Jacob (vv. 5–6a). As Jesus sits by Jacob's well, tired from his journey, one of the main themes of the passage is foreshadowed, namely his relationship to Samaria and its father Jacob.

---

[100]O'Day, 565.

[101]Supporting this interpretation is a statement from Josephus that is in keeping with verse 4. "It was absolutely necessary for those who would go quickly to pass through that country (Samaria), for by that road you may, in three days, go from Galilee to Jerusalem" (*Vita*, 269) (59). Bultmann (176) and Barrett (230) favor this non-theological sense. In the same sense, Schnackenburg interprets the verse as expressing a degree of urgency on the part of Jesus (1.422).

[102]Cf. Brown, 169; Birger Olsson, *Structure and Meaning in the Fourth Gospel: A Text-Linguistic Analysis of John 2:1–11 and 4:1–42*, ConB, New Testament 6 (Lund: C.W. K. Gleerup, 1974), 145; O'Day, *Revelation*, 55–56; Boers, *Neither on this Mountain*, 154–155.

[103]4:1–3 form a transitional passage in the Gospel narrative, rather than the introduction to the conversation. These verses complete the episode with John the Baptist that began in 3:25 and put Jesus on the road to Galilee. His journey finds its completion in 4:43 giving the impression that the Samaritan episode in 4:4–42 is an interruption. Cf. Brown, 164–165; O'Day, *Revelation*, 51–52. However, cf. Lyle Eslinger, ("The Wooing of the Woman at the Well: Jesus, The Reader and Reader-Response Criticism," *JLT* 1 [1987]: 174) who argues that 4:1–3 allude to Moses' flight from Egypt (Ex 2:14–21), accentuating the reader's association of the scene that follows with the betrothal type-scene. He notes that both Moses and Jesus have challenged the authorities, both leave to avoid confrontation with these authorities, and both subsequently sit down by a well in a foreign land.

The description of the setting also includes a temporal reference, ὥρα ἦν ὡς ἕκτε (4:6). The reference may simply serve to explain Jesus' condition; it immediately follows the report that he was tired and sitting by the well.[104] When chapter four is read in isolation, this interpretation seems most probable. However, when considered in relation to chapter three, it is possible that the reference also points ahead to the woman's entrance into the narrative. Note that νυκτός, the temporal reference in chapter three, comes immediately before Nicodemus' actual entrance in the narrative. Yet, if the reference to the noon hour in 4:6 does point ahead to the woman's entrance, it stands out as an unusual time for her to be drawing water, since this chore was not typically done in the heat of the day (v. 7).[105] Both this incongruity and the parallel temporal reference in chapter three suggest that the time of day is significant and should be seen as a point of contrast between the two scenes. As Reinhartz states, "unlike Nicodemus, who came to Jesus by night, she meets Jesus at noon, when the light is strongest."[106] In this sense, the contrast between those who love darkness and those who come to the light in 3:19–21 may provide further commentary on the characters of Nicodemus and the Samaritan woman.

Before moving to a discussion of the conversation itself, another significant issue about the story's setting must be discussed, namely, to what degree it recalls stories in the Hebrew Bible with similar settings. The point is relevant to our discussion since interpreters have frequently drawn conclusions about the characterization of the woman and her relationship to Jesus based on the scene's relationship to the Hebrew betrothal narratives. As mentioned above, there are at least three stories that depict a man stopping at a well and meeting a woman whom he later marries. Robert Alter has greatly aided our understanding of these stories by identifying them as type-scenes, that is, stories that contain certain conventional elements and appear repeatedly in the course of the

---

[104]So Bultmann, 178; Barrett, 231; Schnackenburg, 1.424; O'Day, *Revelation*, 58; Boers, *Neither on this Mountain*, 165. Cf. also 1:39 which contains a similar temporal reference.

[105]Cf. Brown, 169.

[106]Reinhartz, "The Gospel of John," 573. There may also be significance to Calum M. Carmichael's observation that Rachel comes to the well at an odd time of day and there meets Jacob, her future husband (Gen 29:7) ("Marriage and the Samaritan Woman," *NTS* 26 [1980]: 336).

biblical narrative.[107] His description of the elements common to the betrothal type-scene accords well with the setting in chapter four. In his words,

> The betrothal type-scene...must take place with the future bridegroom in a foreign land. There he encounters a girl...or girls at a well. Someone, either the man or the girl, then draws water from the well; afterward, the girl or girls rush to bring home the news of the stranger's arrival;...finally, a betrothal is concluded between the stranger and the girl, in the majority of instances, only after he has been invited to a meal.[108]

By understanding such stories as literary convention—a pattern as embedded in the imagination of ancient Bible readers/listeners as our American understanding of Hollywood westerns—Alter helps us understand the context in which John 4 may have been understood.[109]

Indeed, even before Alter's recognition of this biblical convention, several scholars perceived the similarity between the Hebrew Bible betrothal narratives and the Fourth Gospel's scene. For instance, using the Hebrew Bible imagery, Calum Carmichael suggested that Jesus and the Samaritan woman experience a symbolic marriage, signifying the reunion of the original Israelite community.[110] Others have drawn specifically on Alter to interpret the relationship between Jesus

---

[107]Alter, *Art of Biblical Narrative*, 51. Alter also identifies as type-scenes the annunciation of the birth of the hero to his barren mother, the epiphany in the field, the initiatory trial, danger in the desert, and the discovery of a well or other source of sustenance, and the testament of the dying hero.

[108]Alter, *Art of Biblical Narrative*, 52.

[109]Bultmann's citation of a 2nd or 3rd century Buddhist parallel, although it is not a betrothal scene, suggests that the basic motif of an encounter between a man and women at a well may have been common in other cultures as well (cf. Bultmann, 179). In fact, the Buddhist story, whose meaning concerns the transcendence of class distinctions, is in some respects closer to John 4 than the other biblical stories. Cf. Boers, *Neither on this Mountain*, 150.

[110]Carmichael, "Marriage and the Samaritan Woman," 332–346. In his far-reaching (and far-fetched) interpretation, Carmichael extends the marriage imagery back to the creation story. In his words, "a woman who has experienced marriage in a singularly fragmented way becomes aware, because of the movement of the divine spirit, of the need for an ideal marriage to the God-man, Jesus, that will achieve the ultimate pristine state of creation" (341). According to Carmichael, the woman fulfills the command to "be fruitful and multiply" by bringing the villagers to Jesus.

An earlier reference to the Hebrew Bible stories can be found in John Bligh's "Jesus in Samaria," *HeyJ* 3 (1962): 332. Cf. also Jerome H. Neyrey, "Jacob Traditions and the Interpretation of John 4:10–26," *CBQ* 41 (1979): 425–426.

and the Samaritan woman. Paul Duke sees the relationship between John 4 and the type-scenes as producing a "deep and delightful irony" for the perceptive reader. "An unlikely daughter of God and her outcast people are gently but irresistibly wooed and won by the Stranger...."[111] Lyle Eslinger takes this notion of "wooing" further still, reading the entire first half of the story as sexual innuendo designed to confuse the reader about Jesus' intentions.[112]

The difficulty with this sort of interpretation is that it relies on the reader's recognition of an entire network of meanings existing beneath the surface of the narrative. In other words, while Eslinger makes a convincing argument about the sexual undertones evoked with the talk of drinking, water, wells, and fountains, he admits that the responsibility for perceiving these hidden meanings rests solely on the reader. In his words, "Neither the reader nor the character can be certain that what they hear is what was meant."[113] Precisely for this reason, one should proceed with caution before leaning too heavily on the type-scene to interpret the whole passage. This is especially true since the way in which the pattern is used becomes crucial for perceiving the construction of the story's female character. For example, in Eslinger's reading, the woman is characterized as a coquettish, loose woman who is, in effect, "asking for it." Similarly, Duke labels the woman as a "five-time loser currently committed to an illicit affair," and even more bluntly, "a tramp."[114] Both of these characterizations seem extreme and neither ring true to Jesus' interaction with the woman or to the outcome of the story.

Nevertheless, there are striking similarities between John 4 and the type-scene that Alter describes. Additionally, the repeated reference to Jacob's well (vv. 6, 12) does recall Genesis 29, making the likelihood of an allusion to the betrothal type-scene even stronger. Given this, how might such an allusion inform a reading of John 4, without dominating the entire interpretation? First, the notion of weddings and bridegrooms has been in the air since chapter two, first with the wedding feast at

---

[111]Duke, *Irony*, 103.

[112]Eslinger, "Wooing" 167–183. Eslinger understands the use of the type-sene as a literary strategy designed to place the reader in a position of misunderstanding similar to the Samaritan woman. Others who note especially the way John 4 diverts from the betrothal type scene include: Culpepper, *Anatomy*, 136; P. Joseph Cahill, "Narrative Art in John IV," *RelStB* 2 (1982): 44–47; Reinhartz, "Gospel of John," 572–573; and Brodie, 217–219.

[113]Eslinger, "Wooing," 169–171.

[114]Duke, "Irony," 101–103.

Cana, then with John the Baptist's description of Jesus as "the bridegroom" in 3:29.[115] That chapter four also has both allusions and explicit references to marriage (4:16–18) links these chapters together, encouraging a close look at their relationship. Second, and most significant for our purposes, any allusions to the betrothal type-scene necessarily draw attention to the gendered identity of Jesus the man and his conversation partner, a woman.[116] Just as Jesus' reference to his mother as γύναι accented her gender identity, so now, casting this conversation in the light of an impending betrothal focuses the reader's attention on the male/female dynamic between the characters. Indeed, one could say that before the conversation even begins, the reader is prepared to observe how these two people interact together from a gender critical perspective. In this way, gender is not coincidental to the story, but a major component of the narrative.[117]

The First Round of Conversation (4:7–15)

Following the introduction, the Samaritan woman enters the scene with little fanfare. There are no suggestive epithets surrounding her name; indeed, she is given no proper name at all. In this way, too, she stands in contrast to Nicodemus, whose name we are told. As for the character introduced here, we read only that she is a γυνὴ ἐκ τῆς

---

[115]Cf. Bligh, who notes that marriage is not far from the Evangelist's thoughts ("Jesus in Samaria," 332). See also Eslinger, "Wooing," 174.

[116]Cf. Reinhartz, "Gospel of John," 572.

[117]Contra de Boer, who argues that gender is not a concern in the narrative. Noting that in verses 7–9, the term γυνή is modified three times by a reference to national identity, he contends that the significance of the woman character lies only in her ethnic/national identity. As discussed in the first chapter, according to de Boer, the character is a woman, and not a man, simply to fulfill the law of verisimilitude that characterizes realistic narrative—men did not draw water in ancient Palestine. Jesus needs to be at a well so that he has an opportunity to discourse about living water, a symbol of revelation ("John 4:27," 214–215, nt. 19, 21).

Regarding the first point, one could just as easily argue that the three references actually call attention to gender identity. For instance, Eslinger contends that the inclusion of γυναικός in verse 9 would be extraneous had no gender contrast been intended, "the feminine form Σαμαρίτιδος being grammatically sufficient for the political contrast" ("Wooing," 182, nt. 23). As for de Boer's second point, his explanation is weak when viewed next to the type-scene relationship discussed above. There are many settings which could suitably evoke a discussion about living water (cf. 7:37–38); the fact that this particular setting is used implies that the gender element is indeed significant to the narrative.

Σαμαρείας, a point that is reiterated three times in the opening verses of the story (vv. 7–9). Based on this description, one might argue that in terms of socio-historical setting, this character has two strikes against her—she is a woman and she is a Samaritan.

It is true that from the perspective of at least some first century Jews, neither of these characteristics would stand in her favor. The New Testament evidence suggests that there was mutual contempt between the Samaritans and the Jews (cf. Mt 10:5; Lk 9:53; Jn 8:48).[118] As the story in John 4 illustrates, disagreements over worship and the Temple were major obstacles in Jewish/Samaritan relations. Other evidence attests to the question of the purity of the Samaritans. As one frequently cited Mishnaic ordinance states, "Samaritan women are deemed menstruants from their cradle" (*Niddah* 4:1). The statement implies that Samaritan women were perpetually impure, therefore one should refrain from contact with them at any time.[119] The parenthetical statement in verse 9 may coincide with this idea, if one infers that purity concerns were among the reasons that Jews distanced themselves from Samaritans.[120]

As for the title "woman," we have numerous attestations from both Jewish and Greek literature of the period that in both cultures women were generally regarded as inferior and subordinate to men.

---

[118]To explain the origins of the Samaritans, commentators often turn to the account of the invasion and colonialization of Samaria by the Assyrians depicted in 2 Kings 17. However, as Richard Coggins points out, "this is religious polemic; nothing in Samaritan practice suggests any link with Assyrian or other foreign origin." He argues that the Samaritan's distinctive identity emerged at a later date and was probably not the result of a single schismatic event. (Cf. "Samaritans," *The Oxford Companion to the Bible*, ed. Bruce M. Metzger and Michael D. Coogan [New York: Oxford University Press, 1993]: 671–673).

[119]Note, however, that this ordinance was recorded at a later period than the Johannine text. I have found no evidence to support the 65-66 CE date that is commonly associated with the pronouncement (cf. Brown, 170; Barrett, 232; et. al). One can safely say only that the Mishnaic text reflects the sentiments of one group within Judaism, and that these sentiments likely stem from an earlier period.

[120]In a well known study, David Daube makes a case for this interpretation by arguing from an etymological perspective that συγχρῶνται means "use together with," so that the intended meaning is "Jews do not use vessels together with Samaritans" ("Jesus and the Samaritan Woman: The Meaning of συγχράομαι" *JBL* 69 [1950]: 137–47). Whether or not the meaning of the verse is this specific (the word vessel does not appear in the sentence), purity issues might still be behind the statement since the purity code was so intricately woven into the daily lives of the Jewish community. Cf. Olsson, *Structure and Meaning*, 154–155.

Their principal domain was the home and beyond that they were subject to a great number of restrictions.[121] While there is evidence that the earliest Christian movement gave greater freedom to women (esp. Gal 3:27),[122] the later literature of the New Testament attests to similar restrictions for Christian woman (cf. Eph 5:22–24; Col 3:18–19; 1 Tim 2:9–15; I Peter 3:1–7). By the time of the Church Fathers, there is ample evidence of outright misogyny; women and their fleshly passions were deemed the source of sin.[123] The rabbis were similarly disposed, as illustrated by another Mishnaic text.

> Yose b. Yohanan of Jerusalem says, "Let your house be wide open and seat the poor at your table and don't talk too much with women." (He spoke of a man's wife, all the more so is the rule to be applied to the wife of one's fellow.) In this regard did sages say, "So long as a man talks too much with a woman, he brings trouble on himself, wastes time better spent on studying Torah, and ends up an heir of Gehenna" (Abot 1:5).[124]

In short, from a historical perspective it is safe to say that a Jewish man would indeed have double cause to spurn a γυνὴ ἐκ τῆς Σαμαρείας.

The question is whether this point of view is also reflected in the Gospel. Do the terms γυνή and Σαμαρείας carry a negative connotation in the text? As with the epithets describing Nicodemus, it will be necessary to track the appearance of these terms throughout the Gospel to understand more fully their meanings as character indicators.

Outside of chapter four, the only reference to Samaritans comes in 8:48. In the midst of a dispute, the Jews accuse Jesus of being a Samaritan as well as being possessed by a demon. Obviously, Jesus' opponents hold a low view of Samaritans; their position reflects the historical tension between the two groups. At the beginning of chapter

---

[121]Cf. Eva Cantarella, *Pandora's Daughters: The Role and Status of Women in Greek and Roman Antiquity* (Baltimore: John Hopkins University Press, 1987).

[122]Although more times than not the male/female dyad is absent in this formulaic expression of freedom (cf. 1 Cor. 12:13; Col 3:11).

[123]Cantarella quotes Tertullian's infamous pronouncement, "Woman, you are the gate of the devil" (*De cultu foeminarum* 1.1.2). Also included are   Clement of Alexandria, "women must seek wisdom, like men, even if men are superior and have first place in every field, at least if they are not too effeminate;" Origen, "woman represents the flesh and the passions, while man represents reason and intellect;" and John Chrystotom, "the mind of woman is somewhat infantile" (*Pandora's Daughters*, 169).

[124]*The Mishnah: A New Translation.* trans. Jacob Neusner (New Haven: Yale University Press, 1988).

four, this tension is similarly reflected in the comments of both the Samaritan woman and the narrator (v. 9). However, as the events of chapter four unfold, it will become clear that the narrative does not espouse this view. Indeed, the Samaritans will eventually be regarded as faithful converts to Jesus. In other words, regardless of their historical relationship with the Jews, the Samaritans will show their true worth in their response to Jesus.[125] In this way, historical reality will be overturned by narrative truth. This evolution will carry over to the epithet Samaritan, as a character indicator its meaning will be transformed by the end of the story.

Can the same be said for the epithet γυνή? Unlike the term Samaritan, which is largely confined to this pericope, we have already come across this term earlier in the narrative. In chapter two, we saw how "woman" drew attention to the gender identity of the mother of Jesus, and that as both mother and woman she played a significant role in eliciting the miracle of Jesus, which brought the disciples to belief. In chapter four, the reiteration of γυνή (and even more γύναι in 4:21) reminds us of the mother of Jesus in chapter two. If, as I suggest, there is a narrative link between the female characters of the text, the role that was begun with the "woman" in chapter two will now be picked up by this woman at the well. In the same way that the mother of Jesus plays a crucial part in the initial revelation of Jesus' glory, so, too, the Samaritan woman will have a role in revealing his true identity as messiah, and bringing an entire village to belief. In this way, the concept of γυνή will continue to be defined in the broader context of the entire Gospel.

As with Nicodemus, the introduction of the Samaritan woman is concluded with a description of her arrival. In contrast to Nicodemus, the woman comes not with the express purpose to meet Jesus, but to perform the mundane task of drawing water from the well. Nevertheless, it is this task that is significant for Jesus. Her ability to draw water initiates the conversation, eliciting an abrupt demand from Jesus, δός μοι πεῖν (v. 7). The editorial comment of verse 8 indicates that such a demand should be considered unusual; normally Jesus' disciples would have been present to give him water. Verse 8 emphasizes that Jesus and the woman are alone during their ensuing conversation and prepares the reader for the disciples' subsequent return in verse 27. Additionally, the

---

[125]The Gospel of Luke also demonstrates a more positive attitude toward Samaritans (cf. 10:33–36; 17:15–18).

reference to food foreshadows the discussion about food that will later take place between Jesus and the disciples.[126]

The woman's opening words provide the first opportunity to glimpse her personality. Given her status in relation to Jesus, one might expect quick acquiescence to his imperative. However, rather than obeying his demand for a drink, she puts forth a challenging question, "How is it that you, being Jewish man, ask for a drink from me, a Samaritan woman?" The question reveals a lack of intimidation; indeed, even a degree of boldness on the woman's part. Despite her obvious knowledge of social customs, she does not shy from transgressing them; she readily engages Jesus in conversation.[127] In this way, one could say that the Samaritan woman and Nicodemus are similar—both initially exhibit confidence in their interaction with Jesus.

As Eslinger argues, the woman's initial comment points to two facts, one political, the other sexual. In his words, "Jesus is a Jew, she is a Samaritan; he is a man, she is a woman."[128] To be sure, by focusing on Jewish/Samaritan relations, the editorial gloss that follows tends to suppress the more implicit issue of male/female relations that the woman's question contains. Yet, as I have argued, the scene itself already evokes the issue of Jesus and the woman as gendered characters. In addition, the inclusion of γυναικός in verse 9 works against this suppression, grammatically calling attention to the gender difference between the woman and Jesus.[129] Significantly, as the conversation progresses the epithet "Samaritan" will be dropped altogether, as both the narrator and Jesus refer to the character only as "woman," (vv. 11, 15, 17, 19, 21, 25).[130]

Jesus' responds to the woman using the third person to refer to himself, ... σὺ ἂν ἤτησας αὐτὸν καὶ ἔδωκεν ἄν σοι ὕδωρ ζῶν (4:10). In this way, a certain formality and distance is maintained between the conversation partners. What is more, as in both of the previous scenes, Jesus does not take up the topic offered. In this case, he broaches neither of the controversial differences, but instead turns the conversation to the

---

[126]Cf. O'Day, *Revelation*, 50, 58; Boers, *Neither on This Mountain*, 158.

[127]Cf. Boers, *Neither on this Mountain*, 163.

[128]Eslinger, "Wooing," 176.

[129]Cf. Eslinger's observations discussed in nt. 128 above.

[130]Cahill sees this as a development of the woman's "cosmic role." As he puts it, "the local lore identified as differences between Samaritan and Jew and frequently mentioned by commentators disappears as the formerly described Samaritan woman gradually becomes a prototype of woman" ("Narrative Art," 47).

woman's lack of knowledge about him and about God (v. 10). This knowledge, Jesus contends, would create a reversal of circumstances— she would be asking him for living water.[131] Thus, in both the Nicodemus passage and this one, knowledge of God and of Jesus is a primary issue. Yet, there is a striking difference in the outcome of the two conversations. While Nicodemus remains ignorant to the degree to which he draws a reprimand from Jesus regarding his lack of knowledge (3:10), the Samaritan woman will eventually lead her people to highly significant knowledge of Jesus, οἴδαμεν ὅτι οὗτός ἐστιν ἀληθῶς ὁ σωτὴρ τοῦ κόσμου (4:42).

In verse 11, the woman's boldness continues as she addresses Jesus directly and intimately, using the second person (v. 11). Her response is much like that of Nicodemus. She takes Jesus' comment literally and thinks that actual water is the issue. However, she understands that Jesus is offering something more than well water.[132] To that idea, she responds with sensible matter-of-factness, pointing out that he does not even have the equipment he needs to draw water from the well, let alone provide her with some other superior water.[133] From her perspective, this thirsty man is making a ridiculous claim. She therefore challenges his authority and in the face of his fantastic offer presents her own authority figure—the giver of the well, "our father Jacob."[134]

O'Day points out the irony in the woman's reply. With her first question (v. 11), the woman unwittingly participates in one of the central questions of the Gospel, i.e., the whence (πόθεν) of Jesus and his gifts (cf. 2:9; 3:8; 7:27f; 8:14; 9:29f; 19:9).[135] Likewise, her second question

---

[131]While the background and nuances of the term "living water" is a critical issue in the interpretation of this passage, it is not necessary for our purposes to explore the term in depth. What is significant is that the phrase is linked to the notion of the revelation. For details see Brown, 178–179; Barrett, 233–234.

[132]Haenchen, 1.220.

[133]Cf. Boers, *Neither on this Mountain*, 163; O'Day, *Revelation*, 61.

[134]Boers suggests that the woman's reference to the Jacob tradition illustrates her imagination. "She does not ask him how he thinks he is going to get her the water, but mocks him with the image of Jacob's miraculous provision of water. By posing the question in this way, not merely expressing skepticism, but formulating it in terms of Jesus' lack of a particular ability, she focuses more on Jesus himself, than on the expected performance. In this way she brings into focus the central Christological question concerning the identity of Jesus" (*Neither on this Mountain*, 166).

[135]O'Day, *Revelation*, 61. On the importance of this theme see Paul S. Minear, "We don't know where... John 20:2," *Int* 30 (1975): 125–139. Notably, the theme will reappear in chapter 20, as Mary Magdalene searches for the body of Jesus.

also concerns an important aspect of Jesus' identity (v. 12).
Unbeknownst to the woman, Jesus is indeed greater than Jacob and all
the patriarchs (cf. 8:53).[136] Yet, while her questions are ironically
charged for the reader, it is perhaps too much to say that they reflect a
deep ignorance on her part.[137] At least, one should distinguish her
ignorance from that of Nicodemus. Unlike him, the woman has not
presented herself as knowledgeable about Jesus, nor does her status as
"Samaritan woman" imply that she should know better. With respect to
characterization, the woman's questions seem more suggestive of
reasonableness and loyalty to her ancestral traditions than of ignorance.

When Jesus next addresses the woman, he, too, will speak more
directly, this time using the first person to refer to himself. In this way,
he becomes more intimately engaged in the conversation. He also
responds directly to the woman's challenge, pointing out that the water
he can supply is indeed greater than the well water that Jacob provided
(vv. 13–14). Not only will the one who drinks of this water not thirst
forever, but it will be transformed in the recipient into a fountain of
water gushing up to life eternal. On the one hand, this explanatory,
though enigmatic, response resembles the one that Jesus gave to
Nicodemus (3:5–9). Both are difficult for the reader to understand, let
alone Jesus' conversation partner. On the other hand, Jesus' more direct
style with the woman makes it obvious that he is speaking about a gift
he has to offer. For this reason, the woman's next response differs from
Nicodemus' final, confused question (3:9).

The woman is able to perceive that Jesus is offering something
fantastic. For this reason, she now voices a request, one that echoes the
words that began the conversation, κύριε, δός μοι τοῦτο τὸ ὕδωρ (v.
15. cf. v. 7).[138] Whether this represents a move forward on the woman's
part is debatable.[139] Indeed, it is difficult to determine whether the

---

[136]O'Day, Revelation, 61–62.

[137]O'Day, Revelation, 61.

[138]Cf. O'Day, "With v. 15 we therefore end up where we began—with a request
for water. The request with which the dialogue opened, "give me a drink" (dos moi
pein), is now ironically placed in the mouth of the other dialogue partner, "give me
this water" (dos moi touto to hydor)" (Revelation, 64).

[139]Brown thinks that it does, seeing in the woman's request for water the
fulfilling of one part of Jesus' challenge in verse 10 (177). Haenchen reads in her
request "a genuine, deep desire for salvation on the part of humankind" albeit
obscured (1.221). Brodie points out that Jesus' words spark an interest in the
woman and she begins to take him seriously. With her request, "genuine contact has
been made. Now the conversation can really develop" (222). O'Day argues that by

woman believes Jesus is capable of supplying this fantastic gift, or whether she persists in her skepticism and mockery.[140] The second half of her response indicates that she remains practically minded. She views Jesus' offer as providing a miraculous way out of her daily task of drawing water.[141] In any case, what is clear is that her request does not alienate her from Jesus. Unlike his exchange with Nicodemus, Jesus never mocks the woman, in spite of the fact that she mocks him. Nor does Jesus cut off communication with her even though in his initial attempts he has gotten nowhere. Instead, he persists in his attempts to get through to the woman and takes a new approach in the conversation.

The Second Round of Conversation (4:16–26)

Concerning the character of the woman, verses 16–18 are perhaps the most discussed verses in this entire narrative. Much has been made of the woman's morality, or lack thereof, based on the fact that she has had five husbands, and is with a man who is not her husband. We have already seen how she has been characterized as a "five-time loser" and "tramp."[142] In the face of such characterizations, feminist scholars

---

verse 15 "the woman has gained considerable ground in this conversation. She has moved from seeing Jesus as a thirsty Jew who knowingly violates social convention to seeing him as someone whose gifts she needs" (567).

[140]So Boers, "To reinforce her disbelief she challenges him to a performance for which she is convinced he does not have the ability." Thus, in Boers's view, the first half of the conversation ends in "complete failure" (*Neither on this Mountain*, 167, 169).

[141] Cf. Bultmann, 187; Schnackenburg, 1.432; Beasley-Murray, 61; O'Day, *Revelation*, 64.

[142]I. Howard Marshall states, "What visual image does the word [woman/γυνή] convey to you? To me it is a word which suggests somebody approaching middle-age or even old-age, and it has a faintly derogatory air... 'woman' tends to put her on the shelf, but the story implies that she was possibly youthful and attractive" ("The Problem of New Testament Exegesis," *JEvThS* 17 [1974]: 68). Marshall's image of the woman is a good example of characterization as a fantasy entertained by the reader, but with no basis in the text.

Additionally, the passage cannot be discussed without mention of the allegorical interpretation that has frequently been posited. Cf. e.g., Olsson, *Structure and Meaning*, 186. Barrett sums up the position has follows: "The woman represents Samaria peopled by five foreign tribes each with its god. The one who is 'not a husband' represents either a false god (Simon Magus has been suggested) or the Samaritans' false worship of the true God (v. 22)." While this reading has fallen into disfavor among most exegetes (primarily because of disjunction between the record of seven Samaritan gods in II Kings 7:30–31 compared to the figure of five husbands), it cannot be dismissed purely on the grounds of its allegorical nature, since the Gospel of John lends itself to symbolic readings. In favor of the allegorical

understandably become defensive and attempt to rescue the woman from moral assessments. For example, drawing on the norms of Palestinian culture, Seim notes that "matters of marriage and divorce were primarily men's privilege."[143] Similarly, Luise Schottroff comments,

> In patriarchal societies, marriage is the social norm, and for women, as a rule, it is also an economic necessity. Women must surrender their bodies, their sexuality, and their labor in order to survive. The Samaritan woman is described as a woman in an extreme situation of sexual exploitation. The man with whom she now lives did not even offer her the security of a marriage contract.[144]

While these observations about first century life in a patriarchal society are undoubtedly accurate, as far as the text is concerned, there is no need to rescue the woman from moral judgment. Indeed, although interpreters have concentrated much energy on deciding what the woman's sexuality implies about her character, the narrative gives no attention to this question. This is not to say that the woman's sexual experience is not addressed. If the reader has been conscious of the male/female dynamic up to this point, Jesus' mode of interaction in these verses further sharpens that awareness. The reader cannot avoid being keenly aware of the woman's gender, and in this case, sexual identity. Indeed, what is remarkable about this story is the fact that although the woman is presented as having at least questionable sexual relationships, no moral evaluation accompanies this presentation. Neither Jesus, who calls attention to the intimate details of her personal life, nor the narrator gives any hint of judgment.[145] This aspect of the woman's character is

---

reading is the woman's transition to the question of Jewish and Samaritan worship. Yet, Boers points out that the woman's question concerns only the location of worship, not the god who is worshipped. The assumption is that they worship the same God, which creates serious problems for the allegorical reading (*Neither on this Mountain*, 172).

[143]"Roles of Women in the Gospel of John," 68.

[144]Luise Schottroff, "Sexuality in the Fourth Gospel" (paper presented at the annual meeting of the SBL, Philadelphia, November 1995) 4. In the same vein, O'Day argues, "The popular portrait of the woman in John 4 as a woman of dubious morals, guilty of aberrant sexual behavior, derives from a misreading of John 4:14–16....The text does not say, as most interpreters automatically assume, that the woman has been divorced five times but that she has had five husbands. There are many possible reasons for the woman's marital history, and one should be leery of the dominant explanation of moral laxity. Perhaps the woman, like Tamar in Genesis 38, is trapped in the custom of levirate marriage and the last male in the family line has refused to marry her ("John," in *The Women's Bible Commentary*, 296).

[145]O'Day, *Revelation*, 172.

relevant to the narrative only insofar as it advances the conversation with Jesus.

In this respect, Seim's second observation about Jesus' statement in verse 17 is more to the point. His statement, she argues, "is not to expose her morals but to show his prophetic power through his miraculous knowledge of her special situation."[146] This is precisely what is accomplished through the exchange in verses 16–18 as the woman comes to recognize Jesus as a prophet (v. 19). In O'Day's words, "It is a moment of revelation for the woman, a moment when she is able to see Jesus with new eyes....This exchange...does not delegitimize the woman because of her supposed immorality, but instead shows the woman's growing faith."[147]

In this sense, most important about the exchange is that it leads to her continued conversation with Jesus. As Boers notes "...the effect of the woman's statement that she does not have a husband, is that Jesus continues his conversation with her, not with the husband he asked her to call."[148] In this way, her independent nature, which has been evident already in her bold and mocking questions of Jesus, comes forth even more strongly. To be sure, Jesus responds to the woman's surprising declaration, οὐκ ἔχω ἄνδρα, with a twist of his own, thereby revealing the "truth" of her statement. His acknowledgment of her situation is not accusatory, instead, it contributes to the woman's characterization as independent.[149]

---

[146]Seim, "Roles of Women in the Gospel of John," 68. Seim is not the first to make this observation. Cf. Bultmann, who states, "Jesus' request is only a means of demonstrating his own omniscience" (187). See also Haenchen, 221; O'Day, "John," in *The Women's Bible Commentary*, 296; Boers, *Neither on this Mountain*, 169–170, 172–173.

[147]O'Day, "John," in *The Women's Bible Commentary*, 296. Boers concurs, "The purpose of the reference to the woman's husbands is to reveal Jesus' miraculous knowledge, not to give information about the woman or her husbands. The figure is of no further significance once Jesus has disclosed his miraculous knowledge to the woman" (*Neither on this Mountain*, 171).

[148]*Neither on this Mountain*, 171. Cf. also Boers's later statement, "Unlike Nicodemus...who quietly disappears from the scene as Jesus' partner in conversation, allowing Jesus to turn the conversation into a revelatory monologue, the woman here remains Jesus' partner in a conversation in which true worship is revealed..." (182).

[149]In this regard, cf. Schneiders who observes that the women characters of the Fourth Gospel "do not appear dependent on husbands or other male legitimators, nor as seeking permission for their activities from male officials" ("Women in the Fourth Gospel," 44).

What is most clear is that the woman herself is undaunted by the discussion of her personal life. Indeed, once she recognizes Jesus as a prophet, the dynamics of the conversation shift. Now, the woman assumes the initiative and asks a question of Jesus, a Jewish prophet. It is no trivial question, but a theological issue that lies at the heart of the Jewish/Samaritan conflict. In raising the question of the proper place to worship, the woman exhibits her keen mind in general, and her theological sensitivity in particular. One should note that the woman's interest in the Jewish/Samaritan relations was already evident in her opening comment to Jesus (v. 9). For this reason, her question in verse 20 is not raised to avoid the uncomfortable subject of her "sinful past" as has sometimes been suggested, but rather is a return to her original concern, now with a specific focus.[150] Along this line, Schnackenburg observes,

> Nothing is said of the woman's emotional reactions; the evangelist is not concerned with her psychology or feelings, but with her growing faith. Hence, her next words are not to be taken as a manoeuvre, steering the conversation away from a painful subject, but as a continuation of the dialogue, in which a religious question is discussed.[151]

It is because of the woman's initiative and persistence that Jesus now reveals the true nature of worship. In marked contrast to Nicodemus, the teacher of Israel whose feeble attempts at a conversation evoked scorn from Jesus, he readily takes up the topic the Samaritan woman proposes. Significantly, Jesus' pronouncement is marked with the vocative γύναι. Moreover, as in chapter two, this form of address is again used in the context of "the hour," (4:21-23). Given what we have seen of both words thus far, there is good indication that what follows is more than mere conversation. Since Jesus has no prior relationship to this character, the use of γύναι is not out of place, as in chapter two. Nevertheless, the two appearances of the word inform one another. As we suggested earlier, the use of γύναι in 2:4 implies that the mother of Jesus is more than just a mother. As woman, she is closely

---

[150]According to Brown, for example, the woman "looks to the light, although she would divert the rays away from her life to something less personal (177)."

[151]Schnackenburg,1.434. Cf. also O'Day, "By asking Jesus about the proper place of worship, the woman is not disengaging from Jesus. Rather, her inquiry about worship is an act of deepening engagement with Jesus, because she anticipates that the prophet Jesus will be able to speak an authoritative word on the subject" (567).

linked with Jesus' hour and also connected to the other woman characters in the text. Now in chapter four, we find the two words clustered together again. Once more, "woman" is evoked in the context of the hour. We should again expect that what follows will result in some sort of self-revelation from Jesus.

To begin, Jesus offers to the woman words of revelation in the form of a definition of worship that transcends national boundaries. Neither location will be deemed the appropriate place to worship, instead the manner of worship will be central. True worshippers will worship the Father in spirit and in truth (v. 23). In typical Johannine fashion, Jesus also makes clear that this manner of worship is not some distant reality, but is effective immediately. In short, Jesus eradicates the source of religious conflict between Jews and Samaritans and offers instead a way that all—including the woman (cf. προσκυνήσετε, v. 21)—can be "true worshippers."

A subtler message is also communicated by Jesus, through his use of the title "the Father." In discussing the object of worship (something the woman omits), Jesus three times repeats the title ὁ πατήρ (vv. 21, 22, 23; in v. 24 ὁ θεός is used). As both O'Day and Duke point out, his use of this title recalls the woman's use of the same term in the preceding verses. In the course of the narrative, she refers to "our father Jacob" (v. 12, cf. also v. 4) and to the collective Samaritan fathers (v. 20). "All these referents for father are dramatically undercut, however, by the one expression of Jesus: you will worship the Father."[152]

Significantly, the woman's final words to Jesus concern her knowledge. Recall that Nicodemus opens his conversation with Jesus declaring what he and those whom he represents know. The woman concludes her talk with a similar declaration. She does not fully comprehend what Jesus has told her, but she does sense the revelatory and eschatological nature of his words. For this reason, she is reminded of the messiah whom she knows (οἶδα) is coming and will proclaim "all things" (ἅπαντα) to her people (v. 25). Her comment reveals what she has missed in Jesus' revelation—her understanding of the messiah is still future oriented. Nevertheless, unlike Nicodemus who could only voice an incredulous question by the end of his conversation, the woman remains engaged and receptive to Jesus.[153]

---

[152]O'Day, *Revelation*, 69. Cf. Duke, *Irony*, 70.

[153]Cf. Bultmann, "The woman's answer in v. 25 is correct, inasmuch as she has seen that Jesus is speaking of an eschatological event; but she has not grasped the

Indeed, especially in this second half of the conversation, the woman seems always one step ahead of Jesus, introducing topics that eventually lead to his self-revelation. In this respect, Boers comments, "It is noteworthy that in the first round, in which Jesus made the proposals, they all ended in a failure of communication, whereas in the second round, when the woman raises the issues, Jesus' responses lead to increasing insight...."[154] Her final statement, in which she brings up the topic of the messiah, elicits the most dramatic response yet from Jesus. He takes advantage of the woman's knowledge of the coming messiah and presses upon her once more that the time has now arrived. However, this time he speaks openly about his identity, using the revelatory formula, ἐγώ εἰμι, ὁ λαλῶν σοι. Furthermore, the absolute form of this phrase suggests more than just identification with the woman's statement. As O'Day states, "John is not confirming that he is the messiah expected by the Samaritan woman but is using the ego eimi in its fullest sense to identify himself as God's revealer, the sent one of God."[155] In other words, Jesus gives to the Samaritan woman "the clearest declaration of his messiahship."[156]

Sowing and Reaping (4:27–42)

It is at this dramatic moment of self-revelation that the conversation is interrupted by the return of the disciples to the well. As a result, instead of hearing a response from the woman, the reader is privy to the disciples' internal reaction to the scene before them. They are astonished that Jesus is speaking with a woman, but they leave unasked their questions about the situation (v. 27). Recalling Alter's belief that statements by the narrator about attitudes and intentions of characters are the most reliable method of conveying information about a

---

meaning of the καὶ νῦν ἐστιν, and consequently has also failed to understand what is meant by ἐν πνεύματι καὶ ἀληθείᾳ ...Even so she is not portrayed as being completely unresponsive to the revelation; her expectation makes it possible for Jesus to reveal himself (v. 26)" (192). Cf. also Schnackenburg, "[The woman's] religious yearnings are sincere, she has also perhaps some intimation of the mystery of Jesus, and this provides him with the occasion of revealing himself to her as the expected Messiah (v. 26)" (1.441).

[154] Boers, *Neither on this Mountain*, 182.

[155] O'Day, *Revelation*, 72. Bultmann, however, contends that in 4:26 ἐγώ εἰμι is not a sacred formula, but simply words with which Jesus reveals himself (cf. 192 and 226, nt. 3). For Bultmann's full discussion of the formula in Hellenistic literature, cf. 225–226, nt. 3. For its use in the Gospel and the Hebrew Bible, cf. Brown, 533–538.

[156] Bligh, "Jesus in Samaria," 333, nt. 2.

character's nature, we can count on learning both about the disciples and the woman from verse 27.

There are several things to note about the narrator's comment in v. 27. As mentioned above, it functions in the narrative as an interruption. The opening phrase, καὶ ἐπὶ τούτῳ, provides a direct link with the preceding words of Jesus. This connection is furthered in the twofold repetition of the verb λαλεῖν. No sooner does Jesus reveal his Messianic identity in terms of his act of speaking to the woman, ὁ λαλῶν σοι, than the disciples enter the scene and question this act, τί λαλεῖς μετ' αὐτῆς. The reader knows the answer to their unasked question—Jesus has been speaking with the woman in order to reveal himself to her.

Given this, it is perhaps no coincidence that the disciples' reaction brings the gender issue, which has been present at some level throughout the narrative, into sharp focus. The fact that immediately following Jesus' words of revelation the issue of gender is explicitly addressed, makes it more clear than ever that revelation and women are closely and intentionally connected in this Gospel. This is not to say that revelation is restricted to women. Clearly, male characters also experience revelation in the Fourth Gospel, as we will see especially in the case of the man born blind (9:37–38).[157] The point is that the Gospel tends to highlight the association of women and revelation, as indicated by the comment in 4:27.

Finally, it is significant that the disciples' questions are unvoiced. Their silence before Jesus stands in contrast to the woman's persistent questioning. As O'Day notes,

> ...one important aspect of her response was that through her often blunt questioning she remained engaged in dialogue with Jesus....(S)uch engagement and participation are central elements in the revelatory process. The disciples, by contrast, do not question at this juncture and therefore keep themselves removed from immediate engagement with Jesus. At this moment in the narrative they are outsiders, mere observers of the scene that is taking place.[158]

Following the interruption by the disciples, the woman's response to Jesus' revelation comes in verse 28. It is expressed through both actions and words. One more time she takes the initiative as she leaves her water jar, goes back to the city, and speaks to the people about Jesus

---

[157]Cf. also Nathanael (1:49) and Thomas (20:28).
[158]O'Day, *Revelation*, 74.

(v. 28). Her actions suggest a degree of excitement and urgency on her part, particularly the detail of the water jar. Her mundane task has been forgotten in light of what has taken place in her conversation with Jesus. As Brodie notes, the abandoned jar indicates "the depth of her response to the Revealer's call: having found a new form of living water, she leaves behind her the symbol of her former preoccupation."[159] In its place, she takes on the role of witness, much like that of John the Baptist. Her initial words, "Come, see..." (v. 29) echo Jesus' own words to the disciples in chapter one, as well as Philip's words to Nathanael (1:39, 1:46). Her words thus resonate with the language of witness and discipleship that have already been established in the Gospel.[160] Based on her experience of Jesus' prophetic abilities (vv. 17–18), the woman raises the question of his messianic identity in terms that are familiar to her, and presumably to her people's understanding of the messiah, ἄνθρωπον ὃς εἶπεν μοι πάντα ὅσα ἐποίησα (v. 29 cf. v. 25). To be sure, the formulation of her ultimate question μήτι οὗτος ἐστιν ὁ χριστός, has troubled some interpreters, who point out that the presence of μήτι implies a degree of tentativeness or skepticism on the part of the woman.[161] This need not be the case.[162] Its inclusion may simply be an expression of the woman's excitement and the overall drama of the scene.[163] Certainly, the woman has been led to belief in the

---

[159]Brodie, 224. Similarly, Brown suggests that the detail is "John's way of emphasizing that such a jar would be useless for the type of living water that Jesus has interested her in" (1.173). Schneiders comments that the detail is the "feminine version of the standard Gospel formula for responding to the call to apostleship, namely to 'leave all things,' especially one's present occupation, whether symbolized by boats (e.g., Mt 4:19–22), or tax stall (cf. Mt 9:9), or water pot" ("Women in the Fourth Gospel," 40). Boers argues that "[t]he jar represents the contrary of [Jesus'] living water....In so far as the jar represents the means of satisfying the need for drinking water, dropping it must mean the negation of that need, not in a general way, but in terms of the semantic structure of the story as the implication of affirmation of the quest for the water of life" (*Neither on this Mountain*, 182–183).

[160]Cf. Seim, "Roles of Women," 69.

[161]Cf. Brown, "The Greek question with *meti* implies an unlikelihood...therefore the woman's faith does not seem to be complete" (173). Similarly, Beasley-Murray, "μήτι need not imply a negative answer but 'puts the question in the most tentative and hesitating way'" (58, the quotation is from Moulton, *Prologomena*, 193).

[162]BDF §427(2) notes that the typically negative connotation of μή is modified in this passage, suggesting as possible translations, "that must be the Messiah at last" or "perhaps this is the Messiah."

[163]Schnackenburg notes that the expression suggests a cautious opinion which "is meant to cause reflection (cf. v. 39), and the reader is thereby reminded of

possibility that Jesus is the messiah, or why would she speak at all to the villagers? In any case, even if the question of her full belief must remain ambivalent, there is no denying the positive effect of her question. The Samaritan people are sufficiently motivated to go to Jesus (v. 30).[164]

Indeed, as the conclusion of the narrative makes clear, the woman's testimony has a remarkable impact on the Samaritans. Verse 39 emphasizes that it was her words that are repeated verbatim, which caused many of them to believe in Jesus. Furthermore, the Samaritans ask Jesus to stay with them, which he does for two days (v. 40). As a result, many more hear the word of Jesus and come to understand him in the fullest sense as the "savior of the world." The villagers' words to the Samaritan woman do not downplay the significance of her role as witness, as much as they signal the villagers' personal encounter with the words of Jesus.[165] The importance of the woman's actions are highlighted in metaphorical terms in Jesus' brief discourse with his disciples (4:31–38). The discourse begins with a misunderstanding between Jesus and his disciples concerning food. While there are similarities between their confusion and the earlier misunderstanding of the woman, at this point in the story the disciples and the woman appear in contrast. While they are urging food on Jesus that he does not need

---

Jesus's self-revelation (v. 26)" (1.444). In agreement is O'Day, who sees the woman's words as a tentative confession, the *meti* being neither denial, nor full affirmation. In her view, this tentativeness has an important narrative function. "Because it is not a definite assertion, it leaves room for individual response" (*Revelation*, 76).

[164]Cf. Boers, *Neither on this Mountain*, 183–184.

[165]Cf. Brown, "...this is scarcely because of an inferiority she might have as a woman—it is the inferiority of any human witness compared to encountering Jesus himself. A similar attitude may be found in chap. 17, where Jesus prays that those who believe in him through the word of his disciples may ultimately be with him in order that they may see glory (17:24)" ("Roles of Women in the Fourth Gospel," 691). Cf. also Schneiders, "In John's perspective the witness of a believing disciple brings a person to Jesus but then the disciple fades away as the prospective believer encounters Jesus himself (cf. Jn 1:35–41)" ("Women in the Fourth Gospel," 40). Similarly Seim,

[m]ission in the Gospel of John is not reaching out, but collecting and bringing to Jesus, a gathering into one the scattered children of God as expressed in 11:52. Even at the outset of the gospel story in 1:35–54, the few disciples called by Jesus himself immediately start calling others to come and see, and they bring them to Jesus. In the light of this, the Samaritan woman is assigned a missionary task and the transition from the woman to Jesus in 4:42 means that she fulfilled it ("Roles of Women in the Gospel of John," 69).

(v. 31–34), she is sowing seed for the harvest (v. 29, cf. 37). On this point, Boers' comments are well taken:

> [The woman] is the sower, who is not identical with him who is about to reap the harvest that is ripe in the fields, but she rejoices with him in the harvest....She is Jesus' co-worker in an unprecedented way, more concretely even than John the Baptist, in the sense that John merely pointed to Jesus as "the lamb of God who takes way the sins of the world" (1:92). The woman participates actively with Jesus in doing the will of his Father....[166]

In sum, the Samaritan woman is presented as a practical, bold, and tenacious woman, one who not only holds her own in conversation with Jesus, but drives the dialogue forward with her own thoughtful questions and observations. The result of the woman's persistent engagement with Jesus is a dawning realization of his identity on her part that eventually leads to the conversion of her people. In this way, the woman moves from a mere conversation partner to a partner in Jesus' ministry. It is at this point that her relationship with the mother of Jesus becomes most clear. As the mother of Jesus is the co-worker of God the Father, so the Samaritan woman becomes an "indispensable co-worker" of Jesus.[167] Moreover, as a faithful witness to Jesus, she also contributes to doing the Father's will. In her own way, the Samaritan woman takes up the role played by the mother of Jesus in chapter two and carries it out with respect to her own people. Because of her witness, the Samaritans join the disciples as children of God.

THE MAN BORN BLIND (9:1–41)

Introduction

The story of the man born blind has several unique features. It is the only story in which Jesus is absent for a large portion of the narrative; he is absent for twenty-seven out of forty-one verses. He is present at the beginning of the story (vv. 1–7) and at the end (vv. 35–41), but in between the activity swirls around the man born blind. This leads to another striking feature of the narrative, namely its dramatic

---

[166]*Neither on this Mountain*, 184–185. While Brown includes no suggestion of the woman as sower in his commentary, in "Roles of Women in the Fourth Gospel" he admits that, "whatever [4:37–38] may have meant in reference to the history of the Samaritan church, in the story itself it means that the woman has sown the seed and thus prepared for the apostolic harvest" (692).

[167]Boers, *Neither on this Mountain*, 190, cf. 182, 200.

structure. If one attends to the shifts in characters and dialogue, the chapter falls neatly into seven scenes, each featuring two characters or character groups in conversation.[168]

For our purposes, this narrative presents the premier example of the way the Fourth Evangelist uses dialogue to construct his characters. As the man born blind is variously approached and interrogated, the reader can detect a steady development in his character. He moves from being an object of a theological debate (vv. 1–3) to a subject confessing belief in Jesus as the Son of Man (v. 38). Along the way, he demonstrates increasing insight into the person of Jesus, first perceiving him as a man (v. 11), then a prophet (v. 17), then as one from God (v. 33), and finally as the Son of Man (vv. 35–38).[169] Significantly, this deliberate progression recalls the presentation of the Samaritan woman. As we continue through the analysis, a number of similarities between these two characters will become apparent. One should note from the outset, however, that unlike the Samaritan woman, the character of the man born blind is forged primarily in the context of confrontation with Jesus' opponents, rather than in conversation with Jesus. Moreover, as the analysis will show, he stands alone as the most fully developed and autonomous character in the Gospel.[170]

---

[168]Martyn observes that the narrative thus follows the law of twos from classical Greek drama, in which no more than two characters appear on stage at the same time (*History and Theology*, 6). Cf. also Beasley-Murray, 152. As we will see, a similar dramatic organization is found in the trial of Jesus before Pilate (18:28–19:6a).

[169]The man's progression in faith has been widely recognized (cf., e.g., Bultmann, 334; Brown, 377; O'Day, 660–661).

[170]Since I am interested in the network of meaning created in and between the presentation of characters, it is important to signal the relationship of the chapter nine narrative and 5:1–18. Both are healing narratives and both deal with Sabbath controversy and interrogation by the authorities. Although I will not analyze the "lame" man of chapter five in detail, we should at least raise the questions of relationship to the man born blind. Does the lame man stand in contrast to the man born blind? So Brown, 377, "...this clever and voluble blind man is quite different from the obtuse and unimaginative paralytic of ch. v." More importantly, does he betray Jesus to the authorities in contrast to the blind man's brave defense? (So Brown, 209; Haenchen, 2.147; Culpepper, *Anatomy*, 138). Or is he simply one who announces his healing to the Jews and becomes an unwitting pawn in their scheme? (O'Day, 580). I would suggest that 5:14–15 seem too ominous to allow a positive reading of this character. Cf., however, Jeffrey L. Staley, "Stumbling in the Dark; Reaching for the Light: Reading Character in John 5 and 9," *Semeia* 53 (1991): 55–80.

Scene 1: The Healing (vv. 1–7)

Like the Samaritan woman, the character in chapter nine is introduced only by means of an epithet, ἄνθρωπον τυφλὸν ἐκ γενετῆς, (v. 1)—he is never given a proper name. His blindness is his defining feature and initially the narrator provides no additional information that might distract from this particular characteristic. Also, like the woman, the man born blind does not initiate the encounter with Jesus. In fact, his introduction to the narrative occurs through the eyes of Jesus and then through Jesus' disciples. The latter see the man only as grist for a theological debate.[171] They have no doubt that sin lies behind his condition; the question is who precisely is to blame (v. 2). The disciples' question reveals traditional Jewish beliefs that physical afflictions are the result of sin and that a person may be punished for the sins of his or her parents.[172] Jesus responds to their question with the explanation that in this case the man's affliction is "in order that the works of God might be revealed in him" (v. 3).[173] Note that whereas the disciples are interested in the past cause of the man's blindness, Jesus speaks of its future purpose.[174] Thus, the reader is led to believe from the beginning that consideration of the blind man's past should not be an issue in understanding his character, but only what will unfold in the course of the narrative. In some ways, this is a more explicit expression of what is implicit in the conversation between the Samaritan woman and Jesus regarding her former life, i.e., the reference to her past husbands (4:16–18) has no bearing on her characterization as co-worker with Jesus.

Along this line, Jesus' final words to the disciples are also pertinent. They consist of an exhortation, a warning, and a self-definition, "We must do the works of him who sent me while it is day;

---

[171]Barrett also points to the initial presentation of the man as the theme of a theological debate (358).

[172]Cf. Exod. 20:5 and Deut. 5:9. For references to rabbinic discussions on the notion of a child sinning before birth, cf. Schnackenburg, 2.240–241; Beasley-Murray 154–155.

[173]So Bultmann, "What [Jesus] says does not confute the Jewish position nor does it suggest that there is another way of looking at such cases....The saying is concerned only with the particular case in question at the moment" (331). So also Beasley-Murray, 155.

[174]Cf. Lindars, who points to Lk. 13:2 as another instance in which "Jesus deflects the thought from the cause of suffering to its possibilities for God's purpose." See also Rensberger, *Johannine Faith*, 44; O'Day, 653.

night is coming when no one can work. As long as I am in the world, I am the light of the world" (v. 4). First, the plural "we" in Jesus' statement indicates that he is not the only one who must do the work of God. Moreover, although the exhortation to "do the works of him who sent me" is directed to the disciples, as we will see, it is the man born blind who carries it out. Second, Jesus' statement situates the ensuing events within the categories of light and dark, thereby continuing this theme from the preceding chapter (8:12).[175] We have already pointed out Nicodemus' connection to the dark (3:2, 19–21) and the Samaritan woman's association with light (4:6). Now once more a Johannine character is introduced with these categories at the forefront of the discussion.

Following his pronouncement, Jesus spits on the ground, makes mud, and spreads it on the man's eyes, instructing him, "Go wash in the pool of Siloam."[176] The man does so, and comes back able to see (v. 7). Note that the blind man has not asked for healing, indeed, he says nothing throughout the first scene. Nor does Jesus have much to say to him—his words are limited to his instructions to wash. One is left with the sense that the man is little more than an object lesson at this point of the narrative. Also significant is that after the blind man "washed and came back, seeing," he does not find Jesus waiting for his return.[177] Jesus has left the scene and does not reenter the narrative until the end. In terms of the characterization of the blind man, the events that unfold while Jesus is "off-stage" are highly significant. What follows are four scenes of interrogation involving the man, his neighbors, the Jewish authorities, and the man's parents. It is in the context of this questioning that the character of the man is more fully developed, in preparation for his final meeting with Jesus in verses 35–38.

---

[175]Cf. Brown, "As a sign that he is the light, Jesus gives sight to a man born blind" (203). Brown, along with the majority of commentators, also points to the contrasting presentations of the man coming to vision/light and the Pharisees sinking into blindness/darkness (376–377).

[176]The narrator translates the name Siloam as ἀπεσταλμένος, i.e., "the one sent." The christological connotations are clear, especially given Jesus' reference to the works "of the one who sent me" (τοῦ πέμψαντός με) in v. 4.

[177]Gail O'Day, *The Word Disclosed: John's Story and Narrative Preaching* (St. Louis, MO: CBP Press, 1987) 60.

Scene 2: The Man and His Neighbors (vv. 8–12)

Upon his return from the pool, the man's presence immediately stirs up controversy between his neighbors and others who had seen him before. The point of conflict is the identity of the man, with some arguing about the fact that he is the blind man who used to sit and beg (new information about the character), and others suggesting that while he resembles that person, he is actually someone else. As for the man himself, he does not hesitate to announce to the crowd, "I am the man," or more literally, "I am" (ἐγώ εἰμι, v. 9). It may be more than coincidence that the man employs the same phrase that occurs repeatedly on the lips of Jesus throughout the Gospel. When Jesus says ἐγώ εἰμι, it is in the context of divine self-revelation, as we saw in the conversation with the Samaritan Woman (4:26; cf. also esp. 6:20; 8:58; 13:19; 18:5). As O'Day points out, the reader of the Gospel has come to understand the ἐγώ εἰμι sayings as bold statements of identity.[178] To be sure, coming from the formerly blind man the phrase is not an indication of divinity, but it does have the quality of a bold statement in the face of a skeptical crowd. In addition, as an echo of Jesus' own words the man's expression foreshadows the way he will speak during his confrontation with the Jewish authorities. There, too, the man will sound much like Jesus himself.

Upon hearing that this is the same man they once observed as a blind beggar, the man's neighbors demand to know how such a change has occurred (v. 10). The man answers matter-of-factly, repeating the earthy details of his healing—the mud spread on his eyes, the command to wash in the pool of Siloam from the man called Jesus, and receiving his sight (v. 11). But when asked of Jesus' whereabouts he can only reply, "I do not know" (v. 12). On a mundane level, this is simply a statement of fact. Jesus has disappeared from the narrative and not even the reader knows where he is. At a deeper level, "knowing" and "not knowing" has theological significance throughout the Gospel. Compare for instance, this man's admitted lack of knowledge with Nicodemus' certainty; in the end the latter proved to know very little. Perhaps the man's very lack of knowledge about Jesus is suggestive about his openness to revelation.[179]

---

[178]O'Day, *Word*, 61.

[179]Along this line, Duke has identified "false claims to knowledge" as another ironic category in the Gospel in which "...the opponents of Jesus are constantly

Scene 3: The Man and the Jewish Authorities (vv. 13–18)

Following the man's response, the people bring him to the Pharisees and another round of questioning begins. At this point in the story, the man is designated as τὸν ποτε τυφλός, a reminder for the reader about the change that has occurred in him (v. 13). Only now does the narrator indicate that the healing took place on a Sabbath (v. 14).

Again the man is asked to report how he received his sight. For a second time he states candidly and succinctly, "He put mud on my eyes, and I washed and I see" (v. 15). Staley notes that already in this response, the blind man may be seen as protecting Jesus. His answer spawns a debate between the Pharisees; some view Jesus' apparent disregard for the Sabbath as evidence that he is not from God, while others argue that a sinner could not perform such signs (v. 16). Ironically, they look to the man for clarification (v. 17). The man does not shrink from the question, but again gives his opinion forthrightly, "He is a prophet." As has frequently been noted, his response demonstrates further reflection on the person of Jesus. Whereas earlier he referred to Jesus only as "the man" when questioned by the religious authorities, he readily identifies Jesus as a religious figure, a prophet, similar to the Samaritan woman. Thus, his insight into the nature of Jesus develops gradually, in much the same way as did that of the Samaritan woman (4:19).[180] As in the preceding scene, the man's terse statement ends the conversation and the scene shifts again.

Scene 4: the Jewish Authorities and the Parents (vv. 18–23)

Having spoken with the man, the Pharisees, here referred to more generally as "the Jews,"[181] doubt his veracity and summon his parents to confirm his story (v. 19). From the parents' response, it would appear that whatever boldness the man demonstrates, he did not learn it from them. They confirm that he is indeed their son and that he was born blind, but they will say no more than that. They insist that they do not know how it is that he now sees, nor do they know who opened his eyes (vv. 20–21). However, since the Jews have made no reference to anyone opening his eyes it would seem that they know more than they are

---

claiming to have expertise on the subject of his origin—his parentage and place of birth" (*Irony*, 64).

[180]Bultmann, 334; Beasley-Murray, 157.

[181]Cf. chapter seven for a similar alternation between Pharisees and Jews. See also nt. 57 above.

willing to admit.[182] Rather than bring punishment upon themselves, they encourage the authorities to question their son directly, since he is of age (v. 21, 23). In terms of the characterization of the man born blind, his parents are set up as a foil. Their fear and timidity before the authorities presents a sharp contrast to the courage of their son.

Scene 5: The Man and the Jewish Authorities (vv. 24–33)

The authorities do as the parents suggest and again summon the formerly blind man (v. 24). In this round of conversation, as the man confronts his interrogators for the second time, his character truly unfolds. The authorities begin by pressing him to "give glory to God, " meaning, "Tell us the truth!"[183] Furthermore, they now express their own unified view of the truth about Jesus, stating unequivocally, "We know that this man is a sinner" (v. 24). In contrast to the authorities' confidence in what they know, the formerly blind man answers in bold simplicity, "Whether he is a sinner, I do not know. One thing I do know, that though I was blind, I now see" (v. 25).[184] His statement reflects both his unwillingness to accept the view of Jesus' opponents, and his reliance on his own experience as a measure of truth.

The authorities persist, however, and ask the man a second time to explain how Jesus healed him. The man's reply gives us the opportunity to see that not only is he a man of courage, but also intelligence and wit. In one of the more ironic twists in the Gospel, he inquires about the authorities' avid interest in Jesus and asks in feigned innocence whether they also want to become his disciples (v. 27). With these questions, the man turns the tables of the investigation so that the interrogators become the interrogated. The same sort of move will occur between Jesus and Pilate in chapter 19. Moreover, as this scene continues the man born blind will assume the same unflinching stance that Jesus will demonstrate during his trial.

Significantly, the man's question to the authorities is also the first indication that he may understand himself to have become a disciple of Jesus. The retort from the authorities accents this fact as they point out,

---

[182]O'Day, *Word*, 65.

[183]For this idiomatic use, cf. Josh. 7:19; 1 Esdras 9:8; 2 Esdras 10:11.

[184]Cf. Brown, "Three times the former blind man, who is truly gaining knowledge, humbly confesses his ignorance (12, 25, 36). Three times the Pharisees, who are really plunging deeper into abysmal ignorance of Jesus, make confident statements about what they know of him (16, 24, 29)" (377).

"You are his disciple, but we are disciples of Moses" (v. 28).[185] Their next statement gets to the heart of their problem and to one of the central issues of the Fourth Gospel, the origin of Jesus. The Jewish authorities claim ignorance regarding Jesus' origin, unable or unwilling to perceive that he comes from God (v. 29).[186]

To this, the man gives his longest and most clever reply of the chapter. He first expresses amazement (v. 30), a reaction that recalls Jesus' own ironical surprise at Nicodemus in 3:10.[187] Significantly, Lindars notes, "At this point the man himself becomes the teacher, echoing the kind of argument used by Jesus himself in other discourses."[188] Jesus' works should be enough to testify to his divine origin (v. 30; cf. 5:36; 10:25). The man then demonstrates his logic as he argues with the authorities on their own terms; his opponents cannot dispute that God listens "to one who worships him and obeys his will" (v. 31). The man goes on to point out the greatness of Jesus' miracle, boldly claiming, "If this man were not from God, he could do nothing" (v. 33). His tenacity before the authorities stands in marked contrast to the timidity of his parents as well as of Nicodemus (7:50–51). Indeed, Rensberger suggests that the nearest parallel to the man's attitude before the Pharisees is found in Jesus' demeanor before the high priest in 18:19–23. He notes further, "Perhaps this very parallel explains why Jesus can be absent from the central episodes of the story; his role is taken over by the blind man himself."[189] If this is the case, it is also suggestive of why this male figure is given such a positive role.

The success with which the once blind man makes his point is revealed in the final words and actions of the religious authorities. Unable to refute the logic of his argument, they can only resort to a personal attack. In spite of the fact that earlier the authorities had expressly asked the man for his opinion (v. 17), they now revile him,

---

[185]Duke sees some of the irony of this narrative located in the way the opponents of Jesus inadvertently push the man toward faith. Thus, with their response in v. 28, they prod him toward discipleship, and "think of the man's discipleship before he does" (*Irony*, 122–125). While it is true that the man comes to faith in and through his confrontation with the authorities, Duke seems to overlook the man's barb in v. 27, which in fact is what initiates the topic of discipleship.

[186]For the development of this theme in the Fourth Gospel, cf. Paul Minear, " 'We Don't Know Where...' John 20:2," *Interpretation* 30 (1976): 125–139.

[187]Lindars, 348.

[188]Lindars, 348.

[189]Rensberger, *Johannine Faith*, 42.

"You were born entirely in sins, and are you trying to teach us?" As O'Day observes, "The Jewish authorities correctly characterize the man's words to them as teaching; he has indeed taken over their role as teacher of the faith."[190] One might add again, that in doing so, he acts much like Jesus does in his encounters with the authorities. This may also explain the authorities' final action. They drive him out of their presence because they cannot tolerate the truth which he has so forthrightly spoken—he reminds them too much of Jesus. Thus, the interrogation concludes as the man presumably receives the punishment that his parents had feared for themselves (v. 34, cf. v. 22).

Scene 6: Jesus and the Formerly Blind Man (vv. 35–38)

Throughout the narrative, the reader has observed in the man an increased willingness to defend Jesus boldly and cleverly as a prophet, sent from God.[191] For this reason, when Jesus reenters the narrative and asks the man somewhat indirectly, "Do you believe in the Son of Man?" one can readily anticipate what the response will be. The use of this particular title illustrates the completion of the man's progression to faith. He began by identifying Jesus simply as "the man," but by the end of his confrontation with the Pharisees he is prepared to confess his belief in the "Son of Man." Furthermore, in the Johannine context, the use of this title highlights Jesus as the eschatological judge who is now present in the world. The implication is that "just as the Samaritan woman is confronted by Jesus with the possibility of the anticipated Messiah's being already present (4:25–26), so also the healed man is confronted by Jesus with the possibility that the future judge is already present."[192]

Much like the Samaritan woman, the man remains level-headed and logical, inquiring, "And who is he, sir? Tell me, so that I may believe in him" (v. 36, cf. 4:19–26). Duke has identified this scene even more closely with scenes of revelation to both the Samaritan woman (4:19–26) and to Mary Magdalene (20:14–16). All three scenes, he argues, are instances of "irony of identity" in the Gospel.

---

[190]O'Day, 660.

[191]Cf. Beasley-Murray, "His dogged persistence in declaring the fact about his blindness and healing by Jesus, and still more his bold resistance of attempts by the religious authorities to discredit Jesus are remarkable" (161).

[192]O'Day, 660.

In all three cases, a character, not knowing who Jesus is, addresses him as *kurie* and makes reference to Messiah/Son of man/Jesus—thought to be absent. In all three Jesus then quickly reveals his identity in the most appropriate way. To the woman at the well who is given to misunderstandings he speaks directly, "I am he, the one speaking to you (4:26). With his dear friend at the tomb, he need only call her name (20:16). Now to the man born blind Jesus beams and says, "You have seen him and he is the one speaking to you" (vs. 37).[193]

Thus, Jesus' response to the blind man is a strong echo of his revelation to the Samaritan woman and a foreshadowing of his revelation to Mary Magdalene. Upon hearing Jesus' words, the man offers his confession of faith which is also his final statement in the Gospel, "Lord, I believe" (v. 38). As Beasley-Murray rightly notes, "The effect of this revelation is as overwhelming as that to the Samaritan woman: the latter runs to her village to proclaim the advent of the Messiah, the former prostrates himself before Jesus."[194] As in the case of Nicodemus' sudden departure, the formerly blind man, following his confession and worship of Jesus, drops out of the narrative.[195] Whereas Nicodemus' exit occurs after his last confused and feeble question (3:9), the formerly blind man leaves the narrative with words and actions that indicate his unequivocal faith in Jesus.

Scene 7: Jesus and the Pharisees (vv. 39–41)

The man's confession does not conclude the story, however. There is one final exchange between Jesus and the Pharisees, which, although not involving the man directly, puts the finishing touch on the presentation of his character. Jesus uses the man's confession as an opportunity to explain his mission, "I came into this world for judgment so that those who do not see may see, and those who do not see may become blind" (v. 39). The reader then discovers that the Pharisees are present in the background and overhear the statement. The author cannot resist one more ironic and condemning question from the Pharisees, "Surely, we are not blind; are we?" (v. 40). The Pharisees, insisting on their ability to see spiritual truths are unwilling to admit their blindness to the light of the world and will remain in sin (v. 41). They stand in contrast to the formerly blind man, who from the beginning openly

---

[193]Duke, *Irony*, 123.
[194]Beasley-Murray, 159.
[195]O'Day, 661.

admitted that he does not know about Jesus (9:12, 25), but in the end comes to full recognition of him.

Thus, the man's firm stance against the Jewish authorities and his confession of faith in Jesus contribute to his positive characterization. In many ways this positive construction parallels that of the Samaritan woman. This is especially clear in his final exchange with Jesus. It is almost as though, in terms of his emerging faith, he functions as the woman's male counterpart in the narrative. Like her, to a certain degree the man acts as Jesus' co-worker, though in his case the work is not to bring others to Jesus. Instead, he contributes to the negative side of Jesus' mission, i.e., to the judgment of those who do not accept Jesus. In confronting the Jewish authorities, as Jesus does just prior to this narrative, he participates in laying bare their condemnation (8:12–59). Thus, in terms of the question of difference between women and men, the relationship between this male character and the Samaritan woman points more to similarities than differences. However, in another sense this character is truly unique. It is not his interactions with Jesus that bring his character out so strongly; he develops independently of Jesus, achieving an unprecedented degree of autonomy in the narrative. Indeed, for large portions of this scene, the man effectively stands in for Jesus in combating the opposing dark forces in the Gospel.

MARTHA AND MARY OF BETHANY (11:1–53; 12:1–11)

Introduction

The character of Martha is developed within the longest sustained narrative of the Gospel (11:1–44). Mary of Bethany is also present in this chapter, but she then goes through further development in the opening to the next chapter (12:1–8). Structurally, chapters 11–12 form a pivotal point in the Gospel. They both culminate the first half of the Gospel, the Book of Signs, and foreshadow the events in the second half, the Book of Glory.[196] In other words, this crucial point in the narrative is marked by the most remarkable sign that Jesus has yet performed. However, the meaning of the sign points ahead, toward the crucifixion and resurrection in which God's glory is revealed. So, too, the prophetic act of Mary in 12:1–8, while set in a context that is closely

---

[196]In describing the pivotal nature of these chapters, Lindars notes that by the end of chapter twelve the reader is left "hovering on the brink of the Passion" (379). Cf. also O'Day, 681.

linked to the previous chapter, is interpreted by Jesus as a forward looking event, one that marks his impending death. Thus, as Reinhartz notes,

> The juxtaposed Johannine passages featuring Mary and Martha are among the last, climatic scenes of Jesus' ministry as well as key elements that advance the plot toward the all-important passion narrative. It is consequently not only the particular roles ascribed to Martha and Mary but the crucial juncture at which they appear that compel us to take them seriously both as characters and as vehicles for Johannine theology.[197]

We will examine the two scenes featuring Martha and Mary in turn, once more examining the role which female characters play in relation to Jesus and to the other characters in the Gospel.

The Raising of Lazarus (11:1–53)

There are several ways in which the chapter may be outlined. Bultmann divides verses 1–44 into two basic sections, the introduction (vv. 1–16) and the main part, "The Resurrection and the Life," (vv. 17–44), with each section further subdivided. Verses 45–54, are treated separately under another heading, "The decision of the Sanhedrin that Jesus must die," though Bultmann recognizes a relationship of this section to what precedes.[198] More in keeping with a literary analysis, and the outline I will adopt, is O'Day's suggestion. She divides the chapter into the same three basic parts as Bultmann: the prologue (vv. 1–16), the story proper (vv. 17–44) and an epilogue (vv. 45–53), with the story proper further divided into several sections, as seen in the following outline.[199]

I.	Prologue	11:1–16
II.	The Story	11:17–44
	A. On the Way to the Tomb	11:17–44
	1. Jesus and Martha	11:17–27
	2. Jesus and Mary	11:28–37
	B. The Tomb	11:38–44
III.	Epilogue: The Aftermath	11:45–53

An advantage of this outline is that it graphically illustrates the centrality of the women's encounters with Jesus. Their meetings make up the bulk of the story, while the actual raising of Lazarus is recounted

---

[197]Reinhartz, "The Gospel of John," 583.

[198]Bultmann, 396–409.

[199]O'Day, *Word,* 78.

in just seven verses.[200] Indeed, the traditional title for this story, "The Raising of Lazarus," tends to obscure the major role the sisters play in the narrative. Lazarus is the plot functionary *par excellence* in the Gospel. He is present only as the object of Jesus' miracle. My focus will be on Martha, Mary and Jesus and for this reason, the events on the way to the tomb will demand the most attention. Nevertheless, the scene at the tomb as well as the prologue and epilogue are important for establishing the context in which these characters are constructed, and also for the way in which their story contributes to the larger narrative.

The Prologue (vv. 1–16)

In the prologue, the first six verses introduce the main characters and the basic conflict of the story. The opening verse introduces a certain ill man, Lazarus of Bethany. Notably, this character's hometown is further defined by means of his sisters—Bethany is the village of Mary and her sister Martha. This gives the impression that these sisters should be familiar to the reader. Indeed, the narrator goes on to provide a detailed reminder of the identity of Mary. She is the one who anointed the Lord with perfume and wiped his feet with her hair (v. 2). On an historical level, the recollection of this event before its actual occurrence in the narrative (cf. 12:3) suggests that Mary's act was well known in early Christian tradition and could be referred to before its narration. On a literary level, the proleptic description of Mary conditions the picture of her character in chapter 11. When we read her words to Jesus in verse 32, her subsequent act of devotion comes to mind. Finally, the prolepsis of 11:2 has christological importance as well. By recalling Mary's act of anointing at the beginning of chapter 11, an act that the saying of Jesus in 12:7 associates with his death and burial, the narrator casts the shadow of the Passion over the story of Lazarus.[201]

Following the introduction of the family at Bethany, it is the two sisters who set the story in motion, much like Jesus' mother in chapter 2. They send word to Jesus, stating simply, κύριε, ἴδε ὃν φιλεῖς ἀσθενεῖ (v. 3). They make no specific request,[202] although later in the narrative it becomes clear that they did expect him to take action. Their

---

[200]I would therefore argue, against Stibbe, that the main subjects of the narrator's attention in John 11 are not Jesus and Lazarus, but rather Jesus and the Bethany sisters, with the Jews also playing an important role ("A Tomb with a View: John 11:1–44 in Narrative-Critical Perspective," *NTS* 40 [1994]: 42).

[201]O'Day, *Word*, 80.

[202]O'Day, *Word*, 81.

identification of Lazarus as one whom Jesus loves indicates the intimacy of the relationship between Jesus and the Bethany family. The point is reiterated in verse 5, in which Martha, Mary and Lazarus are all characterized as beloved by Jesus (cf. also v. 36). However, neither the implicit appeal from the sisters, nor the reminder of Jesus' close relationship with the family, provokes him to action. Instead, Jesus reacts with a formal pronouncement that both foreshadows and interprets the rest of the narrative. According to him, Lazarus' illness "is not to death but for the glory of God, so that the Son of God might be glorified through it" (v. 4). As with the sisters' words to Jesus, this prediction points back to the narrative of 2:1–11. There, too, the glory of Jesus was revealed, with the purpose of bringing the disciples to belief (2:11, cf. 11:15).[203] It also recalls the story of the man born blind, especially Jesus' statement in 9:3 regarding the purpose of the man's affliction as revealing the works of God. In addition, the mention of glory in 11:4 points ahead to the Passion narrative, which in the Gospel of John is the "supreme manifestation of the glory of God in Christ."[204]

Verses 5 and 6 close the introductory verses by reminding the reader once more of Jesus' relationship with the main players of the text—he loved Martha, her sister and Lazarus. Notably, the characters are now listed in reverse order from the way they first appeared. This second list is more indicative of the prominence these characters will actually hold in the narrative, with the character of Martha receiving the most narrative space and Lazarus the least. Finally, for the first-time reader, the conclusion to this section is somewhat surprising. Verse six informs us of the action that Jesus takes upon hearing the news of Lazarus' condition; he stays right where he is for two days.[205]

Only after this delay does Jesus inform his disciples of his intention to go to Judea again (v. 7). The ensuing conversation with the disciples provides the occasion for Jesus to explain his intentions

---

[203]O'Day, *Word*, 85.

[204]Lindars, 387.

[205]Though the action is surprising, I do not see, with Giblin, how it is "the equivalent of a negative verbal response." For him, 11:4 fits a pattern of behavior on the part of the Johannine Jesus that he describes as a negative response to a suggestion followed by positive action ("Suggestion," 200). However, Jesus does not respond negatively, but offers an interpretation of the situation which in fact highlights its eventual positive outcome. In this way, the story is similar to the introduction of the chapter nine narrative (cf. 9:3), and very different from his response to his mother in 2:4.

directly (vv. 8–15). The contribution of the disciples, though somewhat obtuse (esp. v. 12), reinforces the connection between this story of death and awakening and Jesus' own death and resurrection (vv. 8, 16). In returning to Judea, Jesus will deal directly with the power of death, both in relation to the illness that overtook Lazarus and ultimately with those who would take his life (cf. 11:53). Significantly, though this section opens and closes with Jesus' exhortation to the disciples, ἄγωμεν (vv. 7, 15), as well as Thomas' identical appeal (ἄγωμεν) to his co-disciples (v. 16), the disciples disappear from the story until verse 54. Perhaps this too is a foreshadowing of Jesus' own experience. In the case of both Lazarus and Jesus, devoted women are present at the tomb to witness the resurrection (cf. 20:14–17) with male disciples conspicuously absent (cf. 20:10).

The Story (11:17–44)

On the Way to the Tomb (11:17–34)

In verse 17 the scene changes. Jesus has arrived at Bethany, just two miles from Jerusalem, the seat of his enemies. Indeed, to the mention of Jerusalem is added that many ἐκ τῶν Ἰουδαίων had come to Martha and Mary to console them (v. 19). There is no indication that "the Jews" should be regarded negatively here, despite their portrayal in chapters eight and nine, and the more immediate reference in 11:8. In fact, mention of the Jews in verse 19 suggests that Martha and Mary remain accepted members of the Jewish community despite their relationship with Jesus.[206] This aspect of their identity will become important later in the narrative.

Martha and Jesus (11:17–27)

Verses 20–27 depict the encounter between Martha and Jesus. At this point in the narrative, a distinction is made between Martha and Mary. Upon hearing that Jesus is coming, Martha takes the initiative to go and meet him, while Mary stays at home (v. 20). Interpreters often

---

[206]Cf. Adele Reinhartz, "From Narrative to History: The Resurrection of Mary and Martha," *"Women Like This": New Perspectives on Jewish Women in the Greco-Roman World* (ed. Amy-Jill Levine; Atlanta: Scholars Press, 1991) 178–179. Reinhartz is interested in the historical observation that "in the time of Jesus, if not of the evangelist, there were women disciples who were integrated into their Jewish communities." For her, this observation adds further information to the discussion of the relation between church and synagogue in the Evangelist's historical setting, a discussion presently dominated by a focus on 9:22.

take this differentiation as a clue to the character of each sister. The tendency is to compare this scene to Luke 10:38–42, and then to assert that in John's Gospel, too, Martha is active, while Mary is contemplative.[207] Alternatively, Mary's inactivity has been viewed as an early indication of her inadequate faith, compared to that of her sister.[208] However, the reason why Mary remains in the house may be viewed as purely practical. Haenchen suggests that she stayed behind to receive mourners and accept condolences.[209] Since the narrative provides no explanation, we will have to read further in the narrative before we suggest reasons why the two sisters are distinguished at this point. For now, the focus shifts exclusively to Martha.

Martha's first words to Jesus express her strong belief that Jesus could have prevented her brother's death (v. 21). Since the reader knows of Jesus' seemingly deliberate delay, there may be a tendency to read a protest or complaint in her statement. Taken alone, however, Martha's statement gives no indication of rancor,[210] and in any case, unlike the reader, she has no knowledge about Jesus' travel plans. Even if we allow for some regret in Martha's opening words, her next comment makes it clear that confidence in Jesus is her overriding emotion. She immediately voices hope in the fact that Jesus is now present, ἀλλα καὶ νῦν οἶδα ὅτι ὅσα ἂν αἰτήσῃ τὸν θεὸν δώσει σοι ὁ θεός (v. 22). Like Nicodemus before her, Martha speaks of what she knows of Jesus (cf. 3:2). Unlike Nicodemus, however, Martha speaks only on behalf of herself; she is not representative of a larger group. That her knowledge of Jesus and God is accurate can be seen in Jesus' own statements to the disciples about asking and receiving from God (cf. 14:13–14; 15:7, 16; 16:23-24). As in her initial message to Jesus (v. 3), Martha does not specify what she wants Jesus to do. She only expresses her conviction in his ability to elicit God's help effectively.

It is Jesus who gives a clue as to what action he will take with Lazarus. His reply to Martha represents a reversal of the pattern of sign followed by interpretive discourse that was established in chapters 5 and 6. He states succinctly, ἀναστήσεται ὁ ἀδελφός σου (v. 23). Martha responds once more with a statement of confidence. However, this time

---

[207]See, for example, the annotation in *The New Oxford Annotated Bible*. ed. Bruce M. Metzger and Roland E. Murphy (New York: Oxford University Press, 1991) 143NT. Cf. also Lindars, 385, 393; Barrett, 394.

[208]Brodie points to Mary's embeddedness in an inert state of mourning (392).

[209]Haenchen, 2.61.

[210]Rena, "Women in the Gospel of John," 141.

what she knows (οἶδα) is not based on the identity of Jesus, but on the Jewish understanding of a resurrection of the dead at the end-time (v. 24). In this way her statement resonates with that of the Samaritan woman in 4:25. Like this woman before her, Martha's knowledge of her own religious tradition provides Jesus with the opportunity for self-revelation. As in chapter four, Jesus responds with a dramatic "I am" statement—ἐγώ εἰμι ἡ ἀνάστασις καὶ ἡ ζωή (v. 25). Also, in both instances, the misunderstandings of the women give Jesus the opportunity for further clarification. He takes what they understand as a future reality and moves it decisively into the present in the form of the revelation of his identity. As we will see, Martha, like the Samaritan woman gains additional insight from Jesus' clarification. In this way, unlike Nicodemus, both women are real partners in conversation with Jesus.

Following Jesus' dramatic pronouncement to Martha, there is no narrative interruption, as was the case in 4:27. Instead, Jesus goes on to explain his statement further and most significantly, to ask Martha directly πιστεύεις τοῦτο. Martha responds with a clear affirmation, ναὶ κύριε, followed by a threefold confession of the identity of Jesus— ἐγὼ πεπίστευκα ὅτι σὺ εἶ ὁ χριστὸς ὁ υἱὸς τοῦ θεοῦ ὁ εἰς τὸν κόσμον ἐρχόμενος. Despite the seeming clarity of Martha's reply, commentators disagree over whether her words represent a faithful response to Jesus. Doubt arises at several points. First, Martha has already misunderstood Jesus' statement in verse 23, the argument goes, so can there be certainty that she understands his pronouncement in verse 24? To be sure, her reply does not coincide precisely with the teaching of Jesus in verse 25. Added to this is Martha's practical protest at the tomb, indicating that an immediate resurrection of her brother is not something she has considered (v. 39).

However, based on the same textual evidence, Martha can also be viewed quite differently, i.e., as a faithful disciple and confessor of Jesus. Note first that Martha uses the perfect tense in her confession, πεπίστευκα, expressing the firmness of her conviction. Second, the fact that the titles that Martha uses for Jesus appear elsewhere in the Gospel suggests that she has indeed understood the essential point, the identity of Jesus. Her confession of Jesus as ὁ χριστός echoes the earlier confession of Andrew in the first chapter (1:41). Likewise, the title ὁ υἱὸς τοῦ θεοῦ appears in the first chapter on the lips of Nathanael (1:49) and later becomes the issue of controversy between Jesus and

Jews (cf. 10:46). Nowhere in these references is there a suggestion that the titles are not appropriate, or are inadequate for Jesus. On the contrary, as is frequently pointed out, belief in Jesus as the Christ, the Son of God, is in accord with the very goal of the Gospel set forth by the narrator in 20:31.[211] Moreover, the identification of Jesus as "the one coming into the world" resonates deeply with the eschatology that is so central to John's Gospel; Jesus is the one sent into the world by the Father. As Bultmann puts it, this title "most plainly affirms the inbreaking of the beyond into this life."[212] In this way, Martha's words represent not inadequate faith, but the fullest confession of Jesus voiced by a character in the Gospel,[213] except perhaps for the confession of the Samaritan villagers for which the Samaritan woman is partly responsible. It is true that Martha does not feed back the words of Jesus verbatim, but this need not be an indication of her lack of understanding. As Barrett correctly points out, "The confession of faith in Christ, or rather the confessional statement about his person that follows, is not a loose variation of verse 26. It is by true belief in Jesus as Christ and Son of God that [people] have life." By focusing on the identity of Jesus in her reply, rather than mere doctrinal assent, Martha actually takes the discourse a step further.[214] Her "Yes, Lord" includes what Jesus has

---

[211]Cf., for example Schneiders who comments, "This is the faith which, according to its conclusions, the Fourth Gospel was written to evoke (20:31)" ("Death in the Community of Eternal Life: History, Theology, and Spirituality in John 11," *Int* 51 [1987]: 3).

[212]Bultmann, 404.

[213]Schneiders, "Death," 53. In Bultmann's view, Martha shows a "genuine attitude of faith" (404). From his perspective "[i]t is incomprehensible how many exegetes can say that Martha did not rightly understand Jesus" (404, nt. 5). Slightly different is Schnackenburg's positive view of Martha. He compares her to Peter in that neither character demonstrates full understanding of Jesus' words (cf. 6:60, 63b, 68b), but both accept his words as those of the bringer of salvation (332). Cf. also Elisabeth Schüssler Fiorenza, "As a 'beloved disciple' Martha becomes the spokeswoman for the messianic faith of the community. Her confession parallels that of Peter (6:66–71) but is a christological confession in the fuller Johannine sense: Jesus is the revealer who has come down from heaven" ("A Feminist Interpretation for Liberation: Martha and Mary: Lk. 10:38–42" *RelIntel* 3 [1986]: 31). Similarly, de Boer, "The confession of Martha...matches, and perhaps even surpasses, that of Peter in chap. 6....Martha models the very belief the gospel seeks to elicit from its readers, whether these be men or women (29:30–31)" ("John 4:27," 209).

[214]Barrett, 397. Schneiders expresses the point well when she states, "...Martha believes not in *what* she understands but in the *one* who has the words of eternal life" ("Death," 53, nt. 26). Similarly, Stibbe states, "With these words [of confession], Martha exhibits complete faith (20.31). She has moved from her two 'I

taught, but more than this; it is a genuine affirmation of who Jesus is. Most significant is that Martha's conversation with Jesus ends not with words of Jesus, but with her confession. Nowhere else in the Gospel does an individual character's confession conclude a conversation in the way that Martha's does. The confessions of Nathanael (1:49), Peter (6:69), and Thomas (20:28) are all followed by some sort of reprimand by Jesus, and even the profession of faith by the formerly blind man (9:38) is followed by a judgment from Jesus. In contrast, Martha's confession is allowed to stand on its own. The only other place where this occurs is in 4:42 where the Samaritan villagers declare their understanding of Jesus as the Savior of the World.

Mary and Jesus (11:28–37)

Following Martha's conversation, the focus changes to her sister, Mary. Returning to the house, Martha tells her sister that "the teacher" is present and calling for her (v. 28). The need for secrecy (λάθρᾳ) reminds the reader of the sisters' companions in mourning (cf. 11:19). The element of secrecy emphasizes the privileged position held by Martha and Mary with respect to Jesus. It also creates a degree of suspense in the narrative, since the Jews are not privy to the arrival of Jesus. When Mary responds to Martha's words and quickly goes out to meet Jesus, the Jews follow, thinking that she is going to the tomb to weep (v. 31). This is our first indication of one of the roles that Mary will play in the narrative. Unbeknownst to the Jews, she is actually leading them to Jesus.[215]

Mary's own encounter with Jesus is brief. It consists of a dramatic act—she fell or knelt (ἔπεσεν) at his feet—and an echo of Martha's opening words to Jesus, "Lord, if you were here our brother would not have died" (The second half of Martha's statement is not included. As with the earlier depiction of Mary remaining in the house, her portrayal at this point has been variously interpreted. On the negative side are those who see her in contrast to Martha. Schnackenburg, for example, believes the narrator's primary purpose in bringing Mary into

---

know's' (vv. 22, 24) to her climactic 'I believe' (27). She has progressed from a propositional to a personal understanding of the resurrection" ("Tomb," 47).

[215]Cf. Haenchen, "Mary departs quickly from the house filled with mourners: this feature is used skillfully as a motivation for all the Jews who are present to come with her to Jesus and thus to become witness to his act of restoring life to the decaying Lazarus" (2.65).

the story is to set up such a comparison, since, according to him, the scene is not necessary to the flow of the narrative. In his view, since Mary does not include Martha's note of confidence in her statement to Jesus, she "gives the impression of being nothing but a complaining woman."[216] Most often, the sisters' faith has been highlighted as the point of comparison. Brodie, for instance, compares Martha's ascending faith with "the sorrowful state of Mary." He goes on to point out, "It is as though, despite [Mary's] eagerness, there is some kind of veil over her perception. The last activity ascribed to her is that of crying."[217] Bultmann also sees a difference between the sisters, though he is kinder to Mary. He understands her to take the first step of faith as she comes to Jesus for consolation, though she has not attained the certainty that Martha demonstrates.[218]

Alternatively, some interpreters argue against reading the two sisters in contrast. For example, Haenchen contends that no contrast between the sisters is intended, and that, instead, Mary appears as the shadow of her sister.[219] Similarly, Seim points out that, unlike in Luke's Gospel, there is no contrast or conflict between Martha and Mary in the Gospel of John. She, too, sees Mary as "a silent shadow, a weak echo of the articulate, confessing and believing Martha."[220] While these interpreters move in the right direction, their insistence on

---

[216]Schnackenburg seems uneasy with this reading, however, since further on he adds that Mary's meeting with Jesus is fairly colorless and that her words to him probably imply no criticism (333–334).

[217]Brodie, 394. Francis Maloney also contrasts the two sisters' faith, but reverses the traditional reading. He understands Mary to be the one reflecting genuine Johannine faith, while Martha falls short ("The Faith of Martha and Mary: A Narrative Approach to John 11,17–40," *Bib* 75 (1994): 471–493). Martha cannot transcend the limitations of her own world, while Mary "responds to the call of the Good Shepherd (see v. 28–29)," placing herself in a position of total trust in him (v. 32a) (483).

[218]Bultmann, 405–406. Rena also suggests that the two sisters represent different types of faith. While Martha believes and confesses on the basis of the word of Jesus, Mary requires a sign before she responds in faith in 12:3. Martha thus models a superior faith; indeed she is the model confessor for a Gospel reader ("Women in the Gospel," 140–143). Slightly different is Stibbe's reading, which focuses on the sisters' different types of grief. "The grief of Martha is one which has room for a growth in resurrection faith. The grief of Mary is a desperate, passionate and forlorn affair" ("A Tomb," 47).

[219]Haenchen, 2.65.

[220]Seim "Roles of Women," 73. Seim also suggests that the reverse is true in 12:1–8. There Mary's actions will overshadow those of her sister.

conceiving Mary as a shadow still does not give credit to her importance in the narrative. Mary has her own role to play in the story.

As already mentioned above, part of Mary's role is to bring the Jews to Jesus, even though she does it unintentionally. Schneiders makes note of this, but concentrates more on the action's negative implications when she states,

> The...scene between Jesus and Mary appears, at first sight, to be a useless and even impoverished duplication of the Martha scene. Such is not the case. The literary function of the episode is to bring onto the stage with some narrative plausibility, Mary's companions in mourning, the Jews, who will report Jesus to the authorities.[221]

While Schneiders is correct about the Jews, one must add the crucial point that not all of them report Jesus; some in fact come to believe in him (11:45).[222] Along this line, O'Day notes a main difference in the two meetings between Jesus and the sisters. Martha's takes place privately, without any witnesses. In the case of Mary, the Jews are part of the encounter—they observe Mary and hear her words. As O'Day puts it,

> The connection [Mary] makes between Jesus' absence and Lazarus' death is no longer a private confessional statement, but becomes the property of all those who are gathered. Mary's words, therefore, despite their repetitiveness, do add something to the story. They provide the Jewish mourners with the insight necessary to share in the central claims of the narrative.[223]

In this respect, note that ἠκολούθησαν in verse 31 may suggest more than the practical act of following Mary out of the house. It may be a subtle foreshadowing of the Jews who, in following Mary, eventually come to belief in Jesus (cf. v. 45). Still, even when this aspect of Mary's character is taken into account, we may be left with the impression that she is purely functional to the plot—she bridges the gap between the Jews and Jesus. However, there is more to her character than this, especially since she reappears in 12:1–8. To get a fuller picture, it is necessary to look beyond her functional role and more closely examine how she is constructed in the narrative.

Consider first Mary's initial reaction upon seeing Jesus, ἔπεσεν αὐτοῦ πρὸς τοὺς πόδας (v. 32). Surely this is not an act of

---

[221]Schneiders, "Death," 53–54.

[222]In her article, "Women in the Fourth Gospel," Schneiders does point to this division among the Jews (40).

[223]Word, 91. See also O'Day, 690.

desperation,[224] but an indication of Mary's devotion to Jesus. Indeed, Barrett suggests that Mary responds with greater devotion than Martha as she prostrates herself at the feet of Jesus.[225] Moreover, her action is consistent with the portrayal of her character in 12:3, where she is depicted in an unmistakably devotional act at the feet of Jesus. Finally, while Mary's comment to Jesus in 11:32 may have an air of regret, it also expresses a certain confidence in Jesus.[226] Like Martha, Mary knows that Jesus has the power to restore health and would have done so if he were present.

Note however that in the case of this sister words are not the primary focus. Unlike Martha, her comment does not lead to a conversation with Jesus. This is not to say that Mary has no effect on him. On the contrary, the last glimpse we have of Mary in the story proper is actually through Jesus eyes, as he is sees her weeping (v. 33). Significantly, in her weeping, Mary is again closely associated with the Jews, who weep along with her. No doubt this association is partly responsible for the negative way in which commentators have interpreted the tears of both Mary and the Jews, i.e., as an indication of faithlessness. Yet, there is still no indication of hostility on the part of the Jews; here they simply join with Mary in her grief (cf. 11:31). Moreover, Jesus himself is moved to tears; should this also be understood negatively? As Schneiders points out, "Mary's function in this narrative is to weep, and Jesus joins her in her sorrow."[227] Along this line, one should also consider the way in which Jesus responds to the weeping of Mary Magdalene in 20:15. Certainly there is no indication of rebuke or anger in that scene. In fact, Mary of Bethany's tears signal another way in which this story may be linked to the story of Jesus. If the death and resurrection of Lazarus serves as a foreshadowing of Jesus' own death and resurrection, so perhaps Mary's tears foreshadow the tears of Mary Magdalene at the tomb.[228]

---

[224]See Stibbe, "Tomb," 47.

[225]Barrett, 398.

[226]Cf. Barrett, "that [Mary] repeats Martha's statement is meant to emphasize the confidence of both women in contrast to the bystanders" (398).

[227]Schneiders, "Death," 54.

[228]Curiously, Brodie sees in Mary an advance sketch of Mary Magdalene, "who, while others advance in believing, will likewise be left behind crying (20:1–18)" (394). While Brodie's interpretation of Mary at Bethany can be derived plausibly from the text, there is no sound basis for this negative view of Mary Magdalene. As

The reaction of Jesus expressed in verses 33 and 35 has been a point of debate among exegetes and is relevant here since it relates closely to the way in which Mary and her fellow Jews have been viewed. The interpretive crux has been the meaning of ἐνεβριμήσατα τῷ πνεύματι in verse 33 and its relationship to ἐδάκρυσεν in verse 35. Does ἐμβριμᾶσθαι indicate deeply felt emotions, so that Jesus is here revealing his humanity by sharing in this display of feeling?[229] Or is he angry at the lack of faith to which their tears attest? The former interpretation, though overly psychological, at least accords with verse 35, which describes Jesus as weeping (ἐδάκρυσεν). The latter reading attempts to take into account a basic meaning of ἐμβριμᾶσθαι which involves an expression of anger (cf. Mk 1:43; 14:5; Mt 9:30). However, it does not explain Jesus' tears in verse 35, unless we are to picture him as emotionally unstable—moving from anger, to tears, and back to anger again (cf. v. 38).[230] Moreover, this reading has had disastrous effects on the interpretation of Mary, since Jesus' expression of anger has been translated into a judgment of her and her fellow Jews—he is angry at their resignation and lack of faith in him,[231] or alternatively, he is angry because their grief is almost forcing a miracle upon him.[232] In a more

a matter of fact, her tears, like the tears of Mary of Bethany, are what evoke a response in Jesus and moves the narrative forward.

[229]Cf. Lindars, 398–399. Stibbe also argues that in chapter 11 the humanity of Jesus is emphasized, as he is portrayed as a man of profound feeling ("A Tomb," 44–45). Haenchen suggests that the Evangelist may have understood that Jesus was deeply moved in the face of death and so wept along with the Mary and the Jews, although he believes the expression of emotion likely came from a source which made use of the typical features of miracle worker" (66).

[230]For discussions of translation, cf. esp. Beasley-Murray, 192–193; Brown, 425–426; Barrett, 399.

[231]E.g., Bultmann who writes, "The wailing of Mary and of the Jews provokes the height of agitation in Jesus (v. 33). In this context it cannot be otherwise interpreted than his wrath over the lack of faith expressed in the wailing that is raised about the death of Lazarus in his presence"(406). Cf. also Schnackenburg, 2.336; Beasley-Murray, 193. Bultmann is consistent in that he attributes the weeping of Jesus in verse 35 to the same agitation, whereas both Schnackenburg (2.337) and Beasley-Murray (194) see in his tears grief over the darkness of the earthly world which ends in death. O'Day posits that Jesus is angry at the Jews for intruding into the scene and sharing in a miracle that was meant to be for his intimate companions (690).

[232]Barrett compares the scene to 2:4 where a request for miraculous activity evokes a rough response (339). Note however, that Martha's words to Jesus in verse 22 evoked no similar expression of anger, although the request for a miracle is more evident there than in the tears of the mourners.

neutral way, others understand Jesus' anger to be directed toward the power of death that still reigns over the present world.[233]

A closer examination of the passage reveals that the interpretation of Jesus' emotion as anger may be incorrect. First, in other New Testament occurrences where ἐμβριμᾶσθαι is used as an expression of anger towards someone or as a rebuke, it is followed by the dative (cf. Mk 1:43; 14:5; Mt 9:30). When used to describe an internal attitude, as in our case, it may indicate more generally a deeply felt emotion.[234] In 11:33 there is no sense that Jesus' emotion is directed outward. Moreover the narrative does not support the idea of anger toward the "representatives of unbelief." Jesus gives no admonishment for unbelief as he does elsewhere in the Gospel (e.g. 8:24, 45–46). Nor should we presume that the mourners could or should anticipate what Jesus will accomplish with Lazarus. In O'Day's words, "Jesus' gift of life is so radical that no one, no matter how faithful, could be expected to have anticipated it."[235]

For these reasons, the first option discussed above— understanding Jesus to be deeply moved by the tears of the mourners— appears to be the most plausible reading. Nevertheless, we should be wary of delving too deeply into the psyche of Jesus with assumptions about his humanity.[236] The narrative offers no indication that illustrating Jesus' humanity is a concern. As a matter of fact, the tears of Mary and the Jews are what motivate Jesus to action, and his action will eventually reveal his divinity more powerfully than any sign he has performed thus far. To this end, Jesus' immediate response is to direct his attention toward Lazarus and the tomb asking the mourners, "Where have you laid him?" (v. 34).

As they invite Jesus to accompany them to the tomb, Jesus himself begins to weep (vv. 34–35). That his emotions are stirred at this point suggests that it is the death of his friend to which he is reacting. Thus, his weeping is an extension of the emotion already attributed to

---

[233]So Brown, 435; O'Day, *Word*, 91–92. Brodie would have it both ways—the immediate reason for Jesus' anger is the unbelief of Mary and the Jews, who represent "the essence of sin." However, because sin and death are inseparable, he concludes with Brown that Jesus' unfolding anger is directed at sin and death and thus against the realm of Satan (395).

[234]So Liddell and Scott, *An Intermediate Greek-English Lexicon* (7th ed.; Oxford: Clarendon Press, 1990).

[235]*Word*, 91.

[236]Cf. O'Day, 691.

him. As for its cause, the Jews themselves offer the most convincing explanation. They understand Jesus' tears as a sign of his love for Lazarus (v. 36). They are clearly not wrong in their assessment, since the story began by twice highlighting this love (vv. 3, 5).[237] The picture is then complicated by some among the Jews who raise a question. Could not this man, who miraculously opened the eyes of the blind man, keep Lazarus from dying? (v. 37). At one level their question expresses a position similar to that of Martha and Mary—had Jesus been present, the outcome would have been different. However, that their question is presented in contrast to the first view (τινὲς δὲ ἐξ αὐτῶν εἶπαν) suggests a more critical edge. The hint of a division between the Jews here will be stated explicitly in vv. 45–46.

At the Tomb (11:38–44)

Verse 38 once more links Jesus' strong emotions directly to the tomb. For our purposes, the details of the miracle are not as important as what has already taken place in the narrative. However, immediately preceding the raising of Lazarus, a final exchange between Martha and Jesus demands some attention. When Jesus issues the command to remove the stone from the tomb, Martha balks at the idea because of her practical concern about the foul odor (v. 39). As we have seen, for some, this protest is a clear indication of Martha's lack of faith. Haenchen, for example, argues that her comment "in its dreadful realism no longer betrays a scintilla of faith."[238] For those who place Martha's faith on a higher plain than her sister's, her hesitation in this scene presents even more problems. If Martha is supposedly superior in her faith, why does she now express such skepticism?

Others argue that Martha's comment need does not necessarily indicate a sudden wavering in her faith. For example Schneiders points out, "She who knows that Lazarus, even though he has died yet lives, has no reason to think the final resurrection will be anticipated in his case."[239] Schnackenburg emphasizes the functional aspect of Martha's words. According to him, her opposition gives Jesus an opportunity to

---

[237]Contra O'Day who argues the interpretation of the Jews is not to be trusted as accurate. It is true that in many places in the Gospel, the Jews "are neither faithful witnesses nor interpreters of Jesus" (691), but this does not appear to be one of them.

[238]Haenchen, 2.67.

[239]Schneiders, "Death," 54.

answer.[240] On this point, Schnackenburg is certainly correct, but it is also clear that Martha's comment stands in tension with her earlier confession. It does not completely negate the strength of her prior conviction, but it does create ambiguity regarding Martha's characterization. What is significant is that this becomes the means by which the narrative recalls the earlier conversation reinforcing its importance in relation to the miracle about to take place.

Jesus' reminder to Martha (οὐκ εἶπόν σοι ὅτι ἐὰν πιστεύσῃς ὄψῃ τὴν δόξαν τοῦ θεοῦ) (v. 40), though it does not repeat their earlier conversation, effectively recalls the whole of it for the reader. In this way, the raising of Lazarus is defined in the context of Jesus' self-revelatory words to Martha, "I am the resurrection and the life." Their conversation becomes key to interpreting Jesus' sign at the tomb. Note also that Jesus' rephrasing of his conversation with Martha in terms of seeing the glory of God recalls his words to the disciples in verse 4. We are once more reminded of the overall purpose of Jesus' actions.

Finally, although Mary is not mentioned at this point, Jesus' prayer to the Father implicitly recalls her role in leading witnesses to Jesus. He gives thanks to the Father, "for the sake of the crowd, so that they may believe that you sent me" (v. 42). This statement makes clear that the presence of the Jews is a crucial element in what is about to unfold. Jesus performs the sign, not simply to restore a dead friend to life, but to convince the Jewish onlookers of his identity.

The Epilogue (11:45–53)

The success of Jesus' action is reported immediately after Lazarus comes out of the tomb. Notably, Lazarus himself receives very little narrative attention. Instead, the focus is on the Jews who, upon seeing what Jesus did, believe in him. Moreover, for the third time the narrative explicitly reinforces Mary's role, albeit an unconscious one, in bringing the Jews to Jesus (11:45, cf. vv. 32–33). Indeed, without Mary's presence the story could not end the way it does, with a number of Jews coming to belief in Jesus. One could say that, taken together, the two sisters accomplish what the Samaritan woman did alone. Martha elicits self-revelation from Jesus and responds in faith. Mary brings the Jews to Jesus, enabling them to witness his power for themselves.

In this way the narrative purpose for the sisters' separate visits to Jesus becomes clearer. In their distinct encounters with Jesus, and in the

---

240Schnackenburg, 2.338.

unique way each woman is characterized, both contribute to the narrative. Martha's meeting with Jesus leads to a theological discourse that results in his self-revelation and her confession. In addition, their conversation forms the hermeneutic through which we are to understand the raising of Lazarus. As for Mary, she leads the Jews to Jesus so that they are present at the resurrection of Lazarus. She also leads them in mourning, which motivates Jesus to action. The importance of both aspects of her role is evident as some Jews who witness the miracle come to believe in Jesus. To be sure, not all the Jews who accompany Mary believe in Jesus. Some go on to report him to the Pharisees, which carries great consequences in the larger narrative. As the story concludes, we learn that on the basis of this information, the Pharisees plan to put Jesus to death. Significantly, as we move to the next scene, we will also see that more than any other character in the narrative, it is Mary who exhibits a particular sensitivity to Jesus' impending death.

THE ANOINTING: MARY OF BETHANY AND JESUS (12:1–8)

Unlike the previously examined texts, this one does not include an extended conversation between Jesus and another character. In fact, the woman featured in the story, Mary, says nothing at all. Instead, she performs what could be called a sign act, which Jesus then interprets for those gathered around him.

Again, the setting is Bethany. Jesus has returned to the home of Lazarus, where a dinner has been prepared for him. Martha and Lazarus are mentioned only briefly, and play no significant role in the account. That Martha is presented as serving suggests the presence of traditional sources behind the narrative (cf. Lk 10:38 ff.). Most likely both Lazarus and Martha are mentioned primarily to connect this passage with the previous chapter and to identify clearly the woman who anoints Jesus as Mary of Bethany. Although the anointing episode is common to all the Gospels in various forms (Mt 26:6–13; Mk 14:3–9; Lk 7:36–50), only the Fourth Gospel makes this identification.[241] Because the scene is directly connected to 11:1–44, it provides further insight into the

---

[241]The history of tradition behind the story is difficult to determine. The depiction of Mary weeping at the feet of Jesus recalls especially Luke's version of the anointing story. However, the Johannine version shares with Matthew and Mark the location of the scene at Bethany and the interpretation of the anointing as anticipation of Jesus' death and burial. The Fourth Evangelist, in typical style, has creatively crafted this particular version of the story.

character of Mary. Indeed, whereas in chapter 11 Martha plays the more extensive role, in this scene the focus is on Mary.

Her act is described in three stages—she took a pound of expensive perfume, anointed the feet of Jesus, and wiped his feet with her hair (v. 3). The extravagance of her act is emphasized both in the detailed description of the oil, and in its effect—the fragrance of the perfume fills the house. Is this in contrast to the stench that Martha feared in 11:39? That Mary anoints the feet of Jesus is unusual, since typically the head is anointed with oil.[242] Even more remarkable is the fact that she then wipes off the oil with her hair. Aside from the tradition-critical reasons that may lie behind this depiction,[243] it is notable that ἐξέμαζεν reappears in the next chapter where Jesus washes the feet of his disciples, and wipes them (ἐκμάσσειν) with a towel (13:5). In chapter 13, Jesus' foot washing is meant as an example of discipleship (cf. 13:14–15). Thus, on one level, Mary's act of devotion anticipates the lesson of Jesus. She demonstrates, in the most extravagant fashion, the qualities of a good disciple.[244]

Juxtaposed to the depiction of Mary in verse 3 is the introduction of Judas in verse 4. He is explicitly described as one of Jesus' disciples, but this is immediately qualified by the phrase, "the one about to betray him." This is the second time in the narrative that Judas is mentioned and both references emphasize his contradictory identity as disciple and betrayer (cf. 6:71). In 12:5–6, Judas is further characterized as an embezzler, who masks his greed with a false concern for the poor. The juxtaposition of these two characters leads Schüssler Fiorenza to argue that in John's Gospel

---

[242]Bultmann suggests that the act indicates Mary's humility (414), though, citing StrB I.427f, he also notes that anointing the feet of a guest is attested in rabbinic literature (414–415, 415, nt. 1).

[243]Lk 7:38 depicts a tearful woman who bathes Jesus' feet with her tears, dries them with her hair, and then kisses his feet and anoints them with ointment. As mentioned above, the Evangelist may have had a similar tradition in mind when composing this scene (cf. Bultmann, 415, nt. 1).

[244]See Robert Kysar, *John*, Augsburg Commentary of the New Testament (Minneapolis: Augsburg, 1986) 187; also O'Day, 701. Giblin posits another explanation for Mary's act of wiping off the ointment. He suggests, "[I]f the anointing of Jesus' feet prophetically announces his forthcoming burial, wiping off that ointment (which would never be done in an ordinary burial, since the purpose of the ointment was to mask the stench of decomposition) prophesies his rising incorrupt" ("Mary's Anointing for Jesus' Burial-Resurrection (John 12,1–8)" *Biblica* 73 (1992): 560.

Mary is not portrayed as the opposite of Martha, but the counterpart of Judas. The centrality of Judas both in the anointing and in the footwashing scene emphasizes the evangelistic intention to portray the true female disciple, Mary of Bethany, as the alternative to the unfaithful male disciple, Judas, who was one of the Twelve.[245]

Yet, Judas' challenge to Mary's act does more than set up a contrast between the two figures, important as that may be to their characterization. It also provides Jesus with an opportunity to interpret Mary's action on another level. While the grammar is somewhat difficult to follow,[246] the sense of Jesus' statement is clear. Judas' protest is misguided; Mary was right to use the perfume rather than sell it to the poor. Her act was not merely extravagant, but rather an anticipation of the death of Jesus. If there is any doubt remaining as to the faithfulness of Mary based on her portrayal in chapter 11, Jesus' defense of her action should dispel it. Mary has performed a prophetic act that anticipates and prepares for the hour of Jesus. In this, one can see similarities between her portrayal and that of the mother of Jesus; both appear keenly sensitive to the hour of Jesus. A major difference between the two stories, however, is that far from refusing to acknowledge the arrival of his hour, in chapter 12 Jesus provides this interpretative framework for Mary's action. Granted, there is no explicit occurrence of ὥρα in this passage, but in speaking of his death Jesus evokes the theme. In this respect, Schneiders' observation about the Martha and Mary material as a whole is worth noting. As she puts it,

> Chapters 11 and 12 of John constitute a proleptic presentation of the "Hour" of Jesus. The raising of Lazarus both foreshadows Jesus' resurrection and finalizes the intention of the authorities to kill him. The anointing at Bethany foreshadows Jesus' burial and exposes Judas as the one who will precipitate the Hour by his betrayal. Throughout this anticipation of the paschal mystery women disciples play the leading positive roles not only as witnesses but as faithful participants.[247]

---

[245]Schüssler Fiorenza, "A Feminist Interpretation for Liberation" 32.

[246]The ἵνα clause is awkwardly placed and read literally seems to imply that Mary still has oil to keep, which is obviously not the intent of the passage. Lindars suggests that ἵνα may be treated epexegetically, and translates the sentence, "Let her alone! [The reason why she did not sell it and give the proceeds to the poor was] that she might keep it for day of my burial" (419).

[247]"Women in the Fourth Gospel," 42–43.

PILATE (18:28–19:22)

Introduction

From a literary perspective, the account of Jesus before Pilate has much in common with the story of the man born blind in chapter nine.[248] As mentioned before, both narratives are readily divided into seven scenes, indicated by shifts either in character or location. The similarity in structure means that the characterization of the man born blind and of Pilate both occur through a series of interactions with Jesus and with Jesus' opponents. Moreover, in both scenes, these interactions involve interrogation by figures of authority. Most significantly, both stories are replete with irony as the accusers become the accused and the judges become the judged. In the midst of this, Pilate emerges in almost complete contrast to the man born blind.

Scene 1: Outside the Praetorium (18:28–32)

The narrative opens somewhat ambiguously with the statement that "they" took Jesus from Caiaphas to the Praetorium and it is not until verse 31 that we find a specific reference to "the Jews." However, mention of the concern over ritual defilement does indicate that it is indeed the Jews who have brought Jesus to the Roman procurator. That Jesus' opponents are here identified on the basis of their concern for observing Passover is widely recognized as an ironic statement on the part of the Evangelist.[249] In addition, their refusal to enter the palace effectively creates the narrative structure of the trial. The scenes will take place inside and outside of the Praetorium, as Pilate shuttles between Jesus and the Jews.[250] Most importantly for our purposes, does the location of the Jews outside of Pilate's headquarters already suggest something about his characterization? Is he forced from the beginning of the narrative to comply with their demands?[251] To answer this question already at this point may be to predetermine Pilate's character based on traditional New Testament interpretations of the Roman procurator as

---

[248]Cf. Duke, who notes "some striking similarities in form and theme" in these two stories (*Irony*, 117).

[249]E.g., Bultmann, 651–652; Brown, 866; Lindars, 555; Duke, 127–128; O'Day, 815.

[250]According to Culpepper (*Anatomy*, 310), this universally accepted structure was first identified by R. H. Strachan, *The Fourth Gospel: Its Significance and Its Environment* 3rd ed. (London: Student Christian Movement Press, 1941) 310.

[251]So Culpepper, *Anatomy*, 142.

weak and ineffectual before the Jewish leaders.[252] In fact, more recent interpretations of Pilate suggest that the initial exchange between Pilate and the Jews need not indicate compliance on Pilate's part.[253]

To begin, the Evangelist does not provide any initial clues as to how this character should be viewed. He receives no introduction other than his appearance before the Jews in v. 29. The presumption appears to be that the reader is familiar with the figure of "Pilate," but there is no immediate indication as to how he should be regarded. Pilate's first order of business is what one would expect given his position; he inquires about the accusation against Jesus. When the Jews do not provide one, his first inclination is to throw the case back at them (vv. 30–31), not the action of a ruler who easily complies with the whims of his subjects. In fact, his action may be read as a means to humiliate the Jews by reminding them of their powerlessness under Roman rule.[254] In any case, it is only when Pilate discovers that the Jews are seeking Roman execution of Jesus that he is willing to take the case into consideration, and this may say more about his character than anything so far in the narrative. In Rensberger's words, "...in spite of [the Jews] refusal to name any specific charges (18:29–30) he is at once willing to proceed with the hearing when he learns that a crucifixion is in the offing."[255]

Scene 2: Inside the Praetorium (18:33–38)

The narrative continues, therefore, with the first interrogation of Jesus by Pilate. His opening question, "Are you the King of the Jews" (v. 33) comes as a surprise, since the Jews voiced no such charge against Jesus. At the story level, Pilate may best be perceived as attempting to discover whether Jesus' crime is a political one, in which case it would certainly merit his consideration. More importantly, the question also prepares the way for Jesus' response which is, in effect, a searching of Pilate's character. The Johannine Jesus probes Pilate to

---

[252]Cf., e.g., Bultmann who maintains that as a representative of the state, Pilate does not have the strength to maintain neutrality (657).

[253]Cf. esp. Wayne A. Meeks, *The Prophet-King: Moses Traditions and the Johannine Christology* (Leiden: E. J. Brill, 1967); " 'Am I a Jew?'—Johannine Christianity and Judaism," in *Christianity, Judaism and Other Greco-Roman Cults: Studies for Morton Smith at Sixty* 4 vols. (Edited by Jacob Neusner; Leiden: E. J. Brill, 1975) 1.163–186. Also, Rensberger, *Johannine Faith*, 92–95; O'Day, 811–827.

[254]So Schnackenburg, 3.245; Beasley-Murray, 328.

[255]Rensberger, *Johannine Faith*, 92–93.

discern whether he has perceived something of his nature, or whether he is simply repeating a charge brought to him by the Jews (v. 34). With this question, the role reversal between Jesus and Pilate already emerges, and Pilate becomes the one under judgment.[256]

Pilate does not answer Jesus' question directly, but his response nevertheless gives insight into his character. His question to Jesus, "I am not a Jew, am I?" (v. 35), is best understood as a scornful retort. Grammatically, it presupposes a negative answer, so that Pilate distances himself from the Jews—he would not concern himself with their affairs. This does not mean, however, that Pilate sides with Jesus in the dispute.[257] In fact, the scorn with which he speaks of the Jews would also be directed toward Jesus, since from Pilate's perspective, Jesus is included among the Jews. In addition, as Wayne Meeks has argued, Pilate's question, "Am I a Jew," is charged with irony. In Meeks's words,

> This is just the question posed by the trial situation, for "the Jews" represent in John the disbelieving world, the world, seeking to be rid of the Redeemer. Does Pilate belong to the world that rejects Jesus? Grammatically his question expects a negative answer; the development of the trail, however, places him step by step at the disposal of "the Jews."[258]

This is confirmed by his additional statement, "your own nation and the chief priests have handed you over to me" (v. 35b). Elsewhere in the Gospel a distinction has been maintained between the Jewish people and their leaders (cf., e.g., references to the crowd and neighbors vis-à-vis "the Jews" in chapters six and nine). Here, however, the Evangelist accurately presents Pilate's point of view—Jesus' own people and his own leaders have betrayed him. For this reason, Pilate asks again about the charge against him (v. 35c).

At this, Jesus takes up the subject of kingship again, clarifying for Pilate the nature and location of his kingdom—it is "not from this world" (v. 36). Thus in response to Pilate's claim about Jesus' own nation, Jesus explicitly separates himself from "the Jews," (v. 36b). He also points out that his followers have offered no armed resistance

---

[256]Cf. Brown, "Note that the accused criminal asks questions as if he were the judge, and from the first words of Jesus, it is the prefect who is on trial!" (868).

[257]Rensberger, 93; O'Day, 816–817.

[258]Wayne A. Meeks, *The Prophet-King: Moses Traditions and the Johannine Christology* (Leiden: E. J. Brill, 1967) 63.

against his opponents, implying that Pilate has no grounds for a charge of insurrection (though on this point the reader cannot help but recall Peter's misguided attempt in 18:10). Pilate, however, is concerned only with Jesus' admission of his kingship and so returns to that point, οὐκοῦν βασιλεὺς εἶ σύ (v. 37).

Jesus now openly presents Pilate with a succinct summary of his earthly mission, "to testify to the truth," and of the only appropriate response for one who belongs to the truth, "he/she listens to my voice." These are Jesus' words of revelation to Pilate, comparable to his revelation to the Samaritan woman (4:26), and to the man born blind (9:37). Unlike their faithful responses, Pilate can only scoff at the very concept of truth. That his question is not asked with seriousness is shown by his immediate exit from the scene. Dramatically, it is a "curtain line" that rings in the air for the reader,[259] but it is also the decisive indicator of Pilate's negative response to Jesus. As Haenchen puts it, "If Pilate now asks, when face to face with this truth that stands before him, 'What is truth?', it is clear that Pilate does not belong among those whom 'the Father has given to Jesus.' "[260]

Scene 3: Outside the Praetorium (18:38b–40)

All four gospels relate something of the customary release of a prisoner at the Passover (Mk 15:6–11; Mt 27:15–21; Lk 23:18–19), but the Fourth Evangelist gives the least attention to the episode.[261] Nevertheless, aspects of the Johannine Pilate emerge even in this traditional scene. First, Pilate explicitly informs the Jews that he finds no charge against Jesus. However, rather than simply freeing Jesus, as one might expect given his pronouncement, Pilate recalls for the Jews their custom which would have him release a prisoner at the time of the Passover celebration.[262] In the synoptic versions of this episode, it is either the crowd or the chief priests who initiate the request, but in the Fourth Gospel it is Pilate who brings up the subject (v. 39). Are we to

---

[259]Culpepper, *Anatomy*, 142.

[260]Haenchen, 2.180. Cf. also Brown, 869; Schnackenburg, 246–247; Barrett, 538; Rensberger, *Johannine Faith*, 93; O'Day, 817–818.

[261]For a comparative chart of the Barabbas incident, cf. Brown, 870.

[262]The question of the historical accuracy of this tradition is frequently raised, since no clear external witnesses for the custom have been found. C. B. Chavel ("The Releasing of a Prisoner on the Eve of Passover in Ancient Jerusalem," *JBL* 60 [1941]: 273–278) has attempted to prove a connection with an ambiguous Mishnaic reference (*Pesahim* 8.6), but the evidence remains unclear. Cf. the discussion in Beasley-Murray, 333–334; also Barrett, 538; Schnackenburg, 3.252.

understand, therefore, that Pilate is looking for a way for the Jewish leaders to "save face," that is, allow for the release of Jesus without having to reverse their guilty verdict?[263] If so, it is difficult to understand why he would further incite them by referring to Jesus as "the King of the Jews." It seems rather, that Pilate is simply toying with the Jews and deliberately antagonizing them.[264] There is no sense in the passage that Pilate ever expected them to call for Jesus' release.

Scene 4: Inside the Praetorium (19:1–3)

That his words are not to be trusted is made clear by Pilate's actions. In spite of his declaration of Jesus' innocence, he proceeds to have him flogged (19:1). A number of commentators have understood Pilate's action as a warped attempt to satisfy the Jews,[265] but there is no indication of this in the text. On the contrary, the fact that the scene is framed by Pilate's assertions of Jesus' innocence (18:38b, 19:4) serves more to highlight his cruelty and disregard for justice, rather than his sympathy for Jesus. As Rensberger points out, such a beating was reserved for those who had already been formally condemned, it hardly would be appropriate for one who had just been declared innocent.[266] The Evangelist accentuates the point by locating the flogging at the center of the trial instead of at its traditional place immediately prior to the crucifixion.[267]

Scene 5: Outside the Praetorium (19:4–7)

In the fifth scene, all the players in the drama come together for the first time. Pilate announces to the Jews that he is bringing Jesus out to let them know that he finds no charge against him (v. 4). But once more, the action in the narrative betrays the falsity of Pilate's words as Jesus is brought before the Jews still wearing the crown of thorns and

---

[263]So Haenchen, 180; Schnackenburg, 3.252.

[264]O'Day, 818.

[265]Bultmann, 659; Barrett, 530; Brown, 132; Haenchen, 2.180; Duke, *Irony*, 132.

[266]Rensberger, *Johannine Faith*, 93. Cf. Barrett, 539; Lindars, 563–564.

[267]The deeper significance of this scene is found in the mock coronation of Jesus. All of the Gospels present this ironic episode in which the Roman soldiers unknowingly crown the true King of Israel. However, the Fourth Evangelist develops the theme of kingship even more strongly by placing this scene at the center of the trial. No mention is made of the stripping of Jesus following the mockery so that in the next scene Jesus will be presented to the Jews in royal garb, a point emphasized in 19:4 (cf. O'Day, 818–819).

purple robe. Interpreters have variously suggested that in the Fourth Gospel, Pilate's intention in bringing Jesus before the Jews was to evoke their sympathy by presenting them with the beaten and humiliated Jesus[268] or to illustrate his harmlessness by displaying him as an absurd figure.[269] However, this seems an unlikely depiction of Pilate, since it implies his expectation that the Jews would be moved to sympathy for a man they are seeking to put to death. Yet, the Johannine Pilate has shown no genuine concern for Jesus. Indeed, more in keeping with his presentation thus far is the suggestion that he flaunts his authority and parodies the political claims and aspirations of the Jewish leadership.[270] As O'Day puts it, "the purpose of his words and actions seems to be to taunt the Jews and their messianic pretensions."[271] Along this line, Pilate's celebrated words, "Behold, the man!" are also better understood as continuing the mockery that began with the soldiers in the preceding scene rather than an attempt to evoke sympathy from the Jews.

That Pilate seems intent on taunting the Jews is confirmed in the next exchange. The Jews are enraged at Jesus' appearance and shout for Pilate to crucify him. At this, Pilate replies that they should crucify Jesus themselves, since he finds no charge against him (19:7). Note that while this is the third time that Pilate has proclaimed Jesus' innocence, he does not hesitate to urge the Jews to crucify him. These are not the words of a man with great sympathy for the accused. Moreover, Pilate knows full well that the Jews have no authority to crucify Jesus; they have admitted as much already in the beginning of the narrative (18:31b). Pilate is once more flaunting his power and authority over his Jewish subjects. Only at this point do the Jews present a formal charge against Jesus—he has claimed to be the Son of God (19:7). From their perspective, this is blasphemy, a crime against God, punishable by death.

Scene 6: Inside the Praetorium (19:8–12)

At hearing this, Pilate's countenance changes at least momentarily. He is μᾶλλον ἐφοβήθη (v. 8). While this is typically translated as a comparative (e.g., "more afraid than ever" NRSV), it may be better rendered as intensive, i.e., exceedingly afraid, since there has been no mention of Pilate's fear until this point.[272] The narrative

---

[268]So Haenchen, 181.

[269]So Bultmann, 659; Schnackenburg, 3.255–256.

[270]O'Day, 819. Cf. also Rensberger *Johannine Faith*, 94.

[271]O'Day, 819.

[272]So Barrett, 542; Rensberger, *Johannine Faith*, 94; O'Day, 820.

does not provide the reason for Pilate's fear and there are two main interpretive possibilities. The first is that Pilate's fear stems from his perception of the whole proceeding as a threat to his political future. According to Brown, underlying the Jews' charge of blasphemy is a reminder to Pilate that as a Roman administrator he is obligated to honor regional religious customs.[273] Another reading suggests that Pilate's fear "is the numinous terror before the divine.[274] On the one hand, this seems unlikely, since Pilate does not hesitate to return to Jesus' presence, interrogate him further, and even threaten him with crucifixion. Moreover, as O'Day points out, this interpretation "assumes that Pilate would honor and respect "the Jews'" language about God, an assumption that the text does not otherwise support."[275] On the other hand, there is precedence in the Gospel for this sort of fear. At Jesus' arrest the soldiers are momentarily overcome and fall to the ground (18:6), then proceed to arrest Jesus as if nothing had happened. Pilate's fear may be similarly intended to represent the unavoidable reaction to the notion of Jesus' divine identity.[276] Although the question remains open, the latter interpretation seems more plausible than the subtleties of Brown's political reading.

In any event, it is Pilate's fear which brings him once more into the Praetorium to ask Jesus, "Where are you from?" Jesus, however, makes no second attempt to reveal his identity to Pilate, as he did, for instance, to the Samaritan woman. Indeed, his silence suggests that there is nothing further for him to say—Pilate has already been judged. In light of this, Pilate's final words come across as lame posturing. In fact, Jesus' closing words to him may contain a hint of scorn, "you would have no power over me unless it had been given to you from above" (v. 11), so that the tables have been fully turned at the end of the exchange. Finally, Jesus refers to those who have "greater sin" than Pilate. In the context of the trial narrative, the reference to those who have handed over Jesus obviously means the Jews.[277] That the Johannine Jesus distinguishes Pilate from them has been viewed as an apologetic tendency that would exonerate the Roman authority.[278] However, as

---

[273]So Brown, 794, 891. O'Day, 820–821.

[274]Schnackenburg, 2.260.

[275]O'Day, 820.

[276]Cf. Duke, *Irony*, 133.

[277]Judas, of course, also handed Jesus over (18:2–3), but not specifically to Pilate.

[278] So Schnackenburg, 3.262.

Rensberger points out, while guilty of a lesser sin, Pilate is still guilty.[279] Even more compelling is O'Day's observation that while the Jews may be guilty of the greater sin at this point in the trial, by its end Pilate will share in their sin, as he hands Jesus over to be crucified.[280]

At this point, Pilate at last seems intent on releasing Jesus (v. 12). Notably, his first and only earnest attempt to free Jesus is prompted not by his conviction of Jesus' innocence, but out of fear. Moreover, his effort is short-lived; Pilate quickly drops the idea of releasing Jesus when the Jews once more point out the political nature of Jesus' crime (v. 12). It is as though, upon hearing their political threat, Pilate returns to his senses; his next action is to bring out Jesus for judgment. In other words, as Rensberger notes, Pilate "resumes his former character."[281]

Scene 7: Outside the Praetorium (19:13–16a)

In the final scene, Pilate brings Jesus before the Jews for the last time. In doing so, his disregard for the fate of Jesus as well as his disdain for the Jews is made abundantly clear. Whether Pilate sits on the judge's seat (βήματος) or Jesus is placed on it is unclear. Either reading is possible grammatically,[282] and either would fit in the context of the Johannine trial narrative, although placing Jesus on the βήματος would be quite remarkable. Many scholars favor the intransitive reading, based primarily on the historical likelihood of such a scenario.[283] However, the author has already reshaped the tradition considerably, and it would not be beyond his creative impulse to add this detail. Throughout the narrative, the Evangelist has made clear that Pilate and the Jews were actually the ones under judgment, placing Jesus on the judgment seat would be the ultimate symbol of this irony. Moreover, it would not be outside the character of the Johannine Pilate, who has repeatedly humiliated the Jews, to place Jesus on the judge's seat with the scornful proclamation, "Here is your King!" (v. 14).[284] However, even if Pilate is the one seated on the judgment seat, he would still

---

[279]Rensberger, *Johannine Faith*, 95.

[280]O'Day, 821.

[281]Rensberger, *Johannine Faith*, 95.

[282]The verb ἐκάθισεν can be read intransitively (Pilate sat upon the bench) or transitively (Pilate set Jesus upon the bench).

[283]Bultmann, 664; Brown, 881; Schnackenburg, 265; Lindars, 570.

[284]Ignace de la Potterie ("Jesus, roi et juge d'aprés Jn 19,13," *Biblica* 41 [1960]: 217–247) has argued most thoroughly for the transitive reading. Cf. also Meeks, *The Prophet-King*, 73–76; Haenchen, 2.187; O'Day, 822. Barrett (544) and Duke (*Irony*, 134–135) suggest that the author may have been aware of both meanings.

become subject to the same judgment as the Jews as he hands Jesus over to be crucified.[285] The occasion is marked by a specific reference to place and time in the narrative. In particular the reference to noon on the day of preparation for the Passover seems designed to heighten the calamity of the Jews. Upon seeing Jesus and hearing Pilate's goading they repeat their cry to crucify Jesus. Pilate seemingly cannot resist inciting them even further asking, "Shall I crucify your king?" The question seems designed to force the Jews into the ultimate and tragic betrayal of their heritage as they renounce their messianic hopes and pledge their allegiance to the Roman emperor. From his perspective, Pilate has emerged victorious, exacting submission of a proud and obstinate people. From a narrative perspective, as Meeks suggests, Pilate has aligned himself with the Jews. He has rejected Jesus, refusing to listen to the truth, and instead handed him over to be crucified.

In the immediately following crucifixion scene, Pilate has an inscription placed on the cross above Jesus which reads, "Jesus of Nazareth, the King of the Jews" (19:19). While mention of an inscription is found in all four Gospels, only in the Fourth Gospel do the Jews urge Pilate to rewrite it. Their complaint highlights once again how Pilate goads the Jews with his authority; his refusal to comply with their request underscores the point. Pilate has followed through on the crucifixion that they demanded, but uses it to humiliate them–Jesus will be executed as the King of the Jews.[286]

Pilate's Epilogue

Pilate appears briefly twice more in the narrative, first granting the Jews permission for the legs of the crucified men to be broken (19:31) and finally giving permission to Joseph of Arimathea to remove Jesus' body. Neither of these actions is necessarily indicative of his knowledge or understanding of who Jesus is.[287] They may indicate that the Jews continue to be dependent on the jurisdiction of Pilate regarding even

---

[285]Cf. Duke, "No matter who holds the bench, Jesus is the judge" (5:27) (*Irony*, 135).

[286]The inscription also bears christological significance. It continues the theme of the ironic display of Jesus' kingship from the trial narrative. That the inscription is written in three languages is in keeping with the Johannine notion of Jesus as "savior of the world" (4:42; cf. 3:16; 12:19).

[287]Contra Culpepper, "The title, the permission to hasten death by having the legs broken, and the approval of a proper burial for Jesus can all be construed as Pilate's efforts to atone for his concession to the Jews" (*Anatomy*, 143).

their religious concerns. In other words, in terms of the relationship between the Jews and Roman authority, after the trial business resumes as usual.

In sum, despite traditional interpretations to the contrary, the Johannine Pilate is not presented in a sympathetic light.[288] The Evangelist does not attempt to exonerate the Roman governor but instead, presents him one who rejects the mission and revelation of Jesus, just as the "Jews" do. Thus, he is linked to the dark side of Johannine dualism, much like Nicodemus. On this point, it is significant that the Johannine Jesus' interaction with Pilate is much like it was with Nicodemus. In both cases, Jesus shows disdain for their claims to knowledge and power. In the exchange with the leader of the Jews, it was the claim of knowledge regarding Jesus' origins that was scorned by Jesus. In this case of the Roman leader, the claim to power over Jesus is ridiculed. With Nicodemus, Jesus cuts off the dialogue after pointing to Nicodemus' lack of understanding. In the case of Pilate the situation is more severe. Pilate walks out on "the truth" and hands Jesus over to death. In terms of the trial scene alone, Pilate appears victorious over the Jews. He has wrested from them the ultimate betrayal of their religious and national identity. At the level of the larger narrative, however, he has shown himself to be on the side of the Jews. He thus stands in sharp contrast to the man born blind who in his confrontation of the Jews gradually developed in boldness and insight, asserting himself against them with increasing confidence.

SIMON PETER (1:40–42; 6:60–71; 13:1–38; 18:10–11, 15–18, 25–27; 20:1–10; 21)

Introduction

Scholarly debate around the figure of Peter has centered on his relationship to the beloved disciple and his status in the Gospel as a whole. The driving issue has been whether the Fourth Gospel reflects a decidedly anti-Petrine strain, or whether Peter holds the same preeminent position as he does in the Synoptic Gospels.[289] Behind this issue is the historical question of whether the Johannine community decenters traditional ecclesial authority as represented by Peter, in favor

---

[288]Cf., e.g., Brown, "Pilate is typical of...the many honest, well-disposed men who would try to adopt a middle position in a struggle that is total (864).

[289]Cf. Maynard, "Role of Peter," 532 for a review of the two positions.

of its own local leadership represented by the beloved disciple.[290] My interest in the figure of Peter is not limited to how he compares with the beloved disciple, although that issue can hardly be avoided; I am also interested in how he is characterized compared with the other characters and in particular in his exchanges with Jesus.

Based on the number of times that Simon Peter appears in the Gospel, one could argue that, aside from Jesus, he is the most significant male character in the Gospel.[291] He is present in nine passages throughout the narrative, not counting his appearance with Jesus in chapter twenty-one.[292] In the first half of the Gospel, he appears in 1:40–42 and 6:67–69 and these two sections will be treated first. However, Peter's character is particularly prominent in the second half of the Gospel beginning with chapter 13 (cf. 13: 6–11, 23–24, 36–38; 18:10–11, 15–18, 25–27; 19:25–27; 20:1–10; chapter 21), and much of my analysis will focus on those passages.

An exception to this sequence will be the discussion of 20:1–10. The characters of Peter, the Beloved Disciple and Mary Magdalene are so closely interwoven in this passage that it will be necessary to treat it separately, following the individual discussions of Peter and the beloved disciple. This procedure will avoid a threefold repetition of the material and allow the characters to be analyzed in close relationship to each other, as they appear in the narrative.

Introduction of the Character (1:40–42)

In the first chapter of the Gospel, the name Simon Peter appears before he himself does. His name serves as means of identifying his apparently lesser-known brother, Andrew (1:40). On the one hand, this confirms Peter's familiarity in the tradition. On the other hand, that his brother enters the narrative first, having encountered Jesus before Peter, may be an indication of Peter's diminished status in the Fourth

---

[290]Recall that the downplaying of apostolic leadership was also suggested as a possible explanation for the prominence of women in the Gospel (cf. the discussion of Brown and Rena in chapter 1).

[291]Culpepper identifies him as the most complex figure next to Jesus (*Anatomy*, 120).

[292]1:40–42; 6:67–69; 13:6–11, 23–26, 36–38; 18:10–11, 15–18, 25–27; 20:2–10. I assume, along with the majority of scholarship, that chapter 21 is a later addition to the Gospel. For this reason, I will not treat it in detail, although I will discuss what effect its presence has on the portrait of Peter in the Gospel.

Gospel.[293] When Peter does enter the narrative he plays a completely passive role. He is found (εὑρίσκει) by his brother Andrew, who tells him of another find, εὑρήκαμεν τὸν μεσσίαν (1:42). He is then brought to Jesus, who looks at him, identifies him, and renames him (1:42). Unlike the Matthean version of Peter's renaming, which follows his confession at Caesarea Philippi (Mt 16:16–18), Peter here says nothing to elicit his new name.[294] Furthermore, whereas the Matthean Jesus makes clear that Κηφᾶς is indicative of Peter's founding role in the church, the Johannine Jesus offers no such interpretation.[295] Henceforth in the Gospel, Peter will be known interchangeably either as Simon Peter, or Peter, with no clear distinction between them.[296] Thus, although Peter is the only character to receive a new name from Jesus, the event bears little significance either as an indicator of his character, or as a narrative event.

What is most notable about Peter's appearance in this opening chapter is the lack of individual characterization. In the line of male disciples who are introduced in this chapter, he is the only one who does not speak and attribute some sort of title to Jesus. John the Baptist identifies Jesus as the Lamb of God (vv. 29, 36), Andrew witnesses to Peter that Jesus is the messiah (1:41), Philip refers to the one about whom Moses and the prophets wrote, Jesus, son of Joseph from Nazareth (1:45). The last disciple, Nathanael, commands the most attention. His exchange with Philip and eventual confession of Jesus as

---

[293]The synoptic call stories give Peter the most prominent position (Mk 1:16–19; Mt 4:18–20; Lk 5:3–10).

[294]Mark and Luke have no parallel naming scene.

[295]Arthur J. Droge argues that in the Fourth Gospel "Simon's new name is not symbolic of his potential for 'solid' leadership....On the contrary...Peter is a 'rock' because of his obtuseness and persistent inability to understand Jesus" ("The Status of Peter in the Fourth Gospel," *JBL* 109 [1990]: 308). While this may be an accurate description of Peter's character in the Gospel of John, the text provides no such explanation behind the name. Bultmann suggests, on the basis of the future tense of κληθήσῃ, that what is intended here is a foretelling of the renaming event. According to Bultmann, familiarity with the tradition made it unnecessary to actually relate the scene later in the Gospel (101, nt. 5). Brown rightly disagrees, pointing out that "the future tense is part of the literary style of name changing, even when the name is changed on the spot" as in the LXX translation of Gen 17:5, 15 (80). What is most probable is that the author simply felt obligated to include the tradition, despite the fact that it held little importance for him.

[296]Typically, he is called Simon Peter the first time he appears in a scene, with either name occurring in later references. Cf. Raymond Brown, Karl Donfield, John Reumann eds., *Peter in the Fourth Gospel* (New York: Paulist, 1973) 129, nt. 275.

Son of God and King of Israel adds a degree of depth to his character
(1:49). In contrast, amid this cluster of confessions and titles, Peter says
nothing, making his introduction to the narrative unremarkable. His own
confession of Jesus is reserved for a later time and when it occurs it will
not be without complications.

Peter's Confession (6:60–71)

The next passage in which Peter appears comes at the end of an
extended controversy between Jesus and the Jewish authorities involving
Jesus' claim to be "the bread of life" (cf. 6:35–59).[297] Throughout the
Gospel, Jesus' words and actions are frequently the cause of division
(cf. 7:40–44; 9:16; 11:45–46), and in this passage the division occurs
among his own disciples. Indeed, following Jesus' discourse, many of
the disciples complain exactly like his Jewish opponents (γογγύζουσιν,
6:61, cf. 6:41). Jesus is not surprised at their reaction, since, consistent
with his character, he "knew from the beginning who were the ones who
did not believe and who was the one that would betray him" (6:64).

This context of unbelief and betrayal sets the tone for Peter's
words to Jesus. Upon the desertion of many of his disciples (6:66), Jesus
asks the twelve directly, "You (ὑμεῖς) do not also wish to leave, do
you?" This is the first time the twelve have been distinguished in the
Gospel and when Peter responds, it is clearly as a representative for the
twelve.[298] He repeatedly uses the first person plural in 6:68–69 and
when Jesus replies, it is not to Peter alone, but to the twelve (6:70).
Therefore, these first words of Peter should be examined especially in
light of how Peter functions as spokesman for the twelve male disciples.

---

[297]There is disagreement as to the original position of 6:60–71 in the Gospel and
what precipitates the split between Jesus' disciples. Bultmann, as part of his radical
reconstruction of these chapters, argues that 6:60–71 has been divorced from its
original context and places it at the end of a complex consisting of 11:55–12:33 and
8:30–40 (285–287; 412–451). Brown's main concern is the relationship of verse 63
to the preceding discourse. He suggests that 6:60–71 refers back to 6:35–50, with
verses 51–59 being a later editorial insertion (299–303). The issue is irrelevant for
this study and I will read the text as it stands, assuming that the disciples' response
is to the whole of the Bread of Life discourse, including verses 51–59.

[298]Though the twelve are mentioned twice more in this passage (vv. 70–71),
they are referred to after that only in 20:24, where Thomas is identified as one of the
twelve. The absence of the term suggests both that this was not a significant
category for the Evangelist, and that 6:60–71 may have been included largely on the
basis of tradition. As many commentators have pointed out, the scene appears to be
the Fourth Gospel's version of the synoptic scene at Caesara Philippi (cf. Mk 8:27–
33 and parallels). Cf., e.g., Bultmann, 444; Brown, 310; Schnackenburg, 77–78.

His response to Jesus takes the form of a rhetorical Lord, to whom shall we go (6:68a)—followed by a two part confession—you have words of eternal life and we have come to believe and know that you are the holy one of god. (6:68b–69). The first part of the confession picks up on Jesus' earlier reference to "the words which I have spoken" (6:63), and to the idea of eternal life which is woven throughout the discourse in chapter six (vv. 27, 33, 40, 47, 50–51, cf. also 5:24). It thus stands as an affirmation of the person and teaching of Jesus. The second part of the confession is more difficult to understand.

As is often noted, the title "Holy One of God" occurs only here in John's Gospel and is found elsewhere in the New Testament only in Mark 1:24 and its Lukan parallel, 4:34. In the latter instances, the title is voiced by an unclean spirit whom Jesus quickly rebukes and silences. On the basis of this occurrence some interpreters hear in the Johannine text an echo of the synoptic association of Peter's character with the demonic (Mk 8:33, Mt 16:23, absent in Luke), especially since Jesus goes on to speak about a διάβολός (6:70).[299] While this is an unlikely reading of Peter–the narrator takes pains to point out that Jesus is referring to Judas (v. 71)[300] –there remains a hint of ambiguity about his confession for other reasons.

First, the title with which Peter identifies Jesus is not clearly messianic. Even interpreters who argue for its messianic interpretation, admit that evidence for such a reading is lacking.[301] Aside from the other New Testament occurrences mentioned above, there is no evidence of its use elsewhere in Jewish or Christian literature. For this reason,

---

[299] For example, Snyder argues that the title brings a "strange twist to the scene" which "appears as a sly attack on the validity of Peter's confession ("John 13:16," 11). Cf. also Maynard who notes, "There are no demons in the Fourth Gospel, so their supernatural testimony about Jesus' divine origin is here made by Peter," though Maynard's point is that the title, not Peter, is associated with demons ("Role of Peter," 534) .

[300] Snyder deals with this point by noting the rare use of the epithet "son of Simon Iscariot" (6:71) suggesting that the author is "toying with our imaginations, or that a redactor has redirected the charge from Peter to Judas" ("John 13:16," 11). Others suggest that the evangelist is intentionally disassociating Peter from Satan, thereby presenting a more positive evaluation of Peter than in the Markan tradition (cf. Bultmann, 451, nt. 1; Schnackenburg, 78; Barrett, 308; Lindars, 276; Kevin Quast, *Peter and the Beloved Disciple*, 51).

[301] Cf. Barrett, 307. Schnackenburg argues that even though the title is not messianic, it must refer to Jesus' messiahship based on its association with the synoptic confession of Peter in the history of tradition (76).

Haenchen remains more true to the passage when he states that a messianic title does not appear in the confession.[302] To be sure, this in itself does not imply that Peter's words should be taken negatively. Bultmann also readily admits that "Holy One of God" has "no recognisable tradition at all as a messianic title" but sees this precisely as its virtue. In his words, the title expresses "the newness which is proper to every authentic confession."[303]

Nevertheless, if the Evangelist is drawing on traditions about the twelve in this narrative, why does he not adopt the traditional version of Peter's confession?[304] Even more pressing, why does the confession normally attributed to Peter appear later on the lips of Martha (11:27)? We have seen how Martha's confession is in effect the articulation of the Johannine credo (cf. 20:31). In light to this, Schneiders seems right in her assertion that Peter's statement "lacks the fullness of Johannine faith."[305] Since Peter is serving a representative function in this passage, we cannot simply claim that Peter, a man, is overshadowed by Martha, a woman. Still, the gender contrast may nevertheless be present. The twelve traditionally included a group of male disciples gathered in a privileged position around Jesus, a notion confirmed in the Fourth Gospel by Jesus' talk of election in 6:70. Is the confession of an individual woman intended to take precedence over the corporate confession of a group of men?

As an answer to this question, the response of Jesus to Peter's words may be more telling than the title itself. Recall that Martha's confession stands on its own; it closes the conversation with Jesus in a climactic fashion (11:27). In contrast, Jesus replies to the confession of Peter with a sobering pronouncement. Granted, the first part of his response appears to confirm the appropriateness of Peter's words, "Did I not chose you, the Twelve?" The question corresponds to Jesus' earlier statement regarding those who left him. They were not allowed by the Father to come to Jesus (6:65), whereas those who were chosen by

---

[302]Haenchen, 1.307–308.

[303]Bultmann, 449.

[304]That this question troubled the early church is evident in the various attempts to conform Peter's words to a more traditional messianic confession. Note also that those who would argue that the Evangelist intentionally shifted the Markan reference to Satan away from Peter must then account for a deliberate altering of Peter's confession.

[305]Schneiders, "Women in the Fourth Gospel," 41.

Jesus were given that permission.[306] However, the second part of Jesus' response, "and one among you is a devil," immediately dispels any notion that inclusion among the twelve is equivalent to faithful discipleship.[307] Indeed, these final words of Jesus cast a shadow over the conversation with Peter, so that no matter how we understand his confession, an element of suspicion lingers around the twelve. As Haenchen points out, "The confession of the twelve is depicted here basically in its dubiousness: one of the twelve who allegedly knew and believed in Jesus is not a believer but a devil."[308]

To summarize, in the first half of the Gospel, a picture of Peter as an individual character does not emerge. His introduction to the narrative is unremarkable and his confession in chapter six is not an individual profession of faith as much as a position statement spoken on behalf of the twelve. As their representative, Peter expresses their belief in Jesus and their intention to remain with him. Yet, his performance in this role is not flawless. His words of confession are clouded by the use of a non-traditional designation for Jesus and put into question by the reality of imminent betrayal by one of the disciples. This shadow of betrayal, which is cast over the whole group, will become even more evident in the second half of the Gospel.

---

[306]Haenchen sees even this first part of Jesus' statement as a sharp retort to Peter's declaration, "we have believed and have come to know...." In his words, "Jesus insists that he is the one who chose the twelve. The disciples did not come to Jesus and abide with him by virtue of some human determination. To the contrary, Jesus created the circle of disciples by his own decision. Whatever authority the circle has, it has from him" (1.307).

[307]O'Day offers the following observations, "Instead of embracing Peter's confession (cf. Mark 8:30, 33), Jesus raises again the question of election and choice....Even election into the select group of the Twelve is no guarantee of a faith response because one member of the Twelve is a devil....Election is no substitute for the decision of faith" (611).

[308]Haenchen, 1.308. Cf. also Pheme Perkins, "Though Peter does confess loyalty to Jesus in the name of the Twelve (John 6:68–69), Jesus responds to his words with a reference to Judas' betrayal (v. 70). This response alerts the reader that Jesus' disciples are not trustworthy" (*Peter: Apostle for the Whole Church* [University of South Carolina Press, 1994] 97). Brown, et. al., speak of Jesus' response as neutral or noncommittal compared to his reaction in the synoptic tradition (*Peter in the New Testament*, 132).

Peter at the Last Supper (13:1–38)

Chapter 13 opens the second main division of the Gospel; in it Peter plays a larger role. In addition to maintaining his representative role for the
disciples in this second half, he also becomes discernible as an individual character, beginning with his appearance in chapter 13. In the course of the Last Supper, Peter is mentioned three different times: first in conversation with Jesus about footwashing (13:6–11), second, in communication with the beloved disciple concerning Jesus' betrayer (13:24), and finally, in the context of Jesus' prediction of his denial (13:36–38). None of these episodes places Peter in a particularly favorable light.

The first conversation is the longest exchange between Peter and Jesus. Since Jesus has already washed the feet of several disciples, this time Peter apparently speaks for himself when he asks, "Lord, are you going to wash my feet?" (13:6). The Greek syntax, σύ μου νίπτεις, also stresses the personal nature of the encounter, in addition to Peter's incredulity. As Beasley-Murray notes, "the impression is given of Peter sputtering in astonishment and incomprehension!"[309] This astonishment is based on the demeaning nature of the act in which Jesus, his master, is engaged. In taking on the task of footwashing, Jesus has assumed a posture culturally more appropriate to women or slaves than to a learned master, and Peter cannot understand why.[310]

When Jesus responds, he addresses Peter directly. This time personal pronouns are employed in a way that lends a sharpness to the address (ὁ ἐγὼ ποιῶ σὺ οὐκ οἶδας 13:7). On the whole, however, the statement is not merely a rebuke of Peter, but also a promise that he will eventually understand.[311] Despite this assurance from Jesus, Peter emphatically insists, "You will never ever wash my feet!" (οὐ μὴ...εἰς

---

[309]Beasley-Murray, 233.

[310]Beasley-Murray cites rabbinic examples which illustrate the menial nature of the task. *Mekh. Exod.* 21.2.82a lists footwashing among work that a Jewish slave should not be required to do. Instead, it should be left to Gentile slaves, wives, or children (233). Along this line, it is interesting that 1 Tim 5:10 lists washing the feet of the saints among the merits that attest to a widow's good works and thereby qualify her for enrollment (i.e., communal support). Was this act especially associated with women in the Christian church, along with the others on the list— raising children, showing hospitality and helping the afflicted?

[311]Bultmann suggests that along with rebuking Peter for his ignorance, Jesus is also exonerating him and promising that he will understand later (467).

τὸν αἰῶνα, 13:8). He thus continues the pattern of misunderstanding Jesus, even if the misunderstanding is of a different type than was evident with Nicodemus, the Samaritan woman, and Martha. Peter's own brand of incomprehension is marked by a particular passion that will also be evident in his exchange with Jesus later at the meal (13:37).

Jesus responds by making plain that this emphatic rejection of his service is tantamount to a rejection of himself, "Unless I wash you, you have no part in me" (v. 10).[312] Hearing this, Peter makes a pendulum swing in the other direction, urging Jesus to wash not only his feet, but also his hands and head (13:10). These are Peter's last words in the exchange, leaving the reader with the impression of an eager, overly-enthusiastic and foolish follower of Jesus.[313] For his part, Jesus exhibits a certain patience in dealing with Peter. Unlike his final scornful retort to Nicodemus (3:10), he assures Peter as well as the other disciples (cf. ὑμεῖς, 13:10b) that they are clean.[314] In this way, Peter comes across as a more sympathetic figure than Nicodemus, despite the fact that both characters demonstrate a complete misunderstanding of Jesus' words.

Even so, as with the scene between Peter and Jesus in chapter 6, the footwashing episode concludes on an ominous note. In the same breath with which Jesus affirms the purity of the disciples, he conditions

---

[312]In opposition to the almost universal interpretation of the footwashing scene as an expression of humble service, Snyder offers a compelling argument that the scene actually pertains to the assimilation of Jesus that is necessary to perceive his glory. In his view, as an introduction to the farewell discourse, the footwashing episode describes "that one condition necessary for assimilation of the glory: recognition of need.... The focus of the narrative in vss. 1–9 falls on Peter who refuses to accept the self-giving of Jesus and therefore has blocked any possibility of receiving the glory" ("John 13:16," 6–7). Alternatively, Arland Hultgren suggests that Jesus' footwashing is a symbolic act of eschatological hospitality. Jesus assumes the role of a servant to welcome his disciples into his Father's house ("The Johannine Footwashing (13:1–11) as Symbol of Eschatological Hospitality," *NTS* 28 [1982]: 542). See also O'Day, 722, 727–728.

[313]Brown et. al. see in his behavior a correspondence with the traditionally impulsive Peter of the synoptic Gospels (*Peter in the New Testament*, 132–133). Perkins argues that because Peter's reaction to Jesus' footwashing follows the pattern of Johannine irony and misunderstanding, "[i]t does not provide information about character traits of Peter as an individual, such as his alleged impulsiveness" (*Peter*, 97). However, as I suggest above, the two need not be mutually exclusive. Peter does fit the pattern, but does so in his own distinctive way.

[314]To be sure, the meaning of Jesus' complete statement in verse 10 is not altogether clear. Scholars have long debated the textual and interpretive problems it presents, especially whether the saying concerns baptismal allusions. For a more detailed discussion see Brown, 566–568; also O'Day, 723–724.

his statement with the words ἀλλ᾿ οὐχὶ πάντες (13:10b). Once more the narrator makes reference to the one who would betray him, this time without specifying the name Judas (3:11). As a result, the final impression left with the reader is not of Peter the faithful, if foolish, disciple, but of an unnamed betrayer among the disciples.

Significantly, the second reference to Peter in chapter 13 takes up the issue of betrayal directly. Up to this point, the narrator has warned the reader several times about the impending betrayal by a disciple, but it is not until 13:21 that Jesus makes it known to his disciples. It is not clear to the disciples to whom Jesus is referring and so their response is to look at one another with uncertainty (13:22). It is at this point that another disciple is introduced in the narrative, one designated as ὃν ἠγάπα ὁ Ἰησοῦς and described as ἀνακείμενος ἐν τῷ κόλπῳ τοῦ Ἰησοῦ (13:23). The detailed discussion of this disciple will be taken up in a separate section below, but at this point his effect on the characterization of Peter is worth noting. Whereas earlier Peter clearly serves as spokesperson for the twelve, here that role becomes complicated by the presence of the beloved disciple. Peter certainly acts on behalf of the disciples when he seeks an answer as to the identity of the betrayer. However, in this scene he is not even given voice, but only motions to the beloved disciple to ask Jesus for him (13:24). Jesus makes known how he will disclose the betrayer and then does so by dipping a piece of bread, handing it to Judas, and telling him, "Do quickly what you are going to do" (13:26–27).

What is curious about this disclosure is that there is no indication that as a result the beloved disciple, Peter, or the other disciples are any wiser about Judas. Quite the opposite is indicated by the statement that "no one at the table knew why he said this to him," and by the accompanying speculations on the part of the disciples (13:28). No exception to this ignorance is made for either the disciple whom Jesus loved or Peter; both of these figures have simply receded into the background. All of this suggests that despite the exchange between Peter and the other disciple, the primary focus of the scene is on neither of them, but on the betrayal by Judas.[315] The scene does not provide much additional information about the character of Peter, except to suggest

---

[315]Quast notes the secondary role both characters play in the scene relative to Jesus and Judas. As he puts it, "Whatever other significance they may have, Peter and the Beloved Disciple may be regarded as props which enable the story to proceed with the desired effect" (*Peter and the Beloved Disciple*, 63).

that his position as representative disciple here takes second place to another disciple whose own relationship to Jesus is portrayed in terms of proximity and intimacy. The significance of this will be taken up again in our discussion of the beloved disciple.

Thus far in chapter 13 and also in chapter 6, the appearances of Peter have been in the context of betrayal, though always with reference to Judas. Now, in Peter's final appearance in this chapter, the focus turns exclusively to him and his impending denial of Jesus. The brief dialogue opens with a question from Peter that recalls his lack of understanding in 13:6, "Lord, where are you going?" (13:36). Jesus' response recalls this earlier exchange; Peter cannot follow now, but will follow afterward (cf. 13:7). Peter persists, asking, "Lord, why can I not follow you now? I will lay down my life for you" (13:37). In the face of this bold statement comes Jesus' prediction of Peter's three-fold denial. There may be a degree of sarcasm intended as Jesus asks, "Will you lay down your life for me?" Then come the final words of the exchange, "Amen, amen, I say to you, a cock will not crow until you have denied me three times" (13:38). It is with this sobering prediction that chapter 13 ends. There is no denial of the prediction by Peter, as in Mark and Matthew, nor do the other disciples speak up and take some of the focus away from Peter (Mk 14:31; Mt 26:35). In John's Gospel, the exchange is strictly between Peter and Jesus, so that Peter alone bears the full weight of Jesus' prediction.

Peter in the Passion Narrative (18:10–11, 15–18, 25–27; 20: 1–10)

Following this dire prediction, Peter next appears in chapter 18 at the scene of Jesus' arrest in the garden. The scene is remarkable in its portrayal of Jesus in complete control of his own arrest. When the soldiers and police come to the garden, it is Jesus who approaches them with the question, "Whom are you looking for?" (18:4). When they answer "Jesus of Nazareth," Jesus responds with the dramatic ἐγώ εἰμί (18:5). The theophanic nature of his pronouncement is clear by the reaction of his opponents—they step back and fall to the ground (18:6). It is soon after this dramatic portrayal that Peter enters the scene. He draws his sword and cuts off the ear of the high priest's slave, Malchus (18:10). While all of the Gospels relate a similar event (Mk 14:47; Mt 26:51; Lk 22:50), only the Fourth Evangelist specifically identifies the disciple as Simon Peter. Not only does Peter's action appear ridiculous in contrast to Jesus' own dignified and willing submission to the Jewish authorities, he is instantly rebuked by Jesus. Jesus tells Peter to put away his sword asking, "Am I not to drink the cup which the Father has given me?" (18:17). The comment implies that Peter's action, well-intentioned though it may be, is actually a deterrent to Jesus' mission. In this way, Peter differs from the mother of Jesus, who urges Jesus forward on his mission, and, in a different way, also from the Samaritan woman, who functions as Jesus' co-worker. Indeed, whereas these women act in ways that contribute to the will of the Father, Peter is here interpreted as literally fighting against it.

Aside from misunderstanding Jesus' mission, Peter's action may have even more serious implications for his relationship to Jesus. Droge points out that later in the chapter Jesus tells Pilate, "My kingdom is not of this world; if my kingdom were of the world my subjects would fight, that I might not be handed over to the Jews; but my kingdom is not from this world" (18:36). Droge goes on to note "that Peter *does* fight suggests, at a minimum, that he has a fundamental misunderstanding of Jesus and of the nature of his kingship and kingdom....Worse still, Peter's action reveals that he is not a 'subject' of Jesus' heavenly kingdom...."[316] While Droge's assessment of Peter may seem harsh, the distinct way in which Peter's denial is related later may lend credence to Droge's reading.

After Jesus is arrested, Simon Peter and another unnamed disciple follow Jesus (18:15). Peter is not able to get past the gate of the high priest, until the other disciple, who is an acquaintance of the priest, intervenes on his behalf (18:16).[317] That Peter follows is often regarded as a positive sign of his faithfulness. If this is so, the impression quickly changes as Peter encounters the woman guarding the gate. She asks him, "You are not also one of this man's disciples, are you?" Peter responds with the brief statement, οὐκ εἰμί (18:17). Far from "laying down his life" for Jesus, Peter denies his discipleship. Moreover, as O'Day notes, "The words of Peter's denial...are the antithesis of Jesus' words of self-identification and revelation from 18:1–12, "I am" (ἐγώ εἰμί...vv. 5–6, 8)."[318]

The scene closes with the image of Peter warming himself by the fire along with the soldiers. As Judas stood with the soldiers in the garden (18:5), so now does Peter during Jesus' interrogation.[319] He

---

[316]Droge, "Status of Peter," 311.

[317]See below for a discussion of the characterization of this disciple.

[318]O'Day, 808.

[319]O'Day, 809.

gives an identical response when questioned a second time (18:25). The third time Peter is questioned, it is by one of the high priest's slaves, who asks, "Did I not see you in the garden with him?" (18:26). That the slave is a relative of the man whose ear Peter cut off recalls Peter's act of bravado in the garden at the very moment in which he is denying involvement. With this, Jesus' prediction is fulfilled and the cock crows (18:27). Unlike in the synoptic versions, in the Fourth Gospel there is no record of Peter's weeping at this sound. Seemingly, the detail serves more as a reminder to the reader than to Peter. In fact, Bultmann claims that given the fact that the Evangelist adds nothing further to the account about the fulfillment of scripture, the feelings of Peter or his further behavior, the story has no particular importance for the Evangelist. He has simply related it in accordance with the tradition, and in keeping with the thought of 13:36–38.[320]

To be sure, in the synoptic accounts, Peter's behavior is presented in a more extreme fashion; he curses, swears an oath, denies any knowledge of Jesus, but in the end weeps in remorse. On the other hand, John's Gospel is distinct in its repeated use of μαθητής (18:17, 25), a term that focuses Peter's denial specifically on his identity as a disciple of Jesus. Since true discipleship is one of the most important themes in the Gospel, denial of one's discipleship may be an even more serious indictment of Peter's character.[321] Indeed, Walter Lüthi has called this scene "the death of discipleship,"[322] and Droge goes so far as to argue that "Peter's denial is really his *confession*."[323] If this is the case, Peter stands in sharp contrast with the women in the Gospel. The women have all demonstrated various qualities of discipleship, whereas Peter's status as a follower has been called into question repeatedly.

In considering the picture of Peter presented by the Fourth Gospel thus far, it is not difficult to see where the proponents of an anti-Petrine

---

[320]Bultmann, 648.

[321]Maynard, "Role of Peter," 538.

[322]Walter Lüthi, *St. John's Gospel: An Exposition* (Richmond: John Knox, 1960) 280. Cited in Maynard, "Role of Peter," 538. Similarly, Stibbe argues that Peter (along with Thomas) embodies "a certain kind of false discipleship: the kind which promises much in word (in this case martyrdom) but delivers little in deed...." ("Tomb," 46).

[323]Droge, "Status of Peter," 311. In defense of this harsh judgement on Peter, Droge rightly points out that being described as a "disciple" or "believing in Jesus" does not necessarily mean that a person is one of Jesus' own (cf. 2:23–25; 6:66; 8:31). What Droge does not take into consideration is Peter's confession in 6:68–69.

theory get their support. The scene that puts him in the most positive light, 6:66–71, is filled with ambiguity. Peter makes no individual profession of faith and his corporate confession is obscured by strange terminology and overshadowed by the presence of a betrayer among those whom he represents. The other episodes in which he is featured portray him either as repeatedly misunderstanding Jesus or denying his discipleship outright. He shares the first trait with other characters in the Gospel; the second is his alone. Even Nicodemus, who is pointedly rebuffed by Jesus, remains loyal to Jesus in his own guarded way. Finally, the absence of any reference to Peter's witness of the resurrected Christ is significant. He is not presented as the first witness as in the traditions reflected in I Corinthians 15:5 and Luke 24:34, nor is he mentioned when Jesus does appear to the disciples. Instead, in the Fourth Gospel it is Thomas who is singled out in connection with the Twelve and who offers his personal confession of the resurrected Lord (20:24–29).

Peter in the Epilogue (Chapter 21)

As already mentioned, the majority opinion about this final chapter of the Gospel of John holds that it is a later addition to the text.[324] For most critics, the remaining question is whether the Evangelist or a redactor was responsible for the later material. For our purposes, there is no need to review the discussion here; what is relevant is the treatment of Peter in relation to the rest of the Gospel. It is frequently pointed out that Peter undergoes rehabilitation in chapter 21. The thrice repeated question of Jesus, "Simon, son of John, do you love me?" supposedly corresponds with Peter's three denials in chapter 18.[325] However, if Peter is undergoing rehabilitation it can only be with regard

---

[324]For an alternative view cf. O'Day, 854–855. Also E. C. Hosykns, *The Fourth Gospel* (London: Farber & Farber, 1947); Paul S. Minear, "The Original Functions of John 21, *JBL* (1983): 85–98.

[325]Beasley-Murray, for instance, adds a psychological slant to the theory and argues, "Peter must have been conscious of the fact that he had forfeited all right to be viewed as a disciple of Jesus, let alone a close associate of him in his ministry, through his repeated disavowal of any connection with him...this was a profoundly serious failure, which called for a process of re-establishment commensurable with the seriousness of the defection" (405). Bultmann considers the theory to be highly questionable, arguing that although the author may have understood it in that way, 21:15–17 contains no hint of a relation to the account of the denial. Instead, he sees the story as a variant of Peter's commission to be leader of the community (Mt 16:17–19, cf. Lk 22:32) (712).

to a reputation enjoyed somewhere other than in the Fourth Gospel, where, as we have seen, there is little evidence of an earlier good standing. Indeed, rather than rehabilitation, it may be more accurate to say that Peter's character takes on a new dimension in chapter 21, which seems to compensate for his earlier portrayal. To be sure, Peter still displays his characteristic impulsiveness, as when, upon hearing that Jesus is standing on the beach, he clothes himself and jumps into the sea (21:7). But he is now also portrayed in an intimate exchange with Jesus; indeed, the intimacy expressed between Jesus and Peter here recalls conversations between Jesus and the women characters earlier in the Gospel.

That Jesus' attention is directed only to Peter is emphasized in the opening question in which Jesus distinguishes Peter from the rest of the disciples, Σίμων Ἰωάννου, ἀγαπᾷ με πλέον τούτων (21:15). The development of Peter's character is most notable when Jesus confronts him with the same question for the third time. At this point, the narrator gives us a glimpse at Peter's emotions, ἐλυπήθη, as he again answers affirmatively (21:17). Moreover, it appears that Peter's understanding of Jesus has at last improved as he replies simply, κύριε, πάντα σu οἶδας, σὺ γινώσκεις ὅτι φιλῶ σε.

Jesus responds to Peter's affirmation of love with a commission: He is to become shepherd over his flock (21:15–17). This commission is accompanied with a prediction of Peter's eventual martyrdom and a command to follow Jesus, the latter presumably also being an allusion to Peter's death (21:18–19).[326] The commission and the prediction both highlight Peter as an individual, filling out his character in a way that was absent in the earlier part of the Gospel proper. As we will see below, the same individualizing or even historicizing is also present in the treatment of the beloved disciple in chapter 21.

THE BELOVED DISCIPLE (13:21–26; 19:25–27; 20:2–10)

Introduction

The mysterious character known as the beloved disciple has generated an enormous amount of speculation regarding his identity and

---

[326]The meaning of Peter's commission has long been a point of debate between Catholic and Protestant exegetes. The former tend to see the pastoral commission as an indication of Peter's primacy as leader of the church; the latter do see the commission as exclusive to Peter, but understand it as one among many given to the followers of Jesus.

role in the Gospel. A beginning point for the discussion has been whether this character should be regarded as a historical figure, a symbolic figure, or both. Then, depending on the answer to this question, scholars have attempted to discover who or what this disciple was intended to represent. Scholars pressing for a historical view of the disciple have devoted much energy to identifying the actual figure represented by this character. Theories include John the Presbyter,[327] Lazarus, John Mark, and John the son of Zebedee.[328] Others argue that, at least from the perspective of the Evangelist, this anonymous character should be understood as symbolical. For instance, according to Bultmann, the Evangelist intended the beloved disciple to represent Gentile Christianity, as evident in 13:21–26, 19:25–27 and 20:2–10. Bultmann distinguishes these scenes from 19:35 and chapter 21, which in his opinion are the work of a later redactor, and clearly refer to a historical figure.[329] Although many agree with Bultmann that the disciple is a representative figure, the idea that he represents Gentile Christianity has been rejected by the majority of interpreters.[330] Most critics now view the character more generally as a representative of the ideal disciple.[331] Furthermore, several make the point that a representative interpretation need not exclude the beloved disciple's importance as a

---

[327]Most recently argued by Martin Hengel, *The Johannine Question* (London: SCM Press; Philadelphia: Trinity Press International, 1989). See also Richard Bauckham, "The Beloved Disciple as Ideal Author," *JSNT* 49 (1993): 21–44.

[328]That the Apostle John authored the Gospel was the traditional view of the early church and is still argued by some contemporary scholars. Cf. Brown, LXXXVIII–XCVIII, for a review of the arguments. Brown favors the identification as does Feuillet, *Jesus and His Mother: The Role of the Virgin Mary in Salvation History and the Place of Woman in the Church* (Still River, MA: St. Bede's Publications, 1984) 130–133. Barrett, 116–119.

[329]Bultmann, 484, 673.

[330]But see Margaret Pamment, "The Fourth Gospel's Beloved Disciple," *ExpT* 94 (1983): 363–367.

[331]Lindars, for example, states that the Evangelist "needed an ideal disciple as a foil to Peter and an example for the reader" (457). Cf. also William S. Kurz, "The Beloved Disciple and Implied Readers," *BTB* 19 (1989): 100–107; Brendan J. Byrne, "The Faith of the Beloved Disciple and the Community in John 20," *JSNT* 23 (1985): 83–97. Minear has put forth another creative proposal that "the beloved disciple was in part shaped to conform to the picture of Benjamin in Deut. 33:12." There, in the context of Moses' blessing of the tribes of Israel, Benjamin is spoken of as "beloved of the Lord" who "rests between his shoulders." Cf. "The Beloved Disciple in the Gospel of John: Some Clues and Conjectures," *NovT* 19 (1977): 122.

historical figure.[332] To this end, Culpepper states, "It is now generally agreed that the beloved disciple was a real historical person who has representative, paradigmatic, or symbolic significance in John."[333] For my purposes, whether the beloved disciple was an historical figure is not important for the way in which he is presented in the narrative.

In considering the character of the beloved disciple we must begin with the question where he appears in the narrative. The answer to this question is not obvious. There are three scenes in the Gospel proper which apply the epithet "the one whom he loved" to a disciple of Jesus (13:23; 19:26; 20:2). The same description is also found in 21:7, 20. In addition to these scenes, there are several other places in the Gospel that contain possible allusions to the beloved disciple. Most frequently discussed are 1:37–40 and 18:15–16 both of which contain references to an unnamed disciple. Of the two, the reference to the ἄλλος μαθητής in 18:15–16 is more likely to be a reference to the beloved disciple since, 1) it occurs in the context of Jesus' passion along with the other references to the beloved disciple, 2) the disciple is paired with Peter as in chapters 13 and 20, and 3) the phrase ἄλλος μαθητής is used for the disciple whom Jesus loved in 20:2. Although many commentators tend to include 18:15–16 among the passages that refer to the beloved disciple for these reasons, this conclusion can be drawn only in a tentative way. I am more inclined to agree with Bultmann, who argues against reading 18:15–16 as a reference to the beloved disciple. He notes that unlike the other places where Peter and the beloved disciple appear together, here they do not appear as rivals or contrasting types. As Bultmann sees it, the other disciple's sole reason for existence in 18:15–16 is to enable Peter to enter the high priest's courtyard.[334]

The other passage that is discussed in relation to the beloved disciple is 19:35. Although there is no clue as to the identity of this

---

[332]For example, Schnackenburg states, "He is the ideal disciple with an exemplary faith. May we, therefore deny him flesh and blood?...It is possible for disciples and friends of someone to whom they won many traditions and deep insights, to idealize him and to illustrate his truly deep faith with such stories" (3.312). Despite his conviction that the beloved disciple is grounded in an historical figure, Schnackenburg refrains from trying to identify him by name (cf. his excursus, 3.375–388). Cf. also Beasley-Murray, "That the Beloved Disciple served a representative and symbolic function is entirely consistent with his being a real disciple of Jesus..." (lxxiii).

[333]Culpepper, *Anatomy*, 121.

[334]Bultmann, 645, nt. 4. Cf. also Pamment, "The Fourth Gospel's Beloved Disciple," 366.

eyewitness, commentators have reasonably assumed that he is one and
the same as the beloved disciple who is described as a witness and the
author of the Gospel in 21:24. This may well be the case, but if so,
19:35 must be taken as a later editorial gloss, in keeping with the later
addition of the whole of chapter 21.

Given the uncertain nature of all of the above references, I will
limit my analysis to passages with specific references to the disciple
whom Jesus loved. As mentioned earlier, the analysis of chapter 20 will
be taken up separately, since that particular text demands a close
examination of Peter, the beloved disciple and Mary Magdalene in
relation to one another.

The Beloved Disciple at the Farewell Supper (13:21–26)

As mentioned in the discussion of Peter, the beloved disciple is
first introduced to the Gospel narrative at the Farewell Supper. Notably,
what is mentioned first is not that Jesus loved him, but that he is
ἀνακείμενος...ἐν τῷ κόλπῳ τοῦ Ἰησοῦ (13:23). His appearance in
the story does not occur initially through naming, nor through dialogue
with Jesus, but instead through a description of his position in relation to
Jesus.[335] The expression ἀνακείμενος...ἐν τῷ κόλπῳ is used typically
in the context of dining and refers to physical proximity. This meaning of
the phrase is reflected in the NRSV translation, "reclining next to
him."[336] If, as in this context, the person in question is reclining next to
the dinner host, then the phrase may also indicate a place of honor at the
table.[337]

Yet, in light of the larger Gospel context, ἀνακείμενος...ἐν τῷ
κόλπῳ τοῦ Ἰησου indicates more than physical proximity. It echoes the
early description of Jesus ὁ ὢν εἰς τὸν κόλπον τοῦ πατρός (1:18),
and thereby suggests an analogous relationship between Jesus and his
beloved disciple. Frequently, the basis for this analogy is found in the
beloved disciple's role as revealer of Jesus. For example, Culpepper
states, "Just as Jesus was 'in the bosom' of the Father and is therefore

---

[335]Cf. O'Day who notes, "...the anonymity of this disciple suggests that the
Fourth Evangelist understands the significance of this disciple to rest in his
relationship to Jesus, not in his own identity" (729).

[336]Similarly, Brown translates "at the table close beside Jesus" (573).

[337]Cf. BAG, 55. Note, however, Haenchen, who argues that in this scene the
seating arrangement does not indicate a special relationship since the beloved
disciple is pictured on Jesus' right and customarily the place of honor was on the left
(2.110).

able to make him known, so the Beloved Disciple is uniquely able to make Jesus known."[338] Likewise, Beasley-Murray comments, "The Evangelist introduces the Beloved Disciple as standing in analogous relation to Jesus as Jesus is to the Father with respect to the revelation he was sent to make known; behind this gospel is the testimony of one who was 'close to the heart' of Jesus."[339] One should note, however, that this emphasis on the disciple's revelatory function is dependent on his presentation in chapter 21; nothing in the Gospel proper suggests that he reveals anything. Instead, quite the opposite is true—whatever knowledge the disciple may have of Jesus, he does not communicate it to others.[340]

Thus, rather than revelation, the point of analogy lies in the intimacy shared between the Father, Jesus, and the beloved disciple. As Brown puts it, "...the Disciple is as intimate with Jesus as Jesus is with the Father."[341] This is confirmed by the additional information about the disciple which comes at the end of verse 23—he is ὃν ἠγάπα ὁ Ἰησοῦς. In the context of chapter 13, this identification is highly significant. The chapter begins with a statement which both summarizes the first half of the Gospel and anticipates a major theme of the second half, "having loved his own who were in the world, he loved them to the end (εἰς τέλος) (13:1c). Especially in the farewell discourse, Jesus has much to say about the analogous and reciprocal nature of the love between the Father, himself, and his disciples (e.g., 14:21, 15:9), all of which points to the close relationship between Jesus and his followers. But only in the case of the Bethany family and the unnamed disciple does one find an expression of Jesus' love for particular individuals. Even within the context of the Farewell Discourse, in which Jesus explicitly speaks of his love for his disciples, *individual* disciples are presented primarily as those who misunderstand (cf. 14:5; 14:8–10). Moreover, aside from the Father (cf. 1:18, 3:35, 10:17, 14:31: 17:23–24), the beloved disciple is the only male figure in the Gospel who is presented in such closeness to Jesus. It is true that Jesus loves Lazarus, but Lazarus' purely functional role in the narrative does not permit a

---

[338]Culpepper, *Anatomy*, 121.

[339]Beasley-Murray, 238.

[340]Margaret Pamment observes that in these chapters, the beloved disciple seems to be both present and absent at the same time. That is, while he is present in the narrative, his actions typically have no noticeable effect on the story ("Beloved Disciple," 366).

[341]Brown, 577.

personal expression of this relationship. Instead, the love that Jesus has for the Bethany family is expressed through his interaction with Martha and with Mary.[342]

In fact, although the unique quality of the beloved disciple's relationship with Jesus is often held up as an example of his ideal status in the Gospel, one could argue that several of the women characters also demonstrate intimacy with Jesus. Martha and Mary of Bethany certainly appear as intimate associates of Jesus as they share their grief and tears with him. Mary, in particular, is presented as physically close to Jesus, falling at his feet in 11:32, and wiping his anointed feet with her hair in 12:3. Looking ahead, Jesus and Mary Magdalene will also share an intimate moment together, as he calls her name and she recognizes him through her tears (20:16). Even Jesus' conversation with the Samaritan woman is of an intimate nature, albeit of a different sort, as their discussion concerns the personal history of the woman. Thus, although the text indicates that the relationship between the beloved disciple and Jesus resembles the one shared between the heavenly father with his son, when we look for concrete examples of intimacy with Jesus elsewhere in the text, we are led to women characters. In other words, at the story level, the closeness which the beloved disciple shares with Jesus more nearly resembles the relationships that Jesus has with the female characters of the Gospel.

Furthermore, in chapter 13, the intimacy between the beloved disciple and Jesus appears in contrast to the distance between Peter and Jesus. As we have seen, although Peter was previously portrayed as a representative of the disciples, when the beloved disciple is first introduced, Peter defers to him. The fact that Peter must motion to the disciple to ask Jesus about the betrayer implies distance between Peter and Jesus.[343] In contrast, verse 25 reiterates the disciple's physical proximity to Jesus, ἀναπεσὼν...ἐπὶ τὸ στῆθος τοῦ Ἰησοῦ, as he responds to Peter's request and asks Jesus about the identity of his betrayer. In this way, the beloved disciple appears to act as mediator between Peter and Jesus. To be sure, as far as Peter and the other disciples are concerned, nothing actually results from this mediation.

---

[342]Along this line, Schüssler Fiorenza makes a point of calling Martha "a beloved disciple" (*In Memory of Her*, 329–330).

[343]Recall that the one scene in which we might have found an expression of intimacy between Peter and Jesus, namely, the footwashing in 13:1–20, Peter first rejects Jesus' action and then shows only misunderstanding.

They remain ignorant as to the meaning of Jesus' words and actions (v. 28). Nevertheless, in this table scene, the disciple's intimate relationship with Jesus and his role as spokesperson place him in a superior position to Peter and set him off from the other male disciples in the Gospel.

In this regard, the character who presents the strongest contrast to the beloved disciple is undoubtedly Judas. At the same time that the disciple is reclining in the bosom of Jesus, Judas is identified as the betrayer. As he goes out from the gathering of disciples, his departure is punctuated by the telling note that ἦν δὲ νύξ (v. 30). Significantly, the contrast drawn between the beloved disciple and Judas once more recalls a female character in the Gospel—Mary of Bethany also serves as a positive contrast to Judas (12:1–8). Thus, if we accept the theory that this disciple is intended to represent the ideal of discipleship, it would seem that part of this representation involves a contrast with the male characters of the Gospel, and a commonality with several of the female characters.

The Beloved Disciple at the Cross (19:25–27)

In chapter 19, the disciple's similarity to the female characters is made even more explicit as he appears with the mother of Jesus and several other women at the foot of the cross. Recall that only the Gospel of John places the women in proximity to Jesus as he hangs on the cross. The result is that women characters, along with the beloved disciple, are once again depicted in an intimate scene with Jesus. Notably, interpreters frequently highlight the disciple's gender in this scene, pointing out that he is the only male disciple present at the crucifixion.[344] In this respect, he is once again shown to take precedence over Peter and the other male disciples, all of whom are absent from the crucifixion (as they are likewise absent from the tomb of Lazarus). However, by focusing only on the disciple's male identity, we overlook the significance of the fact that he stands in the company of women witnesses. In other words, in his loyalty and devotion to Jesus, the beloved disciple is again more closely associated with female characters than with male. This is true despite the fact that the scene calls attention to the disciple's male identity, as Jesus declares him to be a son to his mother (19:26).

---

[344]Brown, et. al, *Peter in the New Testament*, 136. Minear, "The Beloved Disciple" 119. Bauckham, "The Beloved Disciple," 37.

As mentioned in the discussion of the mother of Jesus, the significance of Jesus' pronouncement is difficult to determine and many suggestions have been offered. As I argued there, the most plausible interpretation sees in the exchange the creation of a new family of God on earth. Moreover, both the beloved disciple and the mother of Jesus are depicted as obedient and willing adherents to Jesus' words and it is their joint presence at the cross which makes possible the completion of Jesus' earthly mission. In this way, there is a balance with respect to the roles of the disciple and Jesus' mother. Again, if the beloved disciple is to be understood as an ideal figure, then the "ideal" quality of the mother of Jesus must also be considered.

The Beloved Disciple in the Epilogue (Chapter 21)

As with Peter, the final appearance of the beloved disciple occurs in the epilogue. Although there is a list of disciples at the opening of the chapter, the beloved disciple is not identified until v. 7. He is again presented in relation to Peter and, for the first and only time, actually speaks to him. Following the great haul of fish that results from Jesus' instructions, the beloved disciple recognizes Jesus, and tells Peter, "It is the Lord" (v. 7). At this point, the disciple can justifiably be called both witness and mediator. His statement indicates his ability to perceive Jesus on the basis of a sign and he communicates his perception to Peter. However, his characterization goes no further than this. After his pronouncement, the disciple drops from the scene and the focus shifts to Simon Peter.

In verse 20, the disciple appears for the last time. He reenters the narrative through the eyes of Peter, who turns and sees him following. Since Peter has just been told to follow Jesus, the repetition of ἀκολουθειν once more introduces a comparison between the two disciples. At this point, the narrator interrupts the narrative to give a detailed recollection of the disciple's role in chapter 13 (v. 20). That this particular scene is recalled, highlights one last time the disciple's intimacy with Jesus above any other characteristic.[345] Whatever is said of the disciple here, it will be with this image of him in mind. In addition, the expansion of the disciple's question to include the words ὁ παραδιδούς σε (cf. 13:25) evokes the notion of betrayal and with it the recollection of Judas, stressing this contrast once more.

---

[345]Cf. Lindars, 638.

In verse 21, Peter makes the comparison between himself and the disciple explicit as he asks Jesus, "Lord, what about him?" His question results in a rather sharp response from Jesus that delineates the roles these two disciples will play (v. 22). Peter is to follow Jesus, presumably into martyrdom (cf. vv. 18–19). The disciple, on the other hand, is to remain until Jesus comes. While the precise meaning of this statement is unclear it likely refers to the parousia. Verse 23a indicates the significance of this exchange between Peter and Jesus; it is meant to explain the origin of a rumor in the community that said that this disciple would not die. Verse 23b then corrects that rumor, pointing out that Jesus did not deny the death of the disciple. Together, both verses give the impression that the beloved disciple was known to the readers of the Gospel and that, contrary to expectations, he died before Jesus' return. In this regard, verses 22–23 give the clear impression of the disciple as a historical figure.[346]

Finally, verse 24 makes the claim that this figure was behind the witness and writing of the Gospel. The point of the claim is no doubt to add authenticity and authority to the text. While there is no indication that the beloved disciple of the gospel proper was intended to be identified as the author of the Gospel, it is notable that the male character who most closely compares with female characters in the text is granted this authority by the redactor of chapter 21. While I wish to make no claims for female authorship of the Gospel (both Schüssler Fiorenza and Scott raise this possibility),[347] it is nevertheless intriguing that the Johannine tradition looked for authority in a male figure that shares characteristics with female figures in the Gospel.

---

[346]Pamment makes an unconvincing attempt to maintain the disciple's symbolic nature even in this verse, arguing that its meaning is that the fate of Gentile Christianity is uncertain ("Beloved Disciple," 367). Much more likely is Bultmann's suggestion that the chapter 21 redactor understood the beloved disciple historically, although the Evangelist did not (483–484). Lindars makes the cogent point that while those behind chapter 21, especially v. 24, may have assumed the beloved disciple to have been a historical figure, there is no guarantee that they were correct (641).

[347]*In Memory of Her*, 333; Scott, *Sophia*, 239–24, cf. also Kysar, *The Maverick Gospel*, 153.

THE EMPTY TOMB (20:1–18): MARY MAGDALENE, PETER, AND THE BELOVED DISCIPLE

Introduction

Chapter 20:1–18 consists of two stories that are woven together by the presence of Mary Magdalene. One is the story of Peter and the beloved disciple at the empty tomb; the other is the encounter between Mary Magdalene and Jesus at the tomb. The combination of these two stories raises many source critical issues involving the Evangelist's use of traditional passion material and knowledge of the synoptic gospels. Clearly, there has been a blending of two or more traditions in the crafting of 20:1–18.[348] However, since I am interested in a literary reading of the text, I will focus on the story as a single narrative, consisting of three distinct scenes. The first scene, verses 1–2, introduces the narrative. It depicts Mary's discovery of the empty tomb and her urgent communication of that fact to Peter and the beloved disciple. The second scene, verses 3–10, relates the two disciples' race to the tomb and what they find upon their arrival. The third and final scene, verses 11–18, tell of Mary's encounter with the resurrected Jesus. Note that her story surrounds that of the disciples, creating an interpretive framework for their experience at the tomb.

Scene 1: Mary's Discovery (vv. 1–2)

In the opening verses of the narrative, Mary Magdalene comes alone to the tomb, early in the morning, and discovers that the stone covering its entrance has been rolled away. She does not stay to investigate, but hurries to report to the two most prominent male disciples in the Gospel what the evidence clearly suggests—the body of Jesus has been removed.[349] Already in the beginning of the story, Mary Magdalene is presented as the person who communicates information to the male disciples. It is Mary's articulation of the problem in verse 2,

---

[348]For a thorough discussion see Robert Mahoney, *Two Disciples at the Tomb: The Background and Message of John 20:1–10* (Theologie und Wirklichkeit 6; Frankfurt: Peter Lang, 1974) 171–193. See also, Frans Neirynck, "John and the Synoptics: The Empty Tomb Stories," *NTS* 30 (1984): 161–187.

[349]Barrett cites an inscription of an ordinance of Caesar discovered in Nazareth which lends evidence to the problem of grave robbing during this period. According to the ordinance which forbids the disturbance of graves or grave stones under threat of death, the primary motivation for the grave robbing was to dishonor the deceased (*The New Testament Background: Selected Documents*, rev. ed. [San Francisco: Harper and Row, 1989] 15).

"They have taken the Lord from the tomb and we do not know where they have laid him," that provides the catalyst for the events detailed in verses 3–10.[350]

Grammatically, Mary's comment raises the question to whom the plural verbs ἦραν and οἴδαμεν refer. In the case of ἦραν, the third person plural can be read as impersonal, the equivalent of a passive construction, "the body has been taken."[351] Alternatively, Mary may be referring in general terms to the enemies of Jesus. With regard to οἴδαμεν, most commentators answer the question of the first person plural on the basis of redaction criticism: the verb is a remnant from the original source which included several women.[352] This may well be the case, but in its present context the plural pronoun simply serves to situate Mary as one among Jesus' followers, including Peter and the beloved disciple.[353]

The second question Mary's statement raises concerns her use of τὸν κύριον for Jesus. Although the vocative κύριε occurs frequently throughout the Gospel as a respectful form of address, the use of the word as a title is rare. When titles are given to Jesus in the Fourth Gospel, they take many forms, (Son of God, Son of Man, the Christ, Holy One of God, etc.) but "the Lord" occurs only in 6:23 and 11:2, and both of these are considered insertions by the narrator.[354] Although Jesus tells his disciples that they rightly called him both ὁ διδάσκαλος and ὁ κύριος (13:13), Mary Magdalene is the first character in the narrative who actually does so (vv. 2, 16, 18). Significantly, after Mary's use of the title, it appears on the lips of Thomas, ὁ κύριός μου καὶ ὁ θεός μου (21:28), and is then used by the beloved disciple, ὁ κύριός ἐστιν (21:7). These late appearances of ὁ κύριος may suggest that the use of this title is only appropriate after the resurrection. If so, it is fitting that Mary uses it first, since she will be the first to encounter the resurrected Jesus. Significantly, the context for Mary's two uses of ὁ κύριος reflect a progression of understanding on her part. In this introductory section, she is convinced, "They have taken the Lord out of the tomb...." By

---

[350]O'Day, 840.

[351]So Lindars, 600.

[352]So Brown, 1000, Barrett, 563, Schnackenburg, 308, Lindars, 600.

[353]Cf. O'Day's comment that "Mary understands herself to be expressing the puzzle of the empty tomb for all of Jesus' followers, not for herself alone" (840).

[354]The omission of 6:23 in some Western witnesses makes its inclusion in the text questionable. The occurrence of the word in 4:1 is even more questionable. The reference in 11:2 is parenthetical.

verse 18 this misunderstanding will be resolved and Mary will be able to announce to the disciples, "I have seen the Lord!"

Scene 2: Peter and the Beloved Disciple at the Empty Tomb (vv. 3–10)

Upon hearing Mary's report, Peter and the beloved disciple set out running to the tomb. This is the second time that Peter and the disciple are paired together, and, as in 13:23–25, a contrast appears to be drawn between the two. The narrator makes the point three times that the beloved disciple arrives at the tomb ahead of Peter (vv. 4, 6, 8) suggesting that being ahead of Peter is especially relevant to the character of the beloved disciple. Perhaps this is to emphasize once more that the disciple is closer than Peter to Jesus. Yet, the narrator also takes pains to mention that despite arriving ahead of Peter, the disciple does not enter the tomb, but observes from the entrance the linen grave wrappings (v. 5). Instead, it is Peter who first goes into the tomb. Perhaps this is an attempt to balance the presentation of the two disciples, giving them an equal share in the discovery of the tomb.[355] The scene may also suggest something about the character of each of these disciples. That the beloved disciple defers to Peter at this decisive moment may imply that he is not competitive—he does not vie with Peter. Or the scene may be more telling of Peter's impulsive nature, demonstrated elsewhere in the Gospel as when he cuts off the ear of the slave Malchus (18:10, cf. 13:8–9; 21:7).

In any event, when Peter does enter the tomb, he, too, sees the linens, and also the carefully folded σουδάριον, something the beloved disciple had not seen from outside of the tomb (v. 7).[356] It is only then

---

[355]Seim notes that "in the Johannine story of the empty tomb there is a strange and rather entertaining apportionment" between Peter, the beloved disciple and Mary Magdalene which she believes could imply an egalitarian interest in the leadership of the Johannine community ("Roles of Women," 67). While her statement may be accurate with respect to Peter and the beloved disciple, Mary Magdalene is given a decidedly more important role in the narrative as a whole, as I will argue below. Alternatively, Lindars contends that the forestalling of the beloved disciple's entry is a delaying tactic, a literary device designed to build the narrative up to the climax of v. 8 (601). This assumes that v. 8 is the climax of the scene—a debatable point as will be discussed below.

[356]The mention of the cloth recalls chapter 11, in which the same word, σουδάριον, is used to describe the cloth that is wrapped around the face of Lazarus. Regarding this link between these two stories, O'Day comments, "Lazarus emerged from the tomb still wrapped in his grave cloths, and he depended on Jesus' command to free himself from the wrappings; but in 20:6–7, Jesus' grave cloths

that the beloved disciple enters and the narrator reports, καὶ εἶδεν καὶ ἐπίστευσεν (20:8). This verse has been crucial for viewing the beloved disciple as the disciple *par excellence*. Based on the two verbs, the majority of interpreters assume that in the Fourth Gospel, the beloved disciple is the first to believe in the resurrection.[357]

Despite its popularity, this interpretation has problems. In fact, this verse, more than any other concerning the beloved disciple, complicates the notion that he represents the ideal of discipleship. The most obvious problem is that the text does not state what it is the disciple sees and believes. It is simply assumed that the reader will be able to fill in the object of these verbs.

Second, the verses immediately following the statement directly contradict the view that the disciple has come to resurrection faith. Verse 9 implies that neither disciple knew what to make of the empty tomb because "they did not yet understand the scripture that he must rise from the dead." Although interpreters do their best to find a way around the statement,[358] it clearly indicates that both disciples lacked understanding about Jesus' resurrection. The uneventful conclusion of the scene in verse 10 confirms this, as the disciples simply return to their homes. Indeed, those who argue that the beloved disciple came to faith in the resurrection must explain why he did not communicate his

---

remain behind in the empty tomb. The details of the grave cloths thus point to the theological resolution of Mary's misunderstanding: No one has taken Jesus away; he has left death behind" (841). On a more mundane level, mention of the carefully folded wrap may have served an apologetic purpose, providing evidence that the body had not been stolen.

[357]Schnackenburg states the case most emphatically, "To what kind of belief [did the disciple come]? According to the context, undoubtedly to the full faith in the resurrection of Jesus; any kind of diminution, with a view to v. 9 is ruled out. The point of the story lies in the clear and strong faith of the beloved disciple" (3.312). Similarly Barrett, "[The beloved disciple] is the first to believe in the resurrection; he holds, in this sense, a primacy of faith" 561. Cf. also Brown, 987; Haenchen 2.208. Lindars contrasts the faith of the beloved disciple with the skepticism of Thomas. "The Disciple has reached Resurrection faith without an appearance of Jesus....*His* kind of faith will be commended by Jesus himself in verse 29" (602).

[358]Schnackenburg understands the verse to emphasize the faith of the beloved disciple and possibly Peter, who believe *even tough* they do not yet know the scripture, 312–313. Haenchen contends that v. 9 explains why the disciples had to see the empty tomb and the linens in order to believe; they did not yet know that the scripture foretold the resurrection of Jesus (2.208). So also Barrett, 564.

understanding to anyone else, especially to Peter.[359] At best, going home is an understated response for a disciple who has just seen evidence of Jesus' resurrection.[360] In this regard, Minear, who offers an alternative interpretation of what the disciple sees and believes, comments, "Nowhere else in the New Testament is it suggested that faith in the risen Lord produced such indifference, as if nothing at all happened to change things."[361] Indeed, one could argue that the behavior of the disciples is more in keeping with Jesus' prediction, "you will be scattered to your homes" (16:32), than with the response of one who has come to the full knowledge of resurrection faith. Finally, one should note that if the beloved disciple came to full resurrection faith in this scene, there would hardly be any point to the next scene with Mary.

Minear has taken these problems seriously and argues that what the beloved disciple actually saw and believed was that Mary spoke the truth; the body of Jesus was no longer there. Indeed, according to Minear, the basic function of the episode in verses 3–10 is to corroborate Mary's discovery of Jesus' missing body.[362] This explanation, although unconventional, has the advantage of making sense of all the narrative elements. First, it links the introduction of the story, in which Mary announces that the tomb is empty, with the disciples' experience at the tomb. More importantly, it readily explains verses 9–10. Because neither of the disciples knew the scripture, they could not come to resurrection faith, but could only confirm what Mary had already told them.

---

[359]In this regard, the disciple's announcement of Jesus' identity to Peter in 21:7 may be intended as a correction for his complete lack of communication in 20:3–11.

[360]Schnackenburg explains verse 9 as a result of clumsy editorial work on the part of the Evangelist (3.313). Lindars suggests that although the disciple has come to faith, "the substance of his faith has still not been formulated" (602). Does this mean he believes something, but he does not know what? If so, he can hardly be viewed as an ideal disciple.

O'Day recognizes that the beloved disciple could not have come to belief in the resurrection. She rightly notes that to say so "is to rush the story" (841).

[361]Minear, "'We don't know where...'" 127.

[362]Minear, "'We Don't Know Where'" 127–128. This is also the argument of Augustine who after noting the mistaken reading that the disciple believed in the resurrection, writes, "What, therefore, did he see? What did he believe? He saw, of course, the empty sepulcher and he believed what the woman had said, that he was taken from the sepulcher" (*St Augustine: Tractates on the Gospel of John 112–24*, FC 92 (Trans. by John W. Rettig; Washington, D.C.: The Catholic University of America Press, 1995) 54–55.

The only argument against such a reading is that typically "to believe" is invested with more theological content than this interpretation would allow.[363] However, note the reaction of the disciples to the women's report of their experience at the tomb in Lk 24:11. Their words are deemed to be nonsense by the disciples καὶ ἠπίστουν αὐταῖς. Only Peter runs to the tomb to investigate the women's account (24:12). In the Gospel of John, the situation is similar, except that both Peter and the beloved disciple race to the tomb, and here the woman's words are verified by the disciple's reaction, καὶ εἶδεν καὶ ἐπίστευσεν. The fact that "belief" is used in this non-theological sense in this resurrection tradition allows for the feasibility of its similar use in 20:8, especially since it is evident that the Fourth Evangelist is drawing on several traditions in crafting his narrative.

How does such an interpretation affect the way the character of the beloved disciple is perceived? If he is not portrayed as the first to come to faith in Jesus' resurrection, does this diminish what has been viewed as his ideal status? First, it should be said that the interpretation offered above does not necessarily imply a negative view of the disciple. As verse 9 makes clear, he could not be expected to do more than confirm Mary's report since he did not yet understand the scripture.[364] Furthermore, there is something to be said of the fact that "seeing and believing" is attributed to the beloved disciple and not to Peter, even if it does not refer to resurrection faith. Though I would not go so far as to call verse 8 the climax of the story, the disciple's confirmation of Mary's report appears to be an important moment in the narrative. With Mary, he serves as witness to the empty tomb, even though neither he nor she understands its significance at this point in the story. In contrast, there is no indication at all of Peter's response to the tomb; we find no expression of amazement as in the Lukan account (Lk 24:12). Thus, while the disciple may not reach the heights of faith that have been

---

[363]Cf. O'Day, who states, "It is unlikely that the Fourth Evangelist would use the verb 'to believe' to mean simply 'acknowledge' or 'give assent to,' as it has more theological weight than that throughout the Gospel (e.g., 1:12; 3:15, 18; 5:38; 11:25–26; 12:46; 14:1, 10–11)." In her view the disciple believes, "not merely that the tomb is empty, but that its emptiness bears witness that Jesus has conquered death and judged the ruler of this world (12:31; 14:30; 16:33). The beloved disciple's faith is as complete as faith in the evidence of the empty tomb can be" (841).

[364]That the disciples will be able to fully understand Jesus only after he has been glorified is a recurrent theme of the Gospel (cf. 2:22; 12:16; 13:7).

attributed to him at this point, there is still a hint of his superior position to Peter. Nevertheless, as we will see below, when compared to what Mary is about to experience, both disciples appear in a lesser position. While all three of these characters observe the empty tomb, she alone witnesses the resurrected Christ.

In sum, if we consider what verses 3–10 contribute to the narrative of 20:1–18, several aspects appear relevant. First, as mentioned above, the scene confirms Mary's report: the tomb is in fact empty. Second, by once again pairing Peter with the beloved disciple, the scene adds to the impression that these two disciples are to be viewed in close relation to one another. In chapter 13, the beloved disciple appears to have the clear advantage over Peter with respect to his relationship to Jesus. However, in chapter 20 their respective positions are not so obvious. On the one hand, there seems to be an interest in balancing the presentation of the disciples. Both have their share in observing the empty tomb, and like Mary Magdalene, neither of them understand its implications. On the other hand, only the response of the beloved disciple is mentioned as confirmation of Mary's report, suggesting that his witness might hold more authority.

Finally, and most significantly, the disciples' encounter with the empty tomb sets up the third scene between Mary Magdalene and Jesus. Although the beloved disciple confirms the truth of the empty tomb, this does not resolve Mary's major concern, namely, the whereabouts of the body of Jesus. The male disciples visit the tomb and return "empty-handed" so to speak. Their presence at the grave leads to nothing Mary had not already known. We thus move to the third scene.

Scene 3: Mary and Jesus at the Empty Tomb (vv. 11–18)

Once the disciples leave the tomb, the focus of the narrative returns to Mary Magdalene. Her reintroduction stands in contrast to the departure of the disciples in v. 10. They return to their homes, "But Mary stood outside the tomb weeping" (v. 11). Weeping is an essential aspect of Mary's role in the opening half of the story as the four-fold repetition of this verb suggests (vv. 11a, 11b, 13, 15). Although she, like Mary of Bethany, has been criticized for her tears,[365] her weeping fulfills

---

[365]Cf. e.g., Brodie who notes that Mary "is described as *standing, outside, crying*....Faced with the tomb her heart and mind have come to a halt. The result is that she is 'outside,' a word which in the goings-in and goings-out of chaps. 18–20 indicates being outside the revelation, outside the sense of divine life. And the final consequence is that she is crying....Mary...seems embedded in her tears" (565).

the prediction of Jesus in 16:20a, "Very truly, I tell you, you will weep and mourn, but the world will rejoice." In fact, she is the only character of the Gospel who weeps and mourns when she "no longer sees" Jesus (cf. 16:19). As the story proceeds, the second half of Jesus' prediction will also be fulfilled: "you will have pain, but your pain will turn into joy" (16:20b, cf. also 16:22).[366] It is perhaps no coincidence that a woman fulfills this prediction, given the fact that Jesus uses the metaphor of childbirth to describe the human emotions that will accompany his death and resurrection (16:21).

Through her tears, Mary looks for herself to see what the tomb holds. Unlike the disciples, she sees two angels sitting at the head and feet of where Jesus had lain. The angels' question, γύναι, τί κλαίεις (v. 13), allows Mary to articulate once more the problem that is the driving force behind the narrative. This time her expression of concern becomes more personal, "They have taken away my Lord and I do not know where they have laid him." Notably, the angels address Mary as "woman." In this instance, the use of γύναι can certainly be explained as a polite form of address. Nevertheless, the title calls attention to Mary's gender and also recalls previous occurrences of γύναι in the Gospel. In this way, the ensuing encounter between Mary Magdalene and Jesus is situated in the context of earlier appearances between Jesus and women characters. This will be confirmed by Jesus' own use of this form of address in verse 15.

Upon answering the angels, Mary turns around and sees Jesus standing, but she does not yet recognize him (v. 14). There is no reason to speculate as to why she does not. Her lack of recognition adds drama to the story, much like the recognition story in Luke 24:13–35 (cf. also Jn 21:7, 12). In verse 15, Jesus repeats the question of the angels, including the address γύναι that occurs here for the last time in the Gospel. In this instance, his use of the form of address accomplishes several things. First, it contributes to the suspense of the recognition scene; Jesus addresses Mary as he would a stranger. Second, by opening the conversation with this more formal means of address, the Evangelist sets up a contrast with the presentation of Jesus' more intimate call to Mary in verse 16. Finally, based on the situations in which Jesus has used this title before, its appearance here hints at the revelation that is to come. This is the last time that Jesus will use γύναι in the Gospel.

---

[366]Cf. O'Day, 841.

Significantly, for the last time in the Gospel, a woman will once again be privy to the self-revelation of Jesus.

To the angels' question, Jesus adds one of his own, τίνα ζητεῖς (v. 15). This second question recalls the one Jesus asked the two disciples who followed him at the beginning of his ministry (τί ζητεῖτε, 1:38), although in Mary's case the question has been personalized.[367] In both scenes, the responses to Jesus are remarkably similar. The disciples of chapter one want to know where Jesus is staying. The disciple of chapter 20 is keenly interested in the whereabouts of Jesus' body.[368] To be sure, Mary's concern for the body indicates her ignorance about the resurrection, similar to that of the two disciples in verses 8b–9. At the same time, her concern for Jesus' whereabouts leads Jesus to articulate one of the major themes of the Gospel, namely, his return to the Father.

Mary's request to Jesus whom she supposes to be the gardener (cf. 19:41) indicates a final time her desire to find him and perhaps lay his body to rest (v. 15). It is this suggestion which leads to the moment of recognition. Jesus speaks one word to her, "Mary" (v. 16). This is the only place in the Gospel where Jesus refers to a female character with her proper name, and his doing so here conveys the intimacy of the moment.[369] Along this line, Grassi makes the interesting suggestion that

---

[367]Minear comments that Jesus' question "is fully in tune with the theme of seeking the redeemer which is so prominent in John (1:38; 5:44; 7:34, 36; 11:56; 12:20; 13:33; 18:4, 7, 8)" ("'We don't know where,' " 129).

[368]Mary's persistent seeking has been likened to the woman in Song of Songs who seeks her lover in the night (S of S 3:1–4). According to M. Cambre the two have in common: the night atmosphere; the triple searching; the question addressed to the watchmen (the same word as "gardener" in Hebrew); and taking hold of him and not being willing to let him go ("L'Influence du Cantique des Cantique sur le Nouveau Testament," *Revue Tômiste* 62 (1962): 5–26. Cf. also Feuillet, "La recherche du Christ dans la Nouvelle Alliance d'après la Christophanie de Jo 20, 11–18," in *L'homme devant Dieu* (Paris: Aubier, 1963) I, 93–112. Cited in Brown, 1010, 1052. Although I will argue that the heavy emphasis which is placed on Mary's holding on to Jesus distorts the reading of this passage, if the love song is part of the background of this story, it would add to the feeling of intimacy it evokes. Moreover, it would bring the gender identities of these two characters strongly to the fore.

[369]Even the use of male names is rare—Jesus refers to Philip in 14:9 and Simon Peter in 21:15–17. The use of μαριάμ instead of μαρία in 20:16 may be significant if it is intended to correspond to Mary's use of ῥαββουνί, since both are Semitic forms. However, as Brown points out, among the various witnesses there is a great fluctuation between the two names in all five of its occurrences in the Gospel (cf. 19:25, 20:1, 11, 16, 18), making it difficult to prove that this particular reference has special significance (990).

in her intimate relationship with Jesus, Mary Magdalene is a counterpart to the beloved disciple.[370] It is widely recognized that when Jesus calls Mary's name, it recalls the description of "his own" (τὰ ἴδια) in chapter 10. The shepherd "calls his own by name" and they follow him because they know his voice (10:3–4). So it is with Mary, who, upon hearing her name, turns and recognizes Jesus.

Mary responds to Jesus' call with only one word, ῥαββουνί, translated by the narrator as "teacher." Probably too much has been read into her use of the title at this point. Although it is not equivalent to the dramatic confession of Thomas that is to come (20:28), there is no reason to see Mary's use of "teacher" as an indication of her misunderstanding of Jesus.[371] She is simply using a familiar title and one that, as we have seen, Jesus himself has deemed appropriate (13:13). To be sure, the text provides no indication that she has full insight into who Jesus is. However, the mere fact that Jesus appears to her suggests that she has been given a privileged role in the narrative, regardless of her immediate level of understanding.

With this we come to the most perplexing part of the exchange between these two characters. Jesus' words to Mary in verse 17, μή μου ἅπτου, remain an enigma despite the concerted efforts of a great many interpreters.[372] The first problem is how best to translate the present imperative, μή μου ἅπτου. The durative force of the present imperative can imply that something already existing is to stop, and this is the way the majority of interpreters understand its function in v. 16.[373] If this is the case, the phrase implies that Mary has already touched Jesus in some way, and he is telling her to stop. The fact that the women in Matthew's

---

[370] Joseph A. Grassi, *The Secret Identity of the Beloved Disciple* (New York: Paulist Press, 1992), 85–90.

[371] So Bultmann, who argues that Mary's response shows that she does not yet fully know him. "She still misunderstands him, insofar as she thinks that he has simply 'come back' from the dead, and that he is again the man she knew as 'Teacher'; that is to say, she thinks the old relationship has been renewed" (687). Seim likewise argues, "Mary's responding address, ῥαββουνί does not correspond adequately. She sounds as if she has not yet adjusted to the new terms of relationship" ("Women in the Gospel of John," 66). Cf. also Brown, 1010; Barrett, 565; Lindars, 607.

[372] Brown provides a detailed note on the subject, listing a wide range of interpretive proposals, including the "utterly banal explanation that Jesus does not want to be touched because his wounds are still sore" (992).

[373] BDF §336.

Gospel expressly "take hold of" (κρατεῖν) Jesus' feet when he appears to them (28:9) gives additional support to this reading.

Critics who determine from Jesus' comment that Mary has touched Jesus, often go a step further and translate , μή μου ἅπτου as "stop clinging to me"[374] a translation which, as one would expect, does not bode well for Mary. She is pictured as "clinging" to Jesus in the hope that he will remain his earthly self. Her touch threatens to prevent Jesus from ascending and taking his rightful place next to the Father.[375] Slightly different is Minear's proposal that the phrase refers to Mary's desire to place the body of Jesus in a tomb. He notes further, "To restrain him in such a place would interfere with his mission, would place restrictions on his freedom of action."[376] Whether Mary is understood as clinging to Jesus or trying to entomb him, the power that this type of interpretation attributes to her is truly remarkable. Although Jesus has been in complete control of his actions throughout the Gospel, indeed has even risen from a tomb, now the mere touch of a woman is enough to keep him from ascending to the Father![377] Apart from Jesus' admonition, which can be interpreted in a number of ways, the text gives no certain indication that Mary is actually touching Jesus, let alone clinging to him.[378]

In fact, the text does not relate any action whatsoever on the part of Mary, which suggests that the importance of Jesus' statement is to be found not in what Mary is doing, but in the state Jesus claims to be in. In other words, the verse emphasizes the strange, "otherly" and divine nature of Jesus at this ultimate moment. After their intimate greeting, his words come not as a rebuke, but as a warning—"do not touch me." The warning is followed by an explanation, "for I have not yet ascended to the Father." Granted, this explanation is not at all clear, the "not yet" being especially problematic. The statement implies that Jesus is in some

---

[374]BAG, 102, cites the translation with a list of its supporters.

[375]In this regard, Seim views Jesus' words as a rebuke reminiscent of the one directed toward his mother in 2: 4 ("Women in the Gospel of John," 66).

[376]Minear, "'We don't know where,'" 130.

[377]Cf. Brown, however, who notes that she could not actually prevent him from ascending (1012). Regarding the assumptions behind this reading, the comment of Mary Rose D'Angelo is revealing, "the reading 'do not cling' appeals to and reinforces a common societal definition of women: women's love is dependent and holds men back from their true call" ("A Critical Note: John 20:17 and Apocalypse of Moses 21," *JTS* 41 [1990]: 531).

[378]Several of the later witnesses resolve this problem with the addition of "and she ran forth to take hold of him" at the end of v. 16.

sort of liminal state; he has risen from the dead, but has not yet ascended to the father. Though this is the most obvious reading, most commentators do not accept it.[379]

Nevertheless, it seems likely that the text should be taken to mean what most exegetes reluctantly admit it implies. As Mary Rose D'Angelo argues, "John 20:17 is concerned to emphasize exactly what many of the interpreters desire to explain away or in the case of Bultmann to deny: that the state of Jesus is different when he encounters Mary from when he meets the disciples and Thomas and invites Thomas' touch."[380] This does not mean that Mary is granted only "an inferior grade" appearance.[381] On the contrary, as D'Angelo rightly notes, "It is equally possible that the uniqueness of the appearance may award Mary a special status. Far from showing the inadequacy of Mary's faith, the story tends to confer on her a unique privilege in this encounter."[382]

If we allow the verse to be read this way, it coincides well with Jesus' next words, which express the most remarkable aspect of the encounter between these two characters. In verse 17, Jesus commissions Mary to go to his brothers and tell them, "I am ascending to my father and your father, to my God and your God." As Schneiders points out,

---

[379]Bultmann rejects the idea of a transitional stage and suggests that the οὔπω applies to Mary (687), a notion which Brown is also willing to accept (1012). Haenchen exonerates the Evangelist from such a view by arguing that he has relied on a "crude tradition" which he felt to be inappropriate, as seen in the fact that further conversation on the matter is cut short in favor of a commission (2.210). O'Day explains that the awkwardness of the verse stems from the necessity of giving "linear, narrative shape to something that transcends temporal categories" (842–843).

[380]D'Angelo finds support for her reading in a parallel passage in the *Apocalypse of Moses* 31.3–4, which portrays Adam instructing Eve, "let no one touch me" (μεδείς μου ἅψηται), at the time of his death. According to D'Angelo both passages call attention to the unique state of each character, and both describe a liminal period that occurs after death ("John 20:17," 535). Cf. also Wayne Meeks, "We can only observe that, since the fourth evangelist's dramatic compression of exaltation and crucifixion motifs into one has left the traditional Easter appearances in a kind of limbo, this strange statement imparts to that limbo a sacred liminality. Jesus is no longer in the world, but not yet ascended; he belongs to the intermediate zone that violates these categories and renders him untouchable" ("Man from Heaven," 66).

[381]Brown argues that this would be the implication if one accepted the reading of Jesus in a transitional state (1014).

[382]D'Angelo, "John 20:17," 535.

even without a detailed exegesis of this statement, it is clear that the message Jesus gives to Mary to proclaim is the Johannine kerygma.[383] The purpose of the incarnation has been accomplished; Jesus has given his disciples the power to become children of God (1:12) and for this reason he can now return to the father. Without hesitation, Mary Magdalene carries out her commission, going and announcing to the disciples, "I have seen the Lord," and delivering his message to them. Note that in doing so, she assumes the role of mediator which commentators typically attribute to the beloved disciple. Yet, as we have seen, only in chapter 21 does the beloved disciple actually function as a mediator so that what Mary does here is unique. That Jesus asks her to communicate to all of the disciples, accents the fact that he did not appear to Peter and the beloved disciple. Indeed, it is her testimony that prepares the way for the disciples to witness joyfully an appearance of the resurrected Christ (vv. 19–29).

All of this points to the significance of Mary's presence as "woman" in this resurrection scene. Like the women characters before her, she is closely associated with the hour of Jesus. Indeed, she is the only character in the Gospel to witness Jesus at this unique moment, the hour of his return to the Father. That the two male disciples are bypassed in favor of Mary at this point is highly significant. Indeed, the structure of the narrative suggests a deliberate juxtaposition between the men and woman in the story. Moreover, Mary is the only one in the gospel proper to receive a commission by the risen Christ; Jesus' commission to Peter occurs only in the appendix. In this way, the Gospel remains consistent; at its conclusion it is again a woman who plays a central role in receiving the self-revelation from Jesus and male disciples who serve as a contrast.[384] The portrayal of Mary Magdalene completes a pattern that has been woven throughout the Gospel. From the active presence of the mother of Jesus at the initiation of Jesus' hour of glory, to the presence of Mary Magdalene at its final moments, women have been witnesses to and participants in this hour's unfolding.

---

[383]Schneiders, "Women in the Fourth Gospel," 43.

[384]Contra Rena, who contends that the Beloved Disciple is superior to Mary Magdalene as a model of faith. According to him, although Mary is the first eyewitness of the risen Lord, she is not an ideal disciple because she must see before she believes ("Women in the Gospel of John," 144).

Conclusion: Peter, the Beloved Disciple and Mary Magdalene

If we consider what chapter 20:1–18 contributes to the characterization of Peter and the beloved disciple, we find that it essentially builds on their presentation earlier in the gospel narrative. Especially with respect to Peter, the scene offers no indication that he understands the significance of the empty tomb.[385] His last appearance in the gospel proper is in keeping with the impression of him that has been formed in the second half of the Gospel. Peter's dominant character trait remains his inability to understand Jesus. As for the beloved disciple, while this scene does not place him as decisively in a superior position to Peter and the other male disciples as does his appearance in chapter 13, he is still cast in a more favorable light. He is portrayed as first on the scene, before Peter, even if he does allow Peter to enter the tomb before him. Furthermore, the text relates the disciple's reaction to what he finds at the tomb, whereas nothing at all is said of Peter. If the disciples' role is to corroborate Mary's discovery, the beloved disciple's witness appears to hold more authority.

The comparison between the disciples in verses 3–10 is of little account however, when they are viewed together in relation to Mary Magdalene. Compared to Mary's experience at the tomb, the disciples' experience is decidedly lacking. They race to the tomb, find nothing but grave clothes, and return home no wiser than before, except that they are able to confirm what Mary told them. If 20:3–10 was added to an original story concerning only Mary, it suggests even more strongly that the two male disciples were intentionally placed in a secondary position to Mary. She lingers at the tomb, weeping and mourning the loss of Jesus. In contrast to the two disciples, and much like Martha and Mary of Bethany, her expressive devotion is rewarded. It is to her that the risen Jesus first appears.

---

[385] Along this line, Lindars contends that in the Evangelist's source it was Peter alone who went home wondering what had happened (602).

Conclusion

In the introduction to this study, I asked whether there was a difference between the way men and women are presented in the Fourth Gospel. The answer is a qualified yes. All five of the women, the mother of Jesus, the Samaritan woman, Martha and Mary of Bethany, and Mary Magdalene are presented in a positive light, but in the presentation of men there is no consistency. Three of the men, Nicodemus, Pilate and Peter, are presented negatively, in clear contrast to the women, but two of them, the man born blind, and the Beloved Disciple play positive roles. Indeed, the man born blind turns out to be the most outstanding character of all, second only to Jesus.

The mother of Jesus is characterized as a woman who, in spite of her son's harsh rebuke, is determined in her confidence that her son will act. What is striking about this first exchange of Jesus with a woman is that she contributes positively to the narrative, notwithstanding his negative reaction to her. The mother of Jesus initiates the action at the wedding at Cana, and in this way is instrumental in initiating Jesus' ministry. She sets him on the course towards his hour, and he goes on to reveal his glory to his disciples by performing his first sign. In this way, it appears that Jesus' mother knows better than he does what is expected of him as he takes the first major step in his earthly ministry. Indeed, the events in the narrative show the mother of Jesus closely aligned with the will of the Father. That she is designated γύναι by Jesus calls attention to her character as a woman, extending it beyond that of a mother. As the first woman in the narrative to interact with Jesus, she sets the pattern for the Johannine women who come after her.

Having appeared in the first major scene in Jesus' ministry, the mother of Jesus also appears in the last scene before his crucifixion. Along with other women she is present near the cross at the hour of Jesus' crucifixion, the ultimate revelation of his glory. Here, together with the Beloved Disciple, she plays a crucial role in the completion of Jesus' work on earth. Through them a new family of God is created, enabling the continuation of Jesus' ministry after his departure to the Father.

The Samaritan woman appears as the next female character in the Gospel. Her initial presentation draws attention to her supposedly inferior status in relation to Jesus as a woman and as a Samaritan. She is not deterred by her position, but readily takes up the conversation he initiates. Even more, as the discussion progresses she takes the initiative, bringing Jesus to a point at which he can reveal himself to her as the Messiah. This revelation is again explicitly connected to the notion of Jesus' hour when he reveals to her that the hour of true worship of the Father is here, manifested by his own presence and identity as the Messiah. That Jesus addresses her as γύναι recalls his address to his mother and the active role she took in chapter two. Like the mother of Jesus, the Samaritan woman also assumes an active role in Jesus' work. She is the one on whom success in her village depends. As Jesus' mother had been instrumental in bringing about the first manifestation of Jesus' glory, the Samaritan woman is instrumental in bringing the Samaritan villagers to him. In doing so, she becomes Jesus' co-worker, contributing in a significant way to his mission. She thus demonstrates that she too is closely aligned with the will of God.

With Martha and Mary of Bethany, the positive presentation of women continues. Like the Samaritan woman before her, Martha readily engages in a theological conversation with Jesus, enabling him to reveal himself to her as the resurrection and life. She responds by offering a complete confession of his messianic identity. Her confession is unmatched by any other in the Gospel, and is allowed to stand alone as a fitting conclusion to the conversation. In addition, it is Jesus' dialogue with her that provides the interpretive lens through which we are to view the raising of Lazarus.

Mary's role in the narrative takes place more through action than through words. She weeps in sorrow at the feet of Jesus, who responds by turning his attention to the tomb and the sign he will perform there. Mary leads the Jews to the tomb to witness the raising of Lazarus, and as a result many of them come to belief in Jesus. Additionally, Mary of Bethany is presented in intimate devotion to Jesus as she anoints his feet with oil, and wipes his feet with her hair. Although she does not speak in 12:1–12, it is highly significant that Jesus comes to her defense before the protesting Judas by interpreting her actions as preparation for his death. In this way, Mary too is linked to his approaching hour.

Finally, bringing to a climactic conclusion the crucial roles played by women in the narrative, Mary Magdalene expresses her emotions openly at Jesus' empty tomb. Her abiding presence there is rewarded in an unprecedented way when she becomes the first to experience the joy which Jesus promised to the disciples in 16:20–21. Her characterization is not restricted to being the first to witness the resurrected Jesus; he commissions her to bring news of his ascension to the other disciples, which she immediately does. What makes Mary's role at the empty tomb all the more remarkable is that Peter and the Beloved Disciple, even though they rushed to the tomb upon hearing from her that it was empty, do not encounter the risen Christ.

Thus, throughout the Fourth Gospel women are presented in incomparably positive ways as persons who are closely linked to the self-revelation of Jesus and to the coming of his hour. Moreover, the narrative calls attention to their gender in various ways, for example, by the repeated use of γύναι, and by juxtaposing them with male characters—Nicodemus with the Samaritan woman, Mary of Bethany with Judas, Mary Magdalene with the Beloved Disciple and Peter, and perhaps Martha with Peter. This suggests that being female is not coincidental, but a key element in the construction of their characters and in the composition of the Gospel narrative.

When we consider the male characters a different pattern emerges. Nicodemus starts off with self-assurance, confident in what he knows about Jesus, but by the end of his first appearance it becomes clear that his primary feature is ignorance. He is scoffed at by Jesus and then simply fades from the scene. In subsequent appearances the weakness of Nicodemus' character is confirmed, even though, as in his first appearance, he seems intent on showing favor towards Jesus. Most telling is that he never takes the bold step of confession, nor does Jesus offer to him a clear statement of his own identity as he does, for example, to the Samaritan woman, to Martha, and to the man born blind. As a result, Nicodemus' commitment to Jesus remains ambivalent at best.

Peter, too, is a weak character who, like Nicodemus, has the best of intentions, but repeatedly misses the mark in his interactions with Jesus. When he appears with the Beloved Disciple, the latter overshadows him; when he appears alone, he does not fare much better. His most positive moment comes early, in 6:60–71, when as spokesperson for the disciples, he offers a confession of Jesus as the Holy One of God. Not only does the use of this particular title raise questions—e.g. why does he not voice the messianic confession traditionally attributed to him— Peter's confession is eclipsed by Jesus' disclosure that there is a devil among them. After this appearance, Peter's characterization takes a downward slide. In chapter 13, he first refuses Jesus' proposal to wash his feet, and then, when he is corrected by Jesus, he over-compensates by demanding more than what is necessary. At the farewell meal Peter has no direct access to Jesus, but must rely on the beloved disciple as an intermediary. In chapter eighteen, he rashly attempts a violent defense in the garden, which Jesus interprets as interference with his mission. Next he denies his discipleship of Jesus three times, at a time as when Jesus is defending himself before the high priest. In chapter 20, Peter observes the empty tomb and burial linens, but comes to no clear understanding of their significance. Only in chapter 21 do we find a more positive characterization of him. The way he is presented in the epilogue to the Gospel stands in sharp contrast to his previous portrayal. It appears as an attempt to compensate for the way he is characterized in the Gospel proper.

Pilate too is presented in a decidedly negative light. He shows little regard for justice and, more significantly, shows no interest in the truth when it is standing before him. He postures himself as the powerful judge, but in the end becomes the one who is judged. In handing Jesus over to the Jews, he aligns himself with the opposition.

In sharp contrast to these three male characters is the man born blind. Indeed, he is a character who stands apart from all the other characters, male or female. He is the most fully developed of them all, showing clear progression in the narrative as he moves from a mere object of debate to a clever, witty and bold figure. Unlike any other character, the man born blind comes to faith not primarily through conversation with Jesus, but in his confrontation with the Jews. In doing so, he assumes a role similar to Jesus himself. He starts off being judged by the Jews and in the end confidently puts them under judgment. The man's confession of faith in Jesus at the end of the narrative signals the extent to which his character has developed; he becomes a person with true insight into the identity of Jesus. Moreover, it is his insight that, with irony, exposes the blindness of Jesus' opponents.

Finally, the Beloved Disciple, too, is presented positively, as a person who has intimate access to Jesus. Like the mother of Jesus, his defining characteristic is his relationship with Jesus. Moreover, as we have seen, his position alongside the mother of Jesus at the foot of the cross is crucial for the completion of Jesus' earthly mission and the continuation of his ministry after his departure to the Father. On the other hand, both at the farewell meal and at the empty tomb he functions primarily to place Peter in a secondary position, without a great deal of personal significance. In the empty tomb scene his superior position in relationship to Peter is attenuated by Mary Magdalene as the one to whom the resurrected Jesus appears. In the end he appears as an enigmatic figure.

Taken together, what do these ten characters suggest about the author's characterization of men and women in the Gospel? To put it concisely, all five women are consistently presented positively, in contrast to three of the male characters, Nicodemus, Peter and Pilate. This suggests that, contrary to the predominant interpretation, the purpose of the positive characterization of Johannine women cannot be to present them as equal disciples with the men in the Gospel. Regarding these three male characters, the women are clearly superior to the men. That this nevertheless does not represent an anti-male attitude or a gender dualism in the Gospel is shown by the portrayal of the man born blind and to a lesser degree by the beloved disciple. One can only surmise that there is something more than gender involved in the positive characterization of the women in the Gospel.

In sum, at the end of this investigation we are left with a clear answer concerning the positive characterization of women in the Fourth Gospel, but also with a new question regarding the positive presentation of two male characters. Are the anonymous characters of the man born blind and the beloved disciple intentionally presented as figures without ties to established authority? Is this what they share with the women in the Gospel? If this is the case, it may or may not be good news from a feminist perspective. On the negative side, it may imply that the positive presentation of Johannine women depends on a presupposition that women stand outside the bounds of recognized structures of authority. On the positive side, the Gospel may be viewed as a polemic against the "world," not only in the sense of those who reject Jesus, but also of precisely those recognized structures.

In chapter one, I mentioned a questions posed by John Rena in his article on Johannine women, namely, is the author of the Gospel "worried about authority figures?" From a more radical perspective, it may be that the Fourth Evangelist is presenting a challenge to these authority figures through the characterization of men and women in the Gospel.

List of Abbreviations

AB	Anchor Bible
BAG	W. Bauer, *A Greek-English Lexicon of the New Testament* (Translated by W. F. Arndt and F. W. Gingrich, revised by Gingrich and F. W. Danker from Bauer's 5th ed; Chicago: University of Chicago Press, 1979).
BETL	Bibliotheca ephemeridum theologicarum lovaniensium
BDF	F. Blass and A. Debrunner, A Greek Grammar of the New Testament and Other Early Christian Literature. Translated and revised by Robert W. Funk (Chicago: University of Chicago Press, 1961).
Bib	*Biblica*
BRev	*Bible Review*
BibT	*Bible Today*
BJRL	*Bulletin of the John Rylands Library*
BTB	*Biblical Theological Bulletin*
CBQ	*Catholic Biblical Quarterly*
ConB	Coniectanea biblica
EgT	*Église et Théologie*
ExpTim	*Expository Times*
EvT	*Evangelishe Theologie*
FC	Fathers of the Church
FS	*Feminist Studies*
HeyJ	*Heythrop Journal*
Int	*Interpretation*
JAAR	*Journal of the American Academy of Religion*
JBL	*Journal of Biblical Literature*
JEH	*Journal of Ecclesiastical History*
JEvThS	*Journal of the Evangelical Theology Society*
JFSR	*Journal of Feminist Studies in Religion*
JLT	*Journal of Literature and Theology*
JR	*Journal of Religion*
LV	*Lumière & Vie*
Neot	*Neotestamentica*
NovT	*Novum Testamentum*
NTS	*New Testament Studies*
ResQ	*Restoration Quarterly*
RB	*Revue Biblique*

RelIntel	*Religion and Intellectual Life*
RelLi	*Religion in Life*
RelStB	*Religious Studies Bulletin*
RelSRev	*Religious Studies Review*
SBLDS	Society of Biblical Literature Dissertation Series
SBLSP	Society of Biblical Literature Seminar Papers
Str.-B	H. L. Strack and P. Billerbeck, *Kommentar zum NT aus Talmud und Midrasch*, 4 vols. 1922, 1924, 1926, 1928.
ST	*Studia Theologica*
TextsS	Texts and Studies
TToday	*Theology Today*
TRu	*Theologische Rundschau*
TS	*Theological Studies*
WUNT	Wissenschafliche Untersuchungen zum Neuen Testament
WW	*Word & World*
USQR	*Union Seminary Quarterly Review*
ZNW	*Zeitschrift für die Neutestamentiche Wissenschaft*
ZwZ	*Zwischen den Zeiten*

Bibliography

Abel, E. "Editor's Introduction," *Critical Inquiry* 8 (1981): 3-7.

Alter, Robert. *The Art of Biblical Narrative.* New York: Basic, 1981.

Anderson, Janice Capel. "Mapping Feminist Biblical Criticism: The American Scene, 1983–1990," Critical Review of Books in Religion. 1991:21–44.

_____. "Matthew: Gender and Reading," *Semeia* 28 (1983): 3–27.

_____. "Mary's Difference: Gender and Patriarchy in the Birth Narratives." *JR* 67 (1987): 183–203.

_____. "Feminist Criticism: The Dancing Daughter." In *Mark and Method: New Approaches in Biblical Studies.* Edited by Janice Capel Anderson and Stephen D. Moore. Minneapolis: Fortress Press, 1992.

Ashton, John. *Understanding the Fourth Gospel.* Oxford: Clarendon, 1991.

Ashton, John, ed. *The Interpretation of John.* Issues in Religion and Theology 9. Philadelphia: Fortress Press, 1986.

St Augustine: Tractates on the Gospel of John 112–24 . FC 92. John W. Rettig, trans. Washington, D.C.: The Catholic University of America Press, 1995.

Bar-Efrat, Shimon. *Narrative Art in the Bible.* Bible and Literature Series 17; Sheffield: Almond Press, 1989.

Barrett, C. K. *The Gospel According to John: An Introduction with Commentary and Notes on the Greek Text.* 2nd ed. Philadelphia: Westminster, 1978.

_____. *The New Testament Background: Selected Documents* , revised edition. San Francisco: Harper and Row, 1989.

Bass, Dorothy C. "Women's Studies and Biblical Studies: An Historical Perspective," *JSOT* 22 (1982): 6–12.

Bassler, Jouette. "Mixed Signals: Nicodemus in the Fourth Gospel," *JBL* 108 (1989): 635–646.

Bauckham, Richard. "The Beloved Disciple as Ideal Author," *JSNT* 49 (1993): 37.

Baur, Ferdinand Christian. "Uber die Komposition und den Charakter des johanneischen Evangeliums," *Theologische Jahrbücher* 3 (1844): 1–191, 397–475, 615–700.

―――. *Kritischen Untersuchungen über die kanonischen Evangelien, ihr Verhältniß zueinander, ihren Charakter und Ursprung.* Tübingen,1847.

Beardslee, William A. *Literary Criticism of the New Testament* . Philadelphia: Fortress Press, 1969. Beasley-Murray, George R. *John.* Word Biblical Commentary 36. David A. Hubbard, Glenn W. Barker, eds; Waco, TX: Word Books, 1987.

Beck, David R. "The Narrative Function of Anonymity in Fourth Gospel Characterization," *Semeia* 63 (1993): 143–158.

Becker, H. *Die Reden des Johannesevangeliums und der Stil der gnostischen Offenbarungsreden.* Göttingen: Vandenhoeck, 1956.

Becker, Jürgen. "Aus der Literatur zum Johannesevangelium (1978– 1980)," *TRu* 47 (1982): 279–301, 305–47.

―――. "Das Johannesevanglium im Streit der Methoden (1980– 1984)." *TRu* 51 (1986): 1–78.

Berlin, Adele *Poetics and Interpretation of Biblical Narrative.* Bible and Literature 9. Sheffield: Almond Press, 1983.

Bird, Phyllis. "Images of Women in the Old Testament." In *Religion and Sexism: Images of Woman in the Jewish and Christian Traditions.* Edited by Rosemary Radford Ruether. New York: Simon and Schuster, 1974.

Blass F., and A. Debrunner, *A Greek Grammar of the New Testament and Other Early Christian Literature.* Translated and revised by Robert W. Funk. Chicago: University of Chicago Press, 1961.

Bligh, John. "Jesus in Samaria," *HeyJ* 3 (1962): 329–346.

―――. "Four Studies in St John, II: Nicodemus," *HeyJ* 8 (1967): 40– 51.

Boers, Hendrikus. *Neither this Mountain Nor in Jerusalem: A Study of John 4.* SBL Monograph Series 35. Atlanta: Scholars Press, 1988.

Boismard, Marie-Emile. "L'Evolution du Thème Eschatologique dans les Traditions Johanniques," *RB* 68 (1961): 507–524.

―――. *L'Evangile de Jean* . Synopse des Quartres Evangiles en français, ed. M.-E. Boismard and A. Lamouille. Paris: Cerf, 1977.

Bowen, C. "The Fourth Gospel as Dramatic Material," *JBL* 49 (1930): 292–305.

Bratcher, R. J. " 'The Jews' in the Gospel of John," *The Bible Translator* 26 (1975): 401–409.

Braun, F. M. *La Mère des fidèles: Essai de théologie johannique.* Tournai-Paris, 1954.

Brenner Athalya and Fokkelien van Dijk-Hemmes. *On Gendering Texts: Female and Male Voices in the Hebrew Bible.* Leiden: E. J. Brill, 1993.

Bretschneider, Karl. *Probabilia de evangelii et epistolarum Joannis Apostoli indole et origine* [Probabilities concerning the nature and origin of the Gospel and Epistles of John] Leipzig, 1920. First published in J. Ricker'sche Buchhandlund (1889): 41–73.

Brodie, Thomas L. *The Gospel According to John: A Literary and Theological Commentary.* New York: Oxford University Press, 1993.

_____. *The Quest for the Origin of John's Gospel.* New York: Oxford University Press, 1993.

Brooke, A. E. *The Fragments of Heracleon.* Texts and Studies 1. Cambridge: Cambridge University Press, 1896.

Brooten, Bernedette. *Women Leaders in the Ancient Synagogue.* Brown Judaic Studies 36. Chico, CA: Scholars Press, 1982.

Brown, Raymond. E. *The Gospel According to John.* 2 Vols. New York: Doubleday, 1970.

_____. "Roles of Women in the Fourth Gospel," *TS* 36 (1975): 688–699.

_____. *The Community of the Beloved Disciple.* New York: Paulist, 1979.

Brown, Raymond E., Karl Donfield, and John Reumann, eds. *Peter in the Fourth Gospel.* New York: Paulist, 1973.

Bultmann, Rudolf. "Der religionsgeschichtliche Hintergrund des Prologs zum Johannes-Evangelium." In *Eucharistērion: Studien zur Religion und Literatur des Alten und Neuen Testament.* (Göttingen: Vandenhoeck & Ruprecht, 1923) 3–26.

_____. "Die Bedeutung der neuerschlossenen mandäischen und manichäischen Quellen für das Verständnis des Johannesvangeliums," *ZNW* 24 (1925): 100–146.

_____. "Die Eschatologie des Johannesevangelium," *ZwZ* (1928): 4–22.

_____. "Untersuchungen zum Johannesevangelium." *ZNW* 27 (1928): 113–163.

———. *Die Reden des Johannesevangeliums und der Stil der gnostischen Offenbarungsreden.* Göttingen: Vandenhoeck, 1956.

———. *The Gospel of John: A Commentary.* Trans. by G.R. Beasley-Murray. Philadelphia: Westminster, 1971.

Butler, Judith. *Gender Trouble: Feminism and the Subversion of Identity* New York: Routledge, 1990.

———. *Bodies that Matter: On the Discursive Limits of 'Sex'* New York: Routledge, 1993.

Bynum, Caroline Walker, Stevan Harrel, and Paula Richman, eds. *Gender and Religion: On the Complexity of Symbols.* Boston: Beacon Press, 1986.

Byrne, Brendan J. "The Faith of the Beloved Disciple and the Community in John 20," *JSNT* 23 (1985): 83–97.

Cahill, Lisa Sowle. *Sex, Gender and Christian Ethics.* Cambridge/New York: Cambridge University Press, 1996.

Cahill, P. Joseph. "Narrative Art in John IV," *RelStB* 2 (1982): 41–48.

Cambre, M. "L'Influence du Cantique des Cantique sur le Nouveau Testament," *Revue Thomiste* 62 (1962): 5–26.

Camp, Claudia. *Wisdom and the Feminine in the Book of Proverbs* Sheffield: JSOT Press, 1985.

Cantarella, Eva, *Pandora's Daughters: The Role and Status of Women in Greek and Roman Antiquity.* Baltimore: John Hopkins University Press, 1987.

Carmichael, Calum M. "Marriage and the Samaritan Woman," *NTS* 26 (1980): 332–346.

Chavel, C. B. :The Releasing of a Prisoner on the Eve of Passover in Ancient Jerusalem,: *JBL* 60 (1941): 273–278.

Charlesworth, James. "Reinterpreting John: How the Dead Sea Scrolls Have Revolutionized Our Understanding of the Gospel of John," *BRev* 9 (1993): 18–25.

Charlesworth, James and Raymond Brown, eds. *John and the Dead Sea Scrolls* . New York: Crossroad, 1990.

Chatman, Seymour. *Story and Discourse: Narrative Structure in Fiction and Film.* Ithaca: Cornell University Press, 1978.

Clark, Elizabeth. "Theory and Practice in Late Ancient Asceticism: Jerome, Chrysostom, and Augustine," *JFSR* 5 (1989): 25–46.

Collier, Peter and Helga Geyer-Ryan, eds. *Literary Theory Today.* New York: Cornell University Press, 1990.

Collins, Adela Yarbro, ed. *Feminist Perspectives on Biblical Scholarship*. Chico, CA: Scholars Press, 1985.

Collins, Patricia. *Black Feminist Thought: Knowledge, Consciousness, and the Politics of Empowerment*. New York: Routledge, 1991.

Collins, Raymond. "Mary in the Fourth Gospel: A Decade of Johannine Studies." *Louvain Studies* 3 (1970): 99–142.

_____. "The Representative Figures of the Fourth Gospel," *Downside Review* 94 (1976): 26–46; 95 (1976): 118–32. Reprinted in *These Things Have Been Written*. Louvain Theological & Pastoral Monographs 2. Grand Rapids: Eerdmans, 1991.

_____. "Jesus' Conversation with Nicodemus." In *These Things Having Been Written*. Louvain Theological & Pastoral Monographs 2. Grand Rapids: Eerdmans, 1991. First published in *BibT* 93 (1977): 1409–1419.

_____. *These Things Have Been Written: Studies on the Fourth Gospel*. Louvain Theological & Pastoral Monographs 2. Grand Rapids: Eerdmans, 1991.

_____. "From John to the Beloved Disciple: An Essay on Johannine Characters," *Int* 49 (1995): 359–369.

Connick, C. M. "The Dramatic Character of the Fourth Gospel," *JBL* 67 (1948): 159–169.

Conway, Jill K., Susan C. Bourque, and Joan W. Scott. "Introduction: The Concept of Gender," *Dædalus* (1987): XXI–XXX.

Cornillon, Susan Koppelman, ed. *Images of Women in Fiction: Feminist Perspectives*. Bowling Green, OH: Bowling Green University Popular Press, 1972.

Cotterell, F. B. "The Nicodemus Conversation: A Fresh Appraisal." *ExpTim* 96 (1985): 237–242.

Cullman, Oscar. *The Johannine Circle*. Philadelphia: Westminster, 1976.

Culpepper, R. Alan. *The Johannine School: An Evaluation of the Johannine School Hypothesis Based on an Investigation of the Nature of Ancient Schools*. Missoula: Scholars Press, 1975.

_____. *Anatomy of the Fourth Gospel: A Study in Literary Design*. Philadelphia: Fortress Press, 1983.

D'Angelo, Mary Rose. "A Critical Note: John 20:17 and Apocalypse of Moses 21," *JTS* 41(1990): 529–536.

Daly, Mary. *Beyond God the Father: Toward a Philosophy of Women's Liberation*. Boston: Beacon, 1973.

Darr, John. *On Character Building: The Reader and the Rhetoric of Characterization in Luke-Acts* . Louisville: Westminster, 1992.

Daube, David. "Jesus and the Samaritan Woman: The Meaning of sugcravomai," *JBL* 69 (1950): 137–147.

Davies, Margaret. *Rhetoric and Reference in the Fourth Gospel*. JSNT Supplement Series 69. Sheffield: JSOT, 1992.

Day, Peggy. ed. *Gender and Difference in Ancient Israel*. Minneapolis: Fortress Press, 1989.

de Beauvoir, Simone. *The Second Sex*. New York: Knopf, 1953.

de Boer, Martinus C. "John 4:27 - Women (and Men) in the Gospel and the Community of John." In *Women in the Biblical Tradition* . Studies in Women and Religion, no. 31. The Edwin Mellen Press, 1992.

de Jonge, Marinus. "Nicodemus and Jesus: Some Observations on Misunderstanding and Understanding in the Fourth Gospel." In *Jesus: Stranger from Heaven and Son of God, Jesus and the Christians in Johannine Perspective*. Missoula: Scholars Press, 1977. First published in *BJRL* 53 (1971): 337–359.

———. *Jesus: Stranger from Heaven and Son of God*. Missoula: Scholars Press, 1977.

de Lauretis, Teresa. *Technologies of Gender: Essays on Theory, Film, and Fiction*. Bloomington: Indiana University Press, 1987.

Docherty, Thomas. *Reading (Absent) Character: Toward a Theory of Characterization in Fiction*. Oxford: Clarendon Press, 1983.

Dodd, C. H. *The Interpretation of the Fourth Gospel*. Cambridge: Cambridge University Press, 1953, reprinted 1992.

———. "The Portrait of Jesus in John and in the Synoptics." In *Christian History and Interpretation*. Cambridge: Cambridge University Press, 1967.

Dollar, Stephen. "The Significance of Women in the Fourth Gospel," Unpublished Th.D. diss. New Orleans Baptist Theological Seminary, 1983.

Droge, Arthur J. "The Status of Peter in the Fourth Gospel," *JBL* 109 (1990): 307–311.

du Rand, J. A. "The Characterization of Jesus as Depicted in the Narrative of the Fourth Gospel," Neot 19 (1985): 18–36.

Duke, Paul D. *Irony in the Fourth Gospel*. Atlanta: John Knox, 1985.

Dunn, James D. G. "Let John Be John: A Gospel for Its Time." In *Das Evangelium und die Evangelien*. Tübingen: J. C. B. Mohr (Paul Siebeck), 1983.

_____. *Christology in the Making: An Inquiry into the Origins of the Doctrine of the Incarnation*, 2d ed. London: SCM Press, 1989.

Eagleton, Mary. *Feminist Literary Criticism*. London: Longman Press, 1991.

Eslinger, Lyle. "The Wooing of the Woman at the Well: Jesus, The Reader and Reader-Response Criticism," *JLT* 1 (1987): 167–183.

Eusebius, *Ecclesiastical History*, III.28. Fathers of the Church 19; New York, 1953.

Feuillet, André. *Johannine Studies*. New York: Alba House, 1964.

_____. *Jesus and His Mother: The Role of the Virgin Mary in Salvation History and the Place of Woman in the Church*. Still River, MA: St. Bede's Publications, 1984.

Fewell, Danna Nolan. "Reading the Bible Ideologically: Feminist Criticism." In *To Each Its Own Meaning: An Introduction to Biblical Criticisms and their Application*. Edited by Steven McKenzie and Stephen Haynes. Louisville: Westminster/John Knox Press, 1993.

Fewell, Danna Nolan and David M. Gunn. *Gender, Power, and Promise: The Subject of the Bible's First Story*. Nashville: Abingdon Press, 1993.

Finger, Rita Halterman. "Feminist Biblical Interpretation," *Daughters of Sarah* 15 (1989): 4–21.

Flanagan, N. "The Gospel of John as Drama," *BibT* 19 (1981): 264–270.

Forster, E. M. *Aspects of the Novel*. New York: Penguin Books, 1962.

Forsås-Scott, Helena, ed. *Textual Liberation: European Feminist Writing in the Twentieth Century*. London: Routledge, 1991.

Fortna, Robert. *The Gospel of Signs: A Reconstruction of the Narrative Source Underlying the Fourth Gospel*. Cambridge: Cambridge University Press, 1970.

Funk, Robert W. *The Poetics of Biblical Narrative*. Sonoma: Polebridge Press, 1988.

Galef, David. *The Supporting Cast: A Study of Flat and Minor Characters*. University Park, PA: Pennsylvania State University Press, 1993.

Gallop, Jane. *Around 1981: Academic Feminist Literary Theory*. New York: Routledge, 1992.

Gardner-Smith, Percival. *Saint John and the Synoptics*. Cambridge: Cambridge University Press, 1938.

Garrett, Susan. "Revelation." In *The Women's Bible Commentary*. Louisville: Westminster/John Knox, 1992.

Gass, William. *Fiction and the Figures of Life*. New York: Knopf, 1970.

Genette, Gérard. *Narrative Discourse Revisited*. Translated by Jane E. Lewin. Ithaca: Cornell University Press, 1988.

———. *Narrative Discourse: An Essay in Method*. Translated by Jane E. Lewin. Ithaca: Cornell University Press, 1980.

Gibbons, Debbie. "Nicodemus: Character Development, Irony and Repetition in the Fourth Gospel." In *Proceedings: Eastern Great Lakes and Midwest Biblical Societies* 11 (1991) 116–128.

Goblin, Charles H. "Suggestion, Negative Response, and Positive Action in St. John's Portrayal of Jesus," *NTS* 26 (1980): 197–211.

———. "Mary's Anointing for Jesus' Burial-Resurrection (John 12:1–8)," *Bib* 3 (1992): 560–564.

Gifford, Carolyn De Swarte. "American Women and the Bible: The Nature of Woman as a Hermeneutical Issue." In *Feminist Perspectives on Biblical Scholarship*. Edited by Adela Yarbro Collins. Chico, CA: Scholars Press, 1985.

Gilbert, Sandra and Susan Grubar. *The Madwoman in the Attic*. New Haven: Yale University Press, 1979.

Grassi, Joseph A. "The Role of Jesus' Mother in John's Gospel: A Reappraisal," *CBQ* 48 (1986): 67–80.

———. *The Secret Identity of the Beloved Disciple*. New York: Paulist Press, 1992.

Gunn, David M. and Danna Nolan Fewell, *Narrative in the Hebrew Bible*. Oxford: Oxford University Press, 1993.

Gunther, J. J. "Early Identifications of Authorship of the Johannine Writings," *JEH* 31 (1980): 407–427.

Haenchen, Ernst. *A Commentary on the Gospel of John*, 2 vols. Hermeneia, Philadelphia: Fortress, 1984. German original, *Das Johannesevangelium*. Tübingen: Mohr, 1980.

Harvey, W. J. *Character and the Novel*. Ithaca, NY: Cornell University Press, 1966.

Hengel, Martin. "Maria Magdalena und die Frauen als Zeugen." In *Abraham unser Vater*. Festshrift for Otto Michel. Leiden, 1963.

_____. *The Johannine Question* . Philadelphia: Trinity Press International, 1989.

Hitchcock, F. R. M. *A Fresh Study of the Fourth Gospel*. London: SPCK, 1911.

_____. "Is the Fourth Gospel a Drama?" *Theology* 7 (1923): 307–17.

Hochman, Baruch. *Character in Literature*. Ithaca: Cornell University Press, 1985.

hooks, bell. *Feminist Theory: From Margin to Center*. Boston: South End Press, 1985.

Hosykns, E. C. *The Fourth Gospel*. London: Farber & Farber, 1947.

Howard, W. F. *The Fourth Gospel in Recent Criticism and Interpretation*. Revised by C. K. Barrett. London: Epworth, 1955.

Hultgren J. Arland, "The Johannine Footwashing (13:1–11) as Symbol of Eschatological Hospitality," *NTS* 28 (1982) 539–546.

Humm, Maggie. "Feminist Literary Criticism in America and England." In *Women's Writing: A Challenge to Theory*. Edited by Moiré Monteith. Sussex: Harvester Press, 1986.

_____. *Women as Contemporary Critics*. Sussex: Harvester Press, 1986.

Irenaeus, *Against the Heresies*. Ancient Christian Writers. New York: Paulist Press, 1992.

Jehlen, Myra. "Archimedes and the Paradox of Feminist Criticism," *Signs: Journal of Women in Culture and Society* 6 (1981): 575–601.

_____. "Gender." In *Critical Terms for Literary Study*. Edited by Frank Lentricchia and Thomas McLaughlin. Chicago: University of Chicago Press, 1990.

Kaestle, J. D., J. M. Poffet, and J. Zumstein, eds. *La Communauté johannique et son histoire: la trajectoire de l'évangile de Jean aux deux preimers siècles*. Geneva: Labor et Fides, 1990.

Käsemann, Ernst. *The Testament of Jesus: A Study of the Gospel of John in Light of Chapter 17*. London: SCM Press, 1968.

Keck, E. K. "The Drama of the Fourth Gospel," *ExpTim* 65 (1953): 173–176.

Keohane, Nanner O., Michelle Z. Rosaldo, and Barbara C. Gelpi, eds. *Feminist Theory: A Critique of Ideology.* Chicago: University of Chicago Press, 1981.

Kilmartin, E. J. "The Mother of Jesus Was There. (The Significance of Mary in Jn 2:3–5 and Jn 19:25–27)," *Sciences Ecclésiastique* 15 (1963): 213–226.

King, J. S. "Nicodemus and the Pharisees," *ExpT* 98 (1986): 45.

King, Ursula, ed. *Gender and Religion.* Cambridge, MA: Basil Blackwell, 1995.

Koester, Helmut. "The History-of-Religions School, Gnosis, and the Gospel of John," *Studia Theologica* 40 (1986): 115–135.

Kolodny, Annette. "Some Notes on Defining a 'Feminist Literary Criticism,'" *Critical Inquiry* 2 (1975): 75-92.

———. "Dancing through the Minefield: Some Observations on the Theory, Practice, and Politics of a Feminist Literary Criticism," *FS* 6 (1980): 3–25.

———. "A Map for Rereading: Or, Gender and the Interpretation of Literary Texts," *New Literary History* 11 (1980): 451–467.

———. "Turning the Lens on "The Panther Captivity": A Feminist Exercise in Practical Criticism," *Critical Inquiry* 8 (1981): 329–345.

Kopas, Jane. "Jesus and Women: John's Gospel," *TToday* 41 (1984): 201–205.

Kraemer, Ross. "Hellenistic Jewish Women: The Epigraphical Evidence," *SBLSP* (1986): 183–200.

Krafft, Eva. "Die Personen des Johannesevangeliums," *EvT* 16 (1956): 18-32.

Krieger, Murray. *A Window to Criticism: Shakespeare's Sonnets and Modern Poetics.* Princeton, NJ: Princeton University Press, 1964.

Kurz, William S. "The Beloved Disciple and Implied Readers," *BTB* 19 (1989): 100–107.

Kümmel, Werner Georg. *The New Testament: The History of the Investigation of Its Problems.* Nashville: Abingdon, 1970.

Kysar, Robert. *The Fourth Evangelist and His Gospel: An Examination of Contemporary Scholarship.* Minneapolis: Augsburg Publishing House, 1975.

———. "The Gospel of John in Current Research," *RelSRev* 9 (1983): 314–23.

_____. "The Fourth Gospel: A Report on the Current Research," *Aufstieg und Niedergang der Romanischen Welt II*, 25.3. Berlin: Walter de Gruyter, 1985.

_____. *John*, ACNT. Minneapolis: Augsburg, 1985.

_____. *John: the Maverick Gospel*. Rev. ed. Louisville: Westminster/ John Knox Press, 1993.

Laqueur, Thomas. *Making Sex: Body and Gender from the Greeks to Freud* Harvard University Press, 1990.

Lee, Dorothy A. "Partnership in Easter Faith: The Role of Mary Magdalene and Thomas in John 20," *JSNT* 58 (1995) 37–49.

Lemonon, Jean-Pierre. "Chronique Johannique (1981–1992)," *Lumière & Vie* 41 (1992): 95–104.

Levine, Amy-Jill. ed. *"Women Like This" New Perspectives on Jewish Women in the Greco-roman World*. Atlanta: Scholars Press, 1991.

Lindars, Barnabus. *The Gospel of John*. New Century Bible. London: Oliphants, 1972.

_____. *Behind the Fourth Gospel*. London: SPCK, 1971.

Love, Stuart L. "Women's Roles in Certain Second Testament Passages: A Macrosociological View," *BTB* 17 (1987): 50–59.

_____. "The Household: A Major Social Component for Gender Analysis in the Gospel of Matthew." *BTB* 23 (1993): 21–31.

Lüthi, Walter. *St. John's Gospel: An Exposition*. Richmond: John Knox, 1960.

MacRae, G. W. "Theology and Irony in the Fourth Gospel." In *The Word in the World: Essays in honour of F. K. Moriarty*, ed. F. J. Clifford and G. W. MacRae. Cambridge, MA: Weston College, 1973.

Mahoney, Robert. *Two Disciples at the Tomb: The Background and Message of John 20:1–10*. Theologie und Wirklichkeit 6. Frankfurt: Peter Lang, 1974.

Malbon, Elizabeth Struthers. "Fallible Followers: Women and Men in the Gospel of Mark," *Semeia* 28 (1983): 29-48.

_____. "Narrative Criticism: How Does the Story Mean?" In *Mark and Method: New Approaches in Biblical Scholarship*. Minneapolis: Augsburg Fortress Press, 1992.

Malbon, Elizabeth Struthers and Elizabeth Capel Anderson. "Literary–Critical Methods." In *Searching the Scriptures: A Feminist Introduction* . Edited by Elisabeth Schüssler Fiorenza. Crossroad: New York, 1993.

Maloney, Francis. "The Faith of Martha and Mary: A Narrative Approach to John 11,17–40," *Bib* 75 (1994): 471–493.

Marshall, I. Howard. "The Problem of New Testament Exegesis," *JEvThS* 17 (1974): 67–73.

Martyn, J. Louis. *History and Theology in the Fourth Gospel.* New York: Harper, 1968.

———. "Glimpses into the History of the Johannine Community." In *L'Evangile de Jean: Sources, rédaction théologie* , edited by M. de Jonge. Gembloux: Duculot and Louvain: Leuven University Press, 1977.

Mattill, A. J. "Johannine Communities behind the Fourth Gospel: Georg Richter's Analysis," *TS* 38 (1977): 294–315.

Maynard, A. H. "The Role of Peter in the Fourth Gospel," *NTS* (1984): 531–548.

Maynes, Mary Jo, et. al., eds. *Gender, Kinship and Power: A Comparative and Interdisciplinary History.* New York: Routledge, 1996.

Meeks, Wayne A. *The Prophet-King: Moses Traditions and the Johannine Christology.* Supplements to Novum Testamentum 14. Leiden: E. J. Brill, 1967.

———. "The Man from Heaven in Johannine Sectarianism," *JBL* 91 (1972): 44–72.

———. " 'Am I a Jew?'—Johannine Christianity and Judaism," 1.163–186 in *Christianity, Judaism and Other Greco-Roman Cults: Studies for Morton Smith at Sixty.* 4 vols. Jacob Neusner, ed. Leiden: E. J. Brill, 1975.

Metzger, Bruce M. and Michael D. Coogan, ed. *The Oxford Companion to the Bible.* New York: Oxford University Press, 1993.

Meyer, Marvin. "Making Mary Male: The Categories 'Male' and 'Female' in the Gospel of Thomas." *NTS* 31 (1985): 554–570.

Meyers, Carol. "Gender Imagery in the Song of Songs." *Hebrew Annual Review* 10 (1986): 209–223.

———. *Discovering Eve: Ancient Israelite Women in Context.* New York: Oxford University Press, 1988.

Miller, Nancy K., ed. *The Poetics of Gender*. New York: Columbia University Press, 1986.

Millet, Kate. *Sexual Politics*. New York: Avon, 1971.

Minear, Paul S. "We don't know where... John 20:2," *Int* 30 (1975): 125–139.

_____. "The Beloved Disciple in the Gospel of John: Some Clues and Conjectures," *NovT*19 (1977): 105–123.

Moers, Ellen. *Literary Women*. New York: Doubleday & Co., 1976.

Moi, Toril. *Sexual/Texual Politics: Feminist Literary Theory*. New York: Methuen & Co, 1985.

Moltmann-Wendal, Elisabeth. *The Women Around Jesus*. New York: Crossroad, 1988.

Moore, Stephen D. *Literary Criticism and the Gospels: The Theoretical Challenge*. New Haven: Yale University Press, 1989.

Morris, Pam. *Literature and Feminism: An Introduction*. Oxford: Blackwell, 1993.

Moule, C. F. D. "The Individualism of the Fourth Gospel," *NovT* 5 (1962): 171–190.

Muilenburg, James. "Literary Form in the Fourth Gospel," *JBL 51* (1932) 40–53.

Neirynck, Frans. "John and the Synoptics." In *L'Évangile de Jean: Sources, rédaction, théologie*. Bibliotheca ephemeridum theologicarum lovaniensium 44. Louvain: Leuven University Press, 1977.

_____. "John and the Synoptics: The Empty Tomb Stories," *NTS* 30 (1984): 161–187.

Newsom, Carol. "Woman and the Discourse of Patriarchal Wisdom: A Study of Proverbs 1–9." In *Gender and Difference in Ancient Israel*. Edited by Peggy Day. Minneapolis: Fortress Press, 1989.

Neyrey, Jerome H. "Jacob Traditions and the Interpretation of John 4:10–26," *CBQ* 41 (1979): 419–437.

_____. "John III—A Debate over Johannine Epistemology and Christology," *NovT* 23 (1981) 115–127.

Nicol, W. *The Semeia in the Fourth Gospel*. Leiden: Brill, 1972.

Nortjé, S. J. "The Role of Women in the Fourth Gospel," *Neot* 20 (1986): 21–28.

O'Collins, Gerald and David Kendall. "Mary Magdalene as Major Witness to Jesus' Resurrection," *TS* 48 (1987): 631–646.

O'Day, Gail Radcliffe. *Revelation in the Fourth Gospel.* Philadelphia: Fortress Press, 1986.

_____. *The Word Disclosed: John's Story and Narrative Preaching* . St. Louis: CBP, 1987.

_____. "John." In *The Women's Bible Commentary.* Louisville, KY: Westminster, 1992.

_____. "John." *The New Interpreters Bible,* vol. IX. Nashville: Abingdon, 1995, 493–865.

O'Grady, John F. "The Role of the Beloved Disciple," *BTB* 9 (1979): 58–65.

_____. "The Human Jesus in the Fourth Gospel," *BTB* 14 (1984): 63–66.

Olsson, Birger. *Structure and Meaning in the Fourth Gospel: A Text-Linguistic Analysis of John 2:1–11 and 4:1–42.* ConB New Testament 6. Lund: C.W. K. Gleerup, 1974.

Origen. *Commentary on the Gospel According to John,* Books 1–10 Washington DC: Catholic University Press of America, 1989.

Osiek, Carolyn. "The Feminist and the Bible: Hermeneutical Alternatives." *Religion and Intellectual Life* 6 (1989): 96–109.

Pagels, Elaine H. *The Johannine Gospel in Gnostic Exegesis: Heracleon's Commentary on John.* Nashville: Abingdon, 1973.

Painter, John. "Christology and the History of the Johannine Community in the Prologue of the Fourth Gospel," *NTS* 30 (1984): 460–474.

Pamment, Margaret. "The Fourth Gospel's Beloved Disciple," *ExpT* 94 (1983): 363–367.

_____. "Focus in the Fourth Gospel," *ExpT* 97 (1985): 71–75.

Pazdan, Mary Margaret. "Nicodemus and the Samaritan Woman: Contrasting Models of Discipleship," *BTB* 17 (1987): 145–148.

Perkins, Pheme. *Peter: Apostle for the Whole Church.* Columbia: University of South Carolina Press, 1994.

Petersen, Norman R. *Literary Criticism for New Testament Critics.* Guides to Biblical Scholarship. Philadelphia: Fortress Press, 1978.

_____. *The Gospel of John and the Sociology of Light: Language and Characterization in the Fourth Gospel.* Valley Forge, PA: Trinity Press International, 1993.

Philo of Alexandria: The Contemplative Life, The Giants, and Selections. Classics of Western Spirituality. Translated by David Winston. New York: Paulist Press, 1981.

Pierce, E. L. "The Fourth Gospel as Drama," *RelL* 29 (1960): 453–455.

Pinto, E. "Jesus, Son of God in the Fourth Gospel," *BibT* 21 (1983): 393–398.

Pippin, Tina. *Death and Desire: The Rhetoric of Gender in the Apocalypse of John*. Louisville: Westminster/John Knox, 1992.

Powell, Mark Allan. *What is Narrative Criticism?* Guides to Biblical Scholarship. Minneapolis: Fortress Press, 1990.

Propp, Vladimir. *The Morphology of the Folk Tale*. Austin: University of Texas Press, 1968.

Quast, Kevin. *Peter and the Beloved Disciple: Figures for a Community in Crisis*. Sheffield: JSOT Press, 1989.

Rabine, Leslie W. "No Lost Paradise: Social Gender and Symbolic Gender in the Writings of Maxine Hong Kingston." *Signs* 12 (1987): 471–492.

Räisänen, Heikki. *Die Mutter Jesu im Neuen Testament*. Helsinki, 1969.

Ramet, Sabrina Petra, ed. *Gender Reversal and Gender Culture: Anthropological and Historical Perspectives*. New York: Routledge, 1996.

Register, Cheri. "American Feminist Literary Criticism: A Bibliographic Introduction." In *Feminist Literary Criticism: Explorations in Theory*. Edited by Josephine Donovan. Lexington: University Press of Kentucky, 1975.

Reim, G. "Jesus as God in the Fourth Gospel: The Old Testament Background," *NTS* 30 (1984): 158–160.

Reinhartz, Adele. "From Narrative to History: The Resurrection of Mary and Martha." In *"Women Like This": New Perspectives on Jewish Women in the Greco-Roman World* . Edited by Amy-Jill Levine. Atlanta: Scholars Press, 1991.

_____. "The Gospel of John," in *Searching the Scriptures*, ed. Elizabeth Schüssler Fiorenza. New York: Crossroad, 1993.

Rena, John. "Women in the Gospel of John" *EgT* 17 (1986): 131–147.

Rensberger, David. *Johannine Faith and Liberating Community*. Philadelphia: Westminster, 1988.

Rhoads, David. "Narrative Criticism and the Gospel of Mark," *JAAR* 50 (1982): 411–34.

Rhoads, David and Donald Michie. *Mark as Story: An Introduction to the Narrative of a Gospel*. Philadelphia: Fortress, 1982.

Richter, Georg. "Präsentische und futerische Eschatologie in 4. Evangelium," *Gegenwart und kommendes Reich*. A. Vögtle Schülergabe. Edited by P. Fiedler and D. Zeller. Stuttgart: Katholisches Bibelwerk, 1975.

Rimmon-Kenan, Schlomith. *Narrative Fiction: Contemporary Poetics*. London and New York: Metheun, 1983.

_____. *Narrative Fiction: Contemporary Poetics* Methuen & Co. Ltd, 1983.

Ruether, Rosemary Radford. "Feminism and Patriarchal Religion: Principles of Ideological Critique of the Bible," *JSOT* 22 (1982): 54–66.

Ruether, Rosemary Radford, ed. *Religion and Sexism: Images of Woman in the Jewish and Christian Traditions*. New York: Simon and Schuster, 1974.

Sakenfeld, K.D. "Feminist Biblical Interpretation," *Princeton Seminary Bulletin* 3 (1988):179–196.

_____. "Feminist Perspectives on Bible and Theology: An Introduction to Selected Issues and Literature," *Int* 42 (1988): 5–18.

Salvoni, Fausto. "Nevertheless My Hour has Not Yet Come (John 2:4)," *Restoration Quarterly* 7 (1963): 236–241.

Sanders, J. N. *The Fourth Gospel in the Early Church: Its Origin and Influence on Christian Theology up to Irenaeus*. Cambridge: Cambridge University Press, 1943.

Schenke, L. "Das Johanneische Schisma und die Zwölf," *NTS* 38 (1992): 105–121.

_____. *Das Johannesevangelium: Einführung-Text-dramatische Gestalt*. Urban-Taschenbücher 446. Stuttgart: Kohlhamner, 1992.

Schnackenburg, Rudolf. *The Gospel According to John*. 3 vols. New York: Crossroad, 1990. German original, *Das Johannesevangelium*. Freiburg: Herder, 1965.

Schneiders, Sandra M. "Women in the Fourth Gospel and the Role of Women in the Contemporary Church," *BTB* 12 (1982): 35–45.

_____. "The Face Veil: A Johannine Sign (John 20:1–10)" *BTB* 13 (1983): 94–97.

_____. "Born Anew, *TToday* 44 (1987): 189–196.

_____. "Death in the Community of Eternal Life: History, Theology, and Spirituality in John 11," *Int*51 (1987): 44–56.

_____. "Feminist Ideological Criticism and Biblical Hermeneutics," *BTB* 19 (1989): 3–10.

_____. "From John to the Beloved Disciple: An Essay on Johannine Characters," *Int* 49 (1995): 359–369.

Schottroff, Luise. *Der Glaubende und die feindliche Welt. Beobachtungen zum gnostischen Dualismus and seiner Bedeutung für Paulus und das Johannesevangelium.* Neukirchen: Neukirchener Verlag, 1970.

_____. "Sexuality in the Fourth Gospel." Paper presented at the annual meeting of the SBL, Philadelphia, November 1995.

Schultz, Siegfried. *Das Evangelium nach Johannes*   Göttingen: Vandenhoeck and Ruprecht, 1972.

Schürer, Emil. "Uber den Gegenwärten Stand der Johanneischen Frage." In *Johannes und Sein Evangelium.* Wege der Forschung 82. Darmstadt: Wissenschaftlich Buchgesellschaft, 1973.

Schüssler Fiorenza, Elisabeth. *Bread Not Stone.* Boston: Beacon Press, 1984.

_____. "A Feminist Interpretation for Liberation: Martha and Mary: Lk. 10:38–42," *RelIntelL* 3 (1986): 21–36.

_____. *In Memory of Her: A Feminist Theological Reconstruction of Christian Origins.* New York: Crossroad, 1987.

_____. "Text and Reality – Reality as Text: The Problem of a Feminist Historical and Social Reconstruction Based on Texts," *Studia Theologica* 43 (1989): 19–34.

_____. *But She Said: Feminist Practices of Biblical Interpretation.* Boston: Beacon Press, 1992.

_____. *Jesus: Miriam's Child, Sophia's Prophet: Critical Issues in Feminist Christology.* New York: Continnum, 1994.

Schüssler Fiorenza, Elisabeth, ed. *Searching the Scriptures*, 2 vols. New York: Crossroad, 1993.

Scott, Joan W. "Gender: A Useful Category of Historical Analysis." *The American Historical Review* 91 (1986): 1053–1075.

_____. "Deconstructing Equality-Versus-Difference: Or, the Uses of Poststructualist Theory for Feminism," *Feminist Studies* 14 (1988) 33–50.

_____. *Gender and the Politics of History.* New York: Columbia University Press, 1988.

Scott, Martin. *Sophia and the Johannine Jesus.* JSNT Supplement Series 71. Sheffield: Sheffield Academic Press, 1992.

Sedgwick, Eve. *Epistemology of the Closet.* Berkeley: University of California Press, 1992.

Segovia, Fernando. "The Love and Hatred of Jesus and Johannine Sectarianism," *CBQ* 43 (1981): 258–272.

Seim, Turid Karlsen. "Roles of Women in the Gospel of John." In *Aspects on the Johannine Literature.* Edited by Lars Hartman and Birger Olsson. ConB NT Series 18. Stockholm: Almqvist & Wiksell International, 1987.

_____. *The Double Message: Patterns of Gender in Luke-Acts* Nashville: Abingdon Press, 1994.

Selvidge, Marla J. "Nicodemus and the Woman with Five Husbands," *Proceedings: Eastern Great Lakes Biblical Society* 2 (1982): 63–75.

Setel, Drorah T. "Prophets and Pornography: Female Sexual Imagery in Hosea" In *Feminist Interpretation of the Bible,* Edited by Letty M. Russell. Philadelphia: Westminster Press, 1985.

Shepherd, Jr. William H. *The Narrative Function of the Holy Spirit as a Character in Luke-Acts.* SBLDS 147; Atlanta: Scholars Press, 1994.

Showalter, Elaine. *A Literature of Their Own: British Women Novelists from Brontë to Lessing.* Princeton: Princeton University Press, 1977.

_____. "Feminist Criticism in the Wilderness," *Critical Inquiry* 8 (1981): 179–205.

_____. "Toward a Feminist Poetics." In *Women's Writing and Writing About Women.* Edited by Mary Jacobus. London: Croom Helm, 1979.

_____. "Women's Time, Women's Space: Writing the History of Feminist Criticism," *Tulsa Studies in Women's Literature* 3 (1984): 29–34.

_____. "Feminism and Literature." In *Literary Theory Today.* Edited by Peter Collier and Helga Geyer-Ryan. New York: Cornell University Press, 1990.

Showalter, Elaine, ed. *The New Feminist Criticism: Essays on Women, Literature and Theory.* New York: Pantheon Books, 1985.

Showalter, Elaine, ed. *Speaking of Gender.* New York: Routledge, 1989.

Sloyan, Gerard S. *What are they saying about John?* New York: Paulist, 1991.

Smith, D. Moody. *The Composition and Order of the Fourth Gospel.* New Haven: Yale University Press, 1965.

————. "Johannine Christianity: Some Reflections on its Character and Delineation," *NTS* 21 (1976): 222–248.

————. *Johannine Christianity: Essays on its Setting Sources, and Theology.* Columbia: University of South Carolina Press, 1984.

————. *John Among the Gospels: The Relationship in Twentieth-Century Research.* Minneapolis: Fortress Press, 1992.

Smith, Jr., Joseph Daniel. "Gaius and the Controversy Over the Johannine Literature," Ph.D. diss., Yale University Press, 1979.

Snyder, Graydon F. "John 13:16 and the Anti-Petrinisim of the Johannine Tradition," *Biblical Research* 16 (1971): 5–15.

Spacks, Patricia. *The Female Imagination.* New York: Alfred A. Knopf, 1975.

Spector, Judith. "Gender Studies: New Directions for Feminist Criticism," *College English* 43 (1981): 374–78.

Spector, Judith, ed. *Gender Studies: New Directions in Feminist Criticism.* Bowling Green, OH: Bowling Green State University Popular Press, 1986.

Staley, Jeffrey. "The Structure of John's Prologue: Its Implications for the Gospel's Narrative Structure," *CBQ* 48 (1986): 241–264.

————. *The Print's First Kiss: A Rhetorical Investigation of the Implied Reader in the Fourth Gospel.* SBL Dissertation Series 82. Atlanta: Scholars Press, 1988.

————. "Stumbling in the Dark, Reaching for the Light: Reading Character in John 5 and 9," *Semeia* 53 (1991): 55–80.

Stanton, Elizabeth Cady, ed. *The Woman's Bible.* New York: European Publishing Company, 1895.

Steinberg, Naomi. "Gender Roles in the Rebekah Cycle," *USQR* 39 (1984): 175–188.

Sternberg, Meir. *The Poetics of Biblical Narrative: Ideological Literature and the Drama of Reading.* Bloomington: Indiana University Press, 1985.

Stibbe, Mark W. G. *John as Storyteller: Narrative Criticism and the Fourth Gospel.* Cambridge: Cambridge University Press, 1992.

_____. "A Tomb with a View: John 11:1–44 in Narrative-Critical Perspective," *NTS* 40 (1994): 38–54.

Stibbe, Mark W. G. ed. *The Gospel of John as Literature: An Anthology of Twentieth Century Perspectives*. Leiden: E.J. Brill, 1993.

Stockton, Eugene D. "The Fourth Gospel and the Woman." In *Essays in Faith and Culture* . Edited by Neil Brown. Catholic Institute of Sydney, 1979.

Strack, H. L. and P. Billerbeck, *Kommentar zum NT aus Talmud und Midrasch*, 4 vols. 1922, 1924, 1926, 1928.

Strauss, David Friedrich. *The Life of Jesus Critically Examined*. Trans. by George Eliot. Philadelphia: Fortress Press, 1972.

Streeter, B. H. *The Four Gospels: A Study of Origins*. London: MacMillan, 1924.

Swidler, Leonard. *Biblical Affirmations of Woman*. Philadelphia: Westminster, 1979.

Talbert, Charles H. *Reading John: A Literary and Theological Commentary on the Fourth Gospel and the Johannine Epistles*. Crossroad: New York, 1992.

Teeple, Howard M. *The Literary Origin of the Fourth Gospel*. Evanston: Religion and Ethics Institute, 1974.

Thiessen, Karen Heidebrecht, "Jesus and Women in the Gospel of John," *Direction* 19 (1990): 53–64.

The Mishnah: A New Translation. Translated by Jacob Neusner. New Haven: Yale University Press, 1988.

The New Oxford Annotated Bible. Edited by Bruce M. Metzger and Roland E. Murphy. New York: Oxford University Press, 1991.

Thompson, Marianne Meye. *The Humanity of Jesus in the Fourth Gospel*. Philadelphia: Fortress, 1988.

_____. "God's Voice You Have Never Heard, God's Form You Have Never Seen: The Characterization of God in the Gospel of John," *Semeia* 63 (1993): 177–204.

Todd, Mary. *Feminist Literary History*. New York: Routledge, 1988.

Tolbert, Mary Ann. "Defining the Problem: The Bible and Feminist Hermeneutics." *Semeia* 28 (1983): 113–126.

_____. "Protestant Feminists and the Bible: On the Horns of a Dilemma," *USQR* 43 (1989): 1–17.

Trible, Phyllis. "Depatriarchalizing in Biblical Interpretation," *JAAR* 41 (1973): 30–48.

_____. *God and the Rhetoric of Sexuality*. Philadelphia: Fortress, 1978.

Trible, Phyllis, ed. "The Effects of Women's Studies on Biblical Studies." *JSOT* 22 (1982).

Twain, Mark. *Mark Twain's Satires and Burlesques*, Edited by Franklin R. Rogers. Berkeley: University of California Press, 1967.

Van den Hengel, John. "Mary: Miriam of Nazareth or the Symbol of the 'Eternal Feminine,'" *Science et Esprit* 37 (1985): 319–333.

von Wahlde, U. C. "The Johannine 'Jews': A Critical Survey," *NTS* 28 (1982): 33–60.

Vouga, François. "The Johannine School: A Gnostic Tradition in Primitive Christianity?" *Bib* 69 (1988): 371–385.

Wainwright, Elaine. "In Search of the Lost Coin: Toward a Feminist Biblical Hermeneutic," *Pacifica* 2 (1989): 135–150.

Watty, William W. "The Significance of Anonymity in the Fourth Gospel," *ExpTim* 90 (1979): 209–212.

Wead, David W. *Literary Devices in John's Gospel*. Theologischen Dissertationen 4; Basel: Friedrich Reinhart Kommissionsverlag, 1970.

Weissler, Chava. " 'For Women and for Men Who are Like Women': The Construction of Gender in Yiddish Devotional Literature," *JFSR* 5 (1989): 7–24.

Wiles, Maurice F. *The Spiritual Gospel: The Interpretation of the Fourth Gospel in the Early Church* . Cambridge: Cambridge University Press, 1960.

Wilson, Rawdon. "The Bright Chimera: Character as a Literary Term," *Critical Inquiry* 7 (1979): 725–749.

Windisch, Hans. "Der Johanneische Erzählungsstil." In *Eucharisterion: Studien zur Religion und Literatur des Alten und Neuen Testaments, Festschrift für H. Gunkel*. 2 vols. Göttingen: Vandenhoeck & Ruprecht, 1923.

Williams, Brackette F. ed. *Women Out of Place: The Gender of Agency and the Race of Nationality*. New York: Routledge, 1996.

Wire, Antoinette C. "Gender Roles in a Scribal Community," in *The Social History of the Matthean Community: Cross Disciplinary Approaches*. Minneapolis Augsburg/Fortress, 1991.

Wisse, Frederik. "Historical Method and the Johannine Community," *ARC* 20 (1992): 35–42.

Wolff, Virginia. *A Room of One's Own*. London: Hogarth Press, 1929.

Woll, D. Bruce. *Johannine Christianity in Conflict: Authority, Rank, and Succession in the First Farewell Discourse*. SBLDS 60. Chico, CA: Scholars Press, 1981.